Introduction to International Economic Law

International Economic Law (IEL) refers to the rules governing economic relations at the international level and involving States, international organizations and private entities. This textbook explores IEL within the broader context of public international law from the ground up, providing all the foundational principles of international law essential for the study of IEL. The first part of the book is devoted to the analysis of actors and sources of IEL while the second part focuses on the three main sectors of IEL: international investment law, the law of international trade, as developed through the work of the World Trade Organization, and international financial and monetary law. Through references to conventional rules, landmark cases and decisions of international organizations, *Introduction to International Economic Law* provides a clear and concise primer on the main issues in current IEL. It will be an ideal textbook for students taking introductory courses in IEL, as well as a useful guide for anyone wishing to learn about the subject and understand the dynamics behind it.

Fulvio Maria Palombino, Ph.D., is Full Professor of International Law at the University of Rome Tor Vergata and Adjunct Professor of International Law and International Economic Law at Luiss University.

Pierfrancesco Rossi, Ph.D., is Assistant Professor of International Law at the University of Teramo, Adjunct Professor of International Law at Luiss University and Adjunct Professor of International Trade Law at the University of International Studies of Rome.

Domenico Pauciulo, Ph.D., is Assistant Professor of International Law at the University of Trieste and Adjunct Professor of International Trade Law at Luiss University.

Donato Greco, Ph.D., is Assistant Professor of International Law at the University of Naples Federico II and Adjunct Professor of International Organizations and Human Rights at Luiss University.

Giuliana Lampo, Ph.D., is Postdoctoral Research Fellow in International Law and Adjunct Professor of International and EU Economic Law at Luiss University.

Caterina Milo, Ph.D., is Postdoctoral Research Fellow in International Law at the University of Trento and Adjunct Professor of International and EU Economic Law at Luiss University.

Ester Ferriello, Ph.D. Candidate in International Law at the University of Naples Federico II.

Introduction to International Economic Law

Edited by Fulvio M. Palombino

With contributions from

Pierfrancesco Rossi, Domenico Pauciulo, Donato Greco, Giuliana Lampo, Caterina Milo, Ester Ferriello

Routledge
Taylor & Francis Group
LONDON AND NEW YORK

G. Giappichelli Editore

First published 2025
by Routledge
4 Park Square, Milton Park, Abingdon, Oxon OX14 4RN

and by Routledge
605 Third Avenue, New York, NY 10158

Routledge is an imprint of the Taylor & Francis Group, an informa business

and by G. Giappichelli Editore
Via Po 21, Torino – Italia

British Library Cataloguing-in-Publication Data
A catalogue record for this book is available from the British Library

Library of Congress Cataloging-in-Publication Data
A catalog record has been requested for this book

ISBN: 978-1-032-95076-1 (hbk-Routledge)
ISBN: 978-1-003-58309-7 (ebk-Routledge)
ISBN: 978-1-032-95073-0 (pbk-Routledge)
ISBN: 979-12-211-1206-1 (pbk-Giappichelli)

DOI: 10.4324/9781003583097

Typeset in Simoncini Garamond
by G. Giappichelli Editore, Turin, Italy

The title has been subjected to a peer review process prior to publication.

CONTENTS

page

1. Introduction 1

Fulvio Maria Palombino

1.1. A Tentative Definition of International Economic Law 1
1.2. Outline of the Volume 4
References 5

2. The Subjects, Actors and Sources of International Economic Law 7

Pierfrancesco Rossi

2.1. Introduction: The Interplay between Subjects and Sources of International (Economic) Law 8
2.2. States 9
2.2.1. The Role of States in International Economic Law 10
2.2.2. The Equality of States and Its Limits in International Economic Law 13
2.3. International Organizations 16
2.3.1. General Features of International Organizations 16
2.3.2. The Role of International Organizations in International Economic Law 18
2.3.3. The United Nations and the Global Economy 20
2.4. Private Corporations 22
2.4.1. The Status of Private Entities in International Law 22
2.4.2. The International Legal Regime on Private Corporations: Corporate Rights 25
2.4.3. The Problem of Corporate Duties under International Law 26
2.5. Non-Governmental Organizations 29
2.6. An Overview of the Sources of International Law 30

page

2.7. International Treaties 32
2.7.1. The Relevance and Interplay of Treaties in International Economic Law 33
2.7.2. The Interpretation of International Economic Treaties 36
2.8. Customary International Law 38
2.8.1. Elements and Basic Features of International Customs 39
2.8.2. The Interplay between Treaties and Customs in International Economic Law 40
2.9. General Principles 43
2.9.1. General Principles Common to Domestic Legal Systems 43
2.9.2. General Principles of International Law 44
2.10. Decisions of Courts and Tribunals 46
2.11. Acts of International Organizations 49
2.12. Soft Law 50
References 53

3. International Investment Law 55

Giuliana Lampo and Caterina Milo

PART I. *Substantive Rules on the Protection of Foreign Investments*

3.1. The Sources of International Investment Law: From Customary International Law to Investment Treaties 56
3.1.1. The Conclusion of Investment Treaties: The Case of European Union Member States 60
3.2. The Object of International Investment Law: The Notion of Investment 63
3.3. The Rules on the Treatment of Foreign Investments: The Main Standards of Treatment 67
3.3.1. Expropriation and Nationalization 70
3.3.2. Fair and Equitable Treatment 76
3.3.3. National Treatment 80
3.3.4. Most-Favored Nation Treatment 83
3.3.5. Full Protection and Security 88
3.3.6. Umbrella Clauses 91
3.4. Reconciling the Protection of Foreign Investments with Other Public Interests 94

PART II. *The Settlement of Investment Disputes*

3.5. Introduction to the Settlement of Investment Disputes: Fundamental Notions 98

page

3.6. From Disputes between States to Investor-State Dispute Settlement 100
3.6.1. The International Centre for Settlement of Investment Disputes 104
3.6.2. Other Relevant Frameworks 106
3.7. Consent as the Basis of Investment Arbitration 107
3.8. Jurisdiction and Admissibility of Investment Arbitration Claims 111
3.8.1. The Scope of Jurisdiction: A Dispute Arising Out of an Investment Between the Investor and the Host State 113
3.8.1.1. Jurisdiction *Ratione Materiae* 113
3.8.1.2. Jurisdiction *Ratione Personae* 115
3.8.1.3. Jurisdiction *Ratione Loci* 115
3.8.1.4. Jurisdiction *Ratione Temporis* 116
3.9. The Laws Applicable to Investment Disputes 117
3.9.1. The Law Governing the Merits of the Dispute 118
3.9.2. The Law Governing the Arbitral Process and the Law of the Seat of Arbitration 119
3.10. The ICSID Procedure 120
3.10.1. Institution of a Claim 120
3.10.2. Constitution of the Tribunal 121
3.10.3. The Written and Oral Procedure 122
3.10.4. Conclusion of the Procedure 123
3.11. The Award 124
3.11.1. ICSID Awards 124
3.11.2. Non-ICSID Awards 127
3.12. Post-Award Remedies 128
3.12.1. ICSID Awards 128
3.12.2. Non-ICSID Awards 131
3.13. Conclusions: The Ongoing Debate on ISDS 132
References 134

4. The Law of the World Trade Organization 137

Donato Greco and Ester Ferriello

4.1. Introduction 138
4.2. The Historical Origins of the WTO 138
4.3. Objective and Functions 142
4.4. Membership, Accession, and Withdrawal 143
4.5. Sources 144
4.5.1. The GATT 1994 and Other Multilateral Trade Agreements 145
4.5.2. The Single Undertaking Principle 147

page

4.5.3. Plurilateral Trade Agreements 148
4.5.4. Regional Trade Agreements 148
4.6. Interpretation of WTO Law and General International Law 148
4.6.1. The Application of General International Law Norms in the WTO System 152
4.7. The Legal Value of Judicial Precedents 154
4.8. Institutional Structure 155
4.9. The WTO Dispute Settlement System 158
4.9.1. The Dispute Settlement Body 159
4.9.2. Panels 160
4.9.3. The Appellate Body 161
4.9.4. Jurisdiction: Nature and Scope 162
4.9.5. Implementation and Enforcement 164
4.9.6. A Paralyzed System: Current Challenges and Future Perspectives 167
4.10. Substantial Obligations: The Multilateralization of International Trade 169
4.10.1. The Most-Favored-Nation Treatment 170
4.10.2. The National Treatment 175
4.10.2.1. …for Internal Taxation on Like Products 178
4.10.2.2. …for Internal Taxation on Directly Competitive or Substitutable Products 180
4.10.2.3. …for Internal Regulation 181
4.11. Derogations and Flexibilities 184
4.11.1. General Exceptions 184
4.11.2. Security Exceptions 186
4.11.3. Regional Integration 189
4.11.4. Enabling Clause 191
References 192

5. International Financial Law 195

Domenico Pauciulo

5.1. Introduction 195
5.2. The G20 and the Intergovernmental Dimension of International Financial Law 198
5.3. The International Monetary Fund 203
5.3.1. Internal Structure 204
5.3.2. The Functions of the IMF: Surveillance and Capacity Development 207
5.3.3. Lending Activities 208
5.4. The World Bank Group 211

page

5.4.1. The International Bank for Reconstruction and Development 212
5.4.2. Internal Structure 214
5.4.3. The International Development Association 216
5.4.4. Functions of the World Bank: Analytics and Policy Advice 217
5.4.5. Financing Activities 218
5.4.6. The International Finance Corporation and Its Support to the Private Sector 222
5.4.7. The Multilateral Investment Guarantee Agency 223
5.5. The Relationship between the Bretton Woods Institutions and International Law 226
5.5.1. The IMF and Human Rights 231
5.5.2. The World Bank "Environmental and Social Framework" 232
5.6. Accountability of International Financial Institutions 234
5.6.1. The IMF Independent Evaluation Office 236
5.6.2. The World Bank Accountability Mechanism 238
5.6.2.1. The Inspection Panel 240
5.6.2.2. Procedural Steps before the Inspection Panel 241
5.6.2.3. The Dispute Resolution Service 242
5.6.3. The IFC/MIGA Compliance Advisory Ombudsman 244
5.7. Final Remarks 247
References 249

Index 251

Chapter 1
INTRODUCTION

Fulvio Maria Palombino

ABSTRACT: *Starting with a definition of international economic law, this opening chapter will provide a basic introduction to the discipline, analyzing its evolution and the main principles inspiring the regulation of international economic relationships. Accordingly, it will investigate whether international economic law may be regarded as a self-contained regime or, quite the opposite, as a part of public international law. Furthermore, it will provide an overview of the book's structure and a brief introduction to the other chapters.*

KEYWORDS: *International Economic Law – Self-Contained Regimes – Fragmentation – Public International Law.*

SUMMARY: 1.1. A Tentative Definition of International Economic Law. – 1.2. Outline of the Volume. – References.

1.1. A Tentative Definition of International Economic Law

At first glance, the definition of international economic law (IEL) appears relatively straightforward. The notion refers to all those rules pertaining to economic relations that operate on an international level and involve States, international organizations, and private entities. However, two perspectives seem to exist when it comes to IEL's autonomy as a distinct legal discipline. According to a first approach, IEL would embody a discipline on its own, completely isolated from public international law. A second approach, contrarywise, considers IEL as nothing but a branch of public international law. The question does not have a purely theoretical relevance. And the reason is not hard to grasp.

In greater detail, the first approach takes us back to the never-ending debate over the fragmentation of international law as a result of the existence of self-contained regimes. The topic is so controversial that it has been an object of study for the International Law Commission (ILC). Nevertheless, a significant terminological confusion continues to exist. And the fact that the very concept of a self-contained regime may be understood in different ways is evidence of this. If considered narrowly, the term denotes "*a special set of secondary rules [that] claims priority over the secondary rules in the general law of State responsibility*".[1] Alternatively, in a sense which may be called "intermediate", self-contained regimes are supposed to consist of "*interrelated wholes of primary and secondary rules [...] that cover some particular problem differently from the way it would be covered under general law*".[2] Seen this way, "*self-contentedness fuses with international law's contractual bias: where a matter is regulated by a treaty, there is normally no reason to have recourse to other sources*".[3] Lastly, in the broadest sense, the notion here scrutinized alludes to the existence of entire fields of international law being "special" in nature, which means that "*rules of general international law are assumed to be modified or even excluded in their administration*".[4]

On closer inspection, international economic law does not seem to fit any of these definitions as it cannot be entirely isolated from public international law. And there is much evidence to support this stance. First of all, the deep connection between IEL and public international law is rooted in the very foundations and evolution of IEL. In the wake of the Second World War, State representatives convened at Bretton Woods, acknowledging that a closer economic integration among States could help prevent economic warfare and foster long-term global prosperity and peace.[5] In practice, this entailed the proliferation of treaties establishing international institutions dealing with international trade, foreign direct investment and lending and financing activities. States chose to limit their economic freedom, adhering to the international customary rule providing that "*a State is not bound to continue particular trade relations*" unless there is "*a treaty commitment or other specific legal obligation*".[6] This entire process developed within the international legal order, relying on its primary instruments. Indeed, the main sources of IEL are the same as those of public international law, namely treaties, customs and general principles of law. Furthermore, over the years, IEL has progressively opened up to other subfields of international law. It is thus evident that IEL

---

[1] International Law Commission, *Report of the Study Group on "Fragmentation of International Law: Difficulties arising from the Diversification and Expansion of International Law"*, 13 April 2006, UN Doc. A/CN.4/L.682, p. 66, para. 124.

[2] *Ibid.*, p. 68, para. 128.

[3] *Ibid.*

[4] *Ibid.*, para. 129.

[5] See more broadly the reconstruction by V. Vadi, *Cultural Heritage in International Economic Law*, Brill, 2023, p. 90 ff.

[6] International Court of Justice, *Military and Paramilitary Activities in and against Nicaragua (Nicaragua v. United States)*, Judgment, 27 June 1986, ICJ Reports 1986, p. 14, para. 275.

was built and continues to function within the general framework of public international law.

On the other hand, the connection between IEL and public international law has been repeatedly confirmed by several institutions across all the main sectors in which IEL is articulated.

By way of example, in the case of international investment law and the bilateral treaties it is based on, the position was taken whereby a "*BIT [Bilateral Investment Treaty] is not a self-contained closed legal system limited to provide for substantive material rules of direct applicability, but it has to be envisaged within a wider judicial context in which rules from other sources are integrated though implied incorporation methods, or by direct reference to certain supplementary rules, whether of international law character or of domestic law nature*".[7] This approach has been constantly followed by arbitral tribunals and will be further explored in the sections dedicated to international investment law, but, for the moment, it is sufficient to recall the widespread use of general international law to ascertain the existence of a wrongful act.

The same is true insofar as the World Trade Organization (WTO) regime is concerned. The regime is far from complete, and the lack of any specific rules on interpretation or standard of review, to say the least, is evidence of this. Accordingly, with regard to these areas, WTO institutions cannot but refer to rules and principles of general international law. Not surprisingly, the Appellate Body described the GATT as an agreement that "*is not to be read in clinical isolation from public international law*", thus clearly confirming the openness of the regime.[8]

Last but not least, the same approach, although with some peculiarities, may be found in the practice of some of the most important international monetary and financial institutions as well as in some soft law instruments echoing this practice. One needs only mention the "Tilburg Guiding Principles on World Bank, International Monetary Fund and Human Rights".

Having this approach in mind, one should conclude that in terms of

[7] *Asian Agricultural Products Ltd. v. Republic of Sri Lanka*, ICSID Case No. ARB/87/3, Final Award, 27 June 1990, para. 21. See also *Eastern Extension, Australasia and China Telegraph Company, Ltd. (Great Britain) v. United States*, Final Award, 7 November 1923, in *Reports of International Arbitral Awards*, vol. VI, p. 114, where the arbitral tribunal recognized that, even when international law does not contain express rules decisive of particular cases, "*the function of jurisprudence is to resolve the conflict of opposing rights and interests by applying, in default of any specific provision of law, the corollaries of general principles, and so to find – exactly as in the mathematical sciences – the solution of the problem*".

[8] *United States – Standards for Reformulated and Conventional Gasoline*, Report of the Appellate Body, 29 April 1996, WT/DS2/AB/R, p. 17.

sources and subjects, IEL does not differ from public international law considered in its entirety. The sole peculiarity is reflected in the fact that some subjects (like multinational enterprises) and some sources (like equity) may play a more fundamental role in comparison to what generally happens in the framework of other international law fields. Finally, as the book will explore, all the core areas of IEL are significantly shaped by rules of general international law, whose normative impact may be perceived in key aspects such as subjectivity, treaty interpretation and termination, attribution of wrongful acts, circumstances precluding wrongfulness and remedies.

1.2. Outline of the Volume

Following the definition of IEL as provided above, the *fil rouge* between the chapters included in the volume will lie in the analysis of the interaction between the main sectors composing IEL and other areas of public international law. As for its targeted readership, the book is written with students in mind, with the intention of making up for the lack of an English textbook suitable for an entry-level university course. However, it is also aimed at anyone wanting to approach the subject and understand the dynamics behind it.

Moving along these premises, the volume will be articulated into two parts.

The first part will be devoted to the analysis of actors and sources of international economic law. Notably, chapter 2 will first highlight the key role of States and international organizations as subjects of IEL while also exploring the involvement of other actors, such as public and privately owned enterprises, which certainly influence the application, interpretation and evolution of IEL. This will be followed by the analysis of the sources of IEL, scrutinizing the specific role of the main sources of international law in the regulation of international economic relations. This section will also consider the impact of other legal sources, such as decisions of international courts and tribunals, acts of international organizations, and the so-called soft law.

The second part will explore the three areas that most contribute to defining international economic law's content, i.e., international investment law, the law of international trade, as developed through the work of the WTO, and international financial and monetary law. Specifically, chapter 3 will delve into the legal framework governing foreign investments. Having outlined the historical background that led to the development of this area,

Part I will cover substantial rules regarding investment, the standards of treatment and expropriation, whereas Part II will address Investor-State Dispute Settlement (ISDS), focusing on the arbitral procedure, including the specific issue of consent to investment arbitration, the law applicable to the merits of the procedure and the remedies available to parties against an award. Chapter 4 will focus on the WTO system, exploring its historical evolution, the basic normative and institutional framework of the Organization, the main substantive obligations and their exceptions, and the WTO dispute settlement system. Finally, Chapter 5 will analyze monetary and financial cooperation as well as the role and activities of both the International Monetary Fund (IMF) and the World Bank Group in eradicating poverty, promoting international trade and investment flows, supporting development, and providing debt relief. Its sections will also be devoted to exploring the institutional framework of the IMF and of the various organizations and institutions part of the World Bank Group, as well as their policies and rules regarding financial assistance to Member States and the accountability system of the organizations.

References

Vadi, V. (2023). *Cultural Heritage in International Economic Law*, Brill.

Chapter 2
THE SUBJECTS, ACTORS AND SOURCES OF INTERNATIONAL ECONOMIC LAW

Pierfrancesco Rossi

ABSTRACT: *The chapter first explores the subjects and actors that play a role in the application, interpretation and evolution of international economic law. It begins by discussing the pivotal role of states, focusing on their equality and its inherent limitations within the international legal framework, and of international organizations. It also analyzes the legal status of non-state actors, namely private corporations and NGOs, addressing their rights, obligations and growing significance under international economic law. The chapter then examines how the diverse sources of international law apply to the regulation of the world economy and how their interaction shapes international economic governance. A general overview of the sources of international law is followed by a detailed discussion of the role played by international treaties and customary international law in international economic law. Additional discussions cover general principles, judicial decisions, acts of international organizations, and the so-called soft law.*

KEYWORDS: *Subjects of International Law – States – International Organizations – United Nations – Corporations – NGOs – Sources of International Law – Treaties – Customary Law – General Principles – Judicial Decisions – Acts of International Organizations – Soft Law.*

SUMMARY: 2.1. Introduction: The Interplay between Subjects and Sources of International (Economic) Law. – 2.2. States. – 2.2.1. The Role of States in International Economic Law. – 2.2.2. The Equality of States and Its Limits in International Economic Law. – 2.3. International Organizations. – 2.3.1. General Features of International Organizations. – 2.3.2. The Role of International Organizations in International Economic Law. – 2.3.3. The United Nations and the Global Economy. – 2.4. Private Corporations. – 2.4.1. The Status of Private Entities in International Law. – 2.4.2. The International Legal Regime on Private Corporations: Corporate Rights. – 2.4.3. The Problem of Corporate Duties under International Law. – 2.5. Non-Governmental Organizations. – 2.6. An Overview of the Sources of International Law. – 2.7. International Treaties. – 2.7.1. The Relevance and Interplay of Treaties in International Economic Law. – 2.7.2. The Interpretation of International Economic Treaties. – 2.8. Customary International Law. – 2.8.1. Elements and Basic Features of International Customs. – 2.8.2. The Interplay between Treaties and Customs in International Economic Law. – 2.9. General Principles. – 2.9.1. General Principles Common to Domestic Legal Systems. – 2.9.2. General Principles of International Law. –

2.10. Decisions of Courts and Tribunals. – 2.11. Acts of International Organizations. – 2.12. Soft Law. – References.

2.1. Introduction: The Interplay between Subjects and Sources of International (Economic) Law

The initial step in studying any legal discipline typically involves understanding its subjects and sources. The objective of this chapter is to explore this matter within the context of International Economic Law (IEL). However, since IEL is just a fragment of the broader international legal order, the following discussion will primarily trace the subjects and sources of international law and clarify how these notions apply or potentially differ in the economic domain.

"Subjects" and "sources" constitute truly foundational legal concepts. Subjects are generally defined as persons or entities capable of possessing rights and obligations in a particular legal system, while sources as those acts or facts that can give rise to legal obligations. These concepts are universally employed in national legal systems, that is, the internal laws of individual States. It is widely known, for example, that the subjects of national law include human beings, referred to in the legal lexicon as "private individuals" or "natural persons", along with legal entities of a collective character known as "juridical persons", such as associations, societies or corporations. As to the sources, readers will certainly be aware of those – or at least some of those – of their own country's legal system, which will include, among many others, a constitution and the legislation passed by the national Parliament.

International law has, of course, different subjects and sources. As the legal system governing international relations, it has always revolved around States, which are its undisputed main subjects. Thus States possess rights and obligations towards other States. International law also has its peculiar type of juridical person: the international organization, akin to a "society of States". Among the most relevant sources of international law, mention should be made of international treaties, binding agreements stipulated by States and international organizations reminiscent of contracts in national law. Repetition of State behavior over time can give rise to unwritten, or customary, rules known as customary international law. And international organizations are often given the power to adopt legal acts that are binding upon their member States. As we will see, all these and other subjects and sources play a pivotal role in IEL.

The above highlights a very distinctive feature of international law: subjects and sources are traditionally interconnected in a sort of "circularity".

In international law, just like any other legal system, the legal sources apply to the subjects, granting them rights or obligations. However, unlike national law, the legal sources are also created by the subjects themselves through their behaviors. In different manners, this is equally true for treaties, customary law and acts produced by international organizations. This stems directly from the structural features of the international society, where no supreme or central authority exists in the form of a world government or lawmaker. This unique "feedback loop" in which subjects not only are bound by legal sources but also directly contribute to their creation has made it more challenging, at least on a theoretical level, to grant international subjectivity to entities that lack the power to produce international rules like treaties or customs. This matter is still debated in legal scholarship, particularly regarding multinational corporations and private individuals. But regardless of whether these entities should be considered formal subjects of international law, they certainly participate in fundamental ways in the application, interpretation and evolution of legal rules in the economic realm. This is the reason why the title of this chapter refers not only to (formal) "subjects" but also, more generically, to "actors" of IEL.

2.2. States

As mentioned in the introductory section, States are the key players in the creation of international legal rules and the primary recipients of international rights and obligations. International law treats States as a single unit: their internal subdivisions, such as regions or provinces, lack separate international personality, and all their acts are ascribed to the State to which the subdivision belongs. This represents a marked difference from national law, where a State's various organs and components can possess individual legal personalities separate from the central State. Thus, in national law, branches of the same State may initiate proceedings against each other – envision a public university litigating against its own State's government in a dispute over public funding. This would not be possible in international law.

It is not always easy to determine whether a certain entity is, legally speaking, a full-fledged State. While most States undisputedly meet this definition and fully engage in international relations, ambiguity may arise in cases where a certain entity has not received widespread international recognition, often due to the existence of territorial or political disputes. These situations are difficult to resolve due to the lack of a universally accepted theory of statehood in international law. A prominent example of a contested status is the island of Taiwan, also known as the Republic of

China. Despite being *de facto* independent from Mainland China, with distinct political institutions and a separate legal system, Taiwan is claimed by China as part of its national territory under the so-called "One China policy" and is not recognized as a sovereign State by the overwhelming majority of States. This has left it in legal limbo and has generally prevented it from undertaking various functions a "normal" State would perform in the international arena, such as entertaining diplomatic relations with other States, negotiating and concluding international treaties, or becoming a member of the United Nations and other multilateral organizations. Interestingly, though, Taiwan – which has emerged as an economic powerhouse primarily due to its technology industry – still manages to participate in IEL through unconventional means. For example, it has gained admission to the World Trade Organization (WTO) as a non-State entity under the name of "Chinese Taipei". Consequently, it shares a similar standing within the WTO as China's Special Administrative Regions of Hong Kong and Macao. Remarkably, despite the lack of formal recognition, over 60 countries have exchanged economic and trade offices with Taiwan.

2.2.1. The Role of States in International Economic Law

As the main subjects of international law, States also serve as the primary actors of IEL.

Their central role manifests itself first and foremost in the field of lawmaking. States are actively involved in shaping international legal rules in the economic realm, both directly (e.g., by entering into international treaties, influencing the formation and evolution of rules of customary international law, etc.) and indirectly (e.g., by establishing international organizations that generate legal rules). As participants in international organizations, States maintain an influence in their activities in accordance with the internal procedures established within each organization.

The influence of States over the regulation of the global economy extends beyond formal lawmaking. Notably, since 1999, a forum for inter-State cooperation known as the Group of Twenty (G20) has taken up a significant steering role in global economic governance, despite not having formalized legal status (that is, not being an international organization) or binding powers. Initially comprising 19 States representing a mix of industrialized and emerging economies – Argentina, Australia, Brazil, Canada, China, France, Germany, India, Indonesia, Italy, Japan, Mexico, Russia, Saudi Arabia, South Africa, South Korea, Turkey, the United Kingdom and the United States – alongside the European Union, the G20 has expanded to 21 permanent members with the inclusion of the African Union in September 2023. Established as a more representative alternative to the Group of Seven (G7), which only encompasses industrialized Western States, the G20 serves as a forum for the discussion of the most critical issues of the global economy, spanning from trade, finance, development, fiscal matters and monetary policies to efforts in the fight against the financing of terrorism or climate change. While the G20 does not directly produce legal rules, the principles it formulates, adopted by consensus, possess substantial political weight and significantly influence future lawmaking. This is especially true for the principles articulated in the final declarations of the G20 Heads of State or Government summits.[1]

It is not only the role of States in *international* lawmaking and economic governance that is central to IEL; their *internal* lawmaking can be no less relevant to the global economy. National laws and administrative actions constitute the primary instruments through which a State exercises regulatory power over economic activities occurring in its territory. Through their domestic legal systems, States can either implement or breach their obligations under IEL. In due course, for example, we will see that in international investment law, most legal claims against States arise from circumstances where a State's legislative, administrative or judicial actions encroach upon the rights of foreign investors. Member States of the WTO bear a specific obligation to ensure that their laws, regulations and administrative procedures align with their WTO commitments.[2] More generally, it is a well-established principle of international law that a State cannot invoke its internal law as an excuse to justify non-compliance with international obligations.

States play a fundamental role in the managing and exploitation of economic resources within their national borders and, on occasion, beyond. Under international law, States have exclusive sovereignty over their natural resources, meaning they have the right to dispose of them freely. This principle remains valid despite having been the object of some important qualifications in recent times: for example, the exploitation of natural resources should be sustainable and not compromise the environment. Accordingly, States are free to delegate the extraction and use of such resources to other entities. This is frequently done through the conclusion of concession contracts with foreign investors. An example would be a State concluding a contract with a foreign company and granting that company the rights to explore and extract oil and gas in the territories and seas under its jurisdiction.

---

[1] See Chapter 5, Section 5.2.

[2] Article XVI:4 of the Marrakesh Agreement Establishing the WTO.

Finally, States can also directly engage in economic activities in ways similar to private businesses. Most notably, they may own companies and make investments, either directly or through the establishment of sovereign wealth funds. The term "State-owned enterprise" (SOE) is commonly used to refer to a company under either full or partial public ownership, where the public share allows for governmental control over the company. SOEs have historically been important to the economies of not just socialist States – which often embarked on large-scale nationalizations, i.e., acquisitions by the State of entire sectors of the economy – but also capitalist States. For example, State intervention in the economy by means of public companies was key to Italy's post-war economic development. The relevance of SOEs to the world economy has increased significantly in recent times due to the economic growth of China, whose economy relies heavily on government-controlled companies. In the 2023 Fortune Global 500, a ranking of the world's largest corporations by annual revenue, four of the top six positions are occupied by three Chinese and one Saudi SOEs.

The key legal issue surrounding SOEs is the extent to which they should be considered legally distinct from their parent State. If an SOE acts in breach of rules of international law, does it imply that its State owner should be responsible for the violation? The answer is not always straightforward. Possession of a separate corporate personality suggests that, as a general rule, the SOE and its State should be treated as legally independent entities. But this presumption can be overridden where the SOE exercises public powers, as it is provided that a private entity may engage the international responsibility of a State if that entity "*is empowered by the law of that State to exercise elements of the governmental authority*".[3] In such instances, the SOE may be regarded as acting in the guise of a government branch. Additionally, conduct by an SOE (or, for that matter, any private entity) is classified as State conduct also if it was "directed or controlled" by a State.[4] This standard requires direction and control by the State over each specific violation of international law (referred to as "effective control"[5]); mere corporate control is not enough to meet this stringent criterion.

---

[3] International Law Commission, *Articles on Responsibility of States for Internationally Wrongful Acts* (ARSIWA), 2001, Article 5.

[4] Article 8 ARSIWA.

[5] International Court of Justice (ICJ), *Military and Paramilitary Activities in and against Nicaragua (Nicaragua v. United States of America)*, Judgment, 27 June 1986, ICJ Reports 1986, p. 14 ff.

2.2.2. The Equality of States and Its Limits in International Economic Law

In the dynamics of IEL, States are commonly categorized based on their overall economic conditions (developed vs. developing or emerging; industrialized vs. industrializing or non-industrialized) or other politico-economic factors (capitalist vs. socialist), sometimes reflected in their rough geographical position (Western States, "Global North", "Global South", etc.).

Of course, these categorizations must not be regarded as expressing the superior importance of some States over others. In colonial times, a few hegemonic States dominated the international legal order, including the international economy, exercising supremacy over subjugated peoples. The ripple effects of that era are still visible in today's world. Despite the dismantling of colonial empires guided by the process of decolonization, the historical consequences of colonialism persist in the enormous economic and social disparities between and within States. Nonetheless, today all categories of States have a say in the making and application of IEL. The principle of "sovereign equality" of States constitutes one of the foundations of contemporary international law: just like humans are all equal regardless of the massive economic differences between them, so are States.

But the principle of State equality should be taken with a grain of salt in economic matters. First, it should be remembered that it is only a legal construct: you may be legally equal to the world's richest person, but that person's impact on the world economy will still be incomparably larger than yours. Secondly, while it represents a cornerstone of the law insofar as it safeguards the position of the weakest, the idea of the legal equality of all States may also risk overshadowing or perpetuating factual differences between States. With this in mind, categorizing States based on their wealth and other economic factors is pivotal to the architecture of IEL. IEL has never been, and arguably cannot and should not be, "blind" to economic differences among States. States with similar economic conditions inevitably share similar interests and needs, which impacts their stance toward the global economy. In this respect, States can act as representatives of their polities, and joint action on the international plane only increases the weight and influence of their positions.

The content of IEL has been historically shaped by the clash of interests among blocs of States. For example, during the 1960s and 1970s, many developing States called for revising existing IEL and creating a "New International Economic Order" (NIEO) to offset the disparities between poorer and richer countries. In essence, this included a set of proposals to ensure more economic solidarity from the developed States and greater economic sovereignty among developing States. The NIEO project generally struggled to find universal acceptance due to resistance from developed States, but its influence should not be entirely understated. For example, the aforementioned principle of State sovereignty over natural resources was put forward by developing States in this context. Its earlier proclamations were far from uncontentious and encountered rejection by most Western States,[6] but over time the principle made its way into "mainstream" international law. Another well-known example of differing views held by developed and developing States concerns compensation for the takings of foreign property. Developing countries have historically sought to maintain more freedom in expropriating foreign assets in their territories. In international investment law, this has led to debates over whether the compensation due to foreigners should always reflect the property's full value. Where this point is not clarified by more detailed treaty provisions, States frequently argue in favor of reducing the amount of compensation or otherwise prioritizing public over private interests.[7]

A related but distinct point is whether, to level the playing field, it is appropriate for the principle of formal equality to leave the door open to "positive" discrimination in favor of weaker States. While there arguably exists no general obligation under international law to discriminate in favor of the weakest,[8] IEL nonetheless provides for instances of "differential treatment" which find their rationale in the idea that it might be detrimental to an economically deprived State to be subject to the same legal constraints as richer States. A key example of this can be found in the WTO legal regime, where developing countries may benefit from a range of "special and differential treatment" (SDT) provisions that derogate baseline obligations and provide for greater policy space. SDT provisions may, for example, give countries longer timeframes to implement trade commitments or provide technical and economic assistance for capacity-building. The so-called "Enabling Clause" allows developed countries to unilaterally grant more favorable treatment to products from developing countries, for example, canceling or lowering duties on imports, without requiring reciprocity from beneficiary developing countries.[9] This consti-

[6] Permanent sovereignty over natural resources, United Nations General Assembly (UNGA) Res. 1803 (XVII) (14 December 1962).

[7] See Chapter 3, Section 3.3.1.

[8] P. Cullet, "Differential Treatment in International Law: Towards a New Paradigm of Inter-state Relations", in *European Journal of International Law*, 1999, pp. 549-582, pp. 576-9.

[9] Decision by GATT Contracting Parties of 28 November 1979 (L/4903).

tutes a departure from the usual functioning of the WTO, which is based on the principle that trade concessions should be reciprocal. However, it should also be mentioned that these "positive discriminations" are not without their critics. Some have questioned their actual benefit to the economies of developing countries, claiming that they may have the effect of discouraging meaningful reform and economic modernization and perpetuating the *status quo*. Another challenge is determining which States should be able to take advantage of the preferential treatment. In the lack of universal legal definitions of developed and developing countries, States in the WTO decide for themselves via a self-declaration. Around two-thirds of WTO members self-identify as developing countries, including States like Israel, Singapore, South Korea or the United Arab Emirates. [10]

Clearly, attenuating the principle of State equality not only has a "democratizing" effect on the dynamics of IEL but may also cause elitism. Once again, it cannot be denied that wealthier States wield an overwhelming influence over IEL. States are normally equal within international organizations ("one State, one vote"), as is the case, for example, within the WTO. However, this principle finds an important exception in the functioning of some financial institutions, such as the International Monetary Fund (IMF) and the World Bank. In the IMF, each country's voting power and the financial contributions due to the organization are determined according to quotas reflecting the size and ranking of the economies of member States. The formula for determining the quotas has been changed many times. It currently depends 50% on GDP and 50% on other economic factors, including openness to the global economy (30%), economic variability (15%) and international reserves (5%). The largest quota currently belongs to the US (at 16.66% of the total), followed by Japan (with around 6%) and, in decreasing order, China, Germany, France, the UK, Italy, India, Russia and Brazil. World Bank membership operates similarly, with a country's weight depending not directly on the size of its national economy but on the number of shares of the World Bank's capital stock subscribed by that country. The system of "weighted voting" may enhance the effectiveness of these organizations, but it is also the subject of criticism in that it allows more affluent countries to prioritize their policy preferences through the activities of the organizations. [11]

---

[10] The complete list is available at https://tfadatabase.org/en/developing-countries.

[11] See Chapter 5, Sections 5.3.1 and 5.4.2.

2.3. International Organizations

International organizations represent another category of undisputed subjects of international law. They may be regarded as "secondary" subjects because they are set up through the agreement of other subjects. Members of international organizations are primarily States, but international organizations can also become parties to other organizations: the European Union, for example, is a member of the WTO.

2.3.1. General Features of International Organizations

The way international organizations are created and function bears resemblance, to a certain extent, to juridical persons, such as corporations, in national law. Any group of individuals can establish a new corporate legal entity by concluding a contract, by which they will also agree on the basic rules governing the company's operations. Similarly, in international law, any group of States can, by mutual agreement, set up a new legal person – a "society of States" – to pursue common goals. They will do so by concluding not a contract but an international treaty, termed a "constituent treaty" or "charter", which serves as the legal foundation of the new organization. The organization will then be able to engage with other entities in its own name and not in the name of its members. Thus, it will conclude international treaties with member and non-member States or with other organizations; stipulate contracts with private parties, for example, its employees or creditors; and bear responsibility for any violations of the law it commits. However, the analogy between corporate bodies and international organizations should not be pushed too far. International organizations are creations of international law: how they are born, operate and cease to exist is dictated by international rules, not national corporate laws. The functioning of their constituent treaties will depend on the law of international treaties – that will be explored in greater detail in the next chapter – and not on the law of contracts.

Organizations are entities with diverse characteristics. They can be very small, having only two member States, or very large, with the United Nations (UN) standing as the world's largest and most significant organization with its 193 member States. Some organizations, referred to as "regional" organizations, only bring together States from the same area of the world, while others are "universal", not in the sense that all existing States are parties but in the sense that all can be parties without geographical limitations, provided they meet the necessary requirements. The

European Union is an example of a regional organization, while the UN is a universal one. The purposes of organizations also vary widely. Some organizations have very precise or technical objectives, such as managing a common watercourse or a specific natural resource, while others have very broad functions. The purposes of the UN, for example, include the maintenance of international peace and security, the promotion of friendly inter-State relations and international cooperation in economic, social, cultural and other fields. The competencies of an organization are outlined within its constituent instrument and the organization is bound to act within those competencies.

It is important to emphasize that the goals of an organization may differ from or even clash with the interests of individual member States of the organization. Actually, one of the key legal criteria for determining if an international organization possesses its own legal personality is whether or not its purposes are distinct from those of the member States. [12] As seen above, for example, the G20, which has no international legal personality, does not have any "will" of its own. Rather than an international organization, it is simply a platform for discussion among its members. By contrast, it is not uncommon to see an organization and its participating States bicker over issues of policy or law: think of the often conflicting relations between EU institutions and EU member States. Such disagreements are entirely physiological if kept within normal range – that is, if they do not go to the point of disrupting the organization's functioning. An example of disagreements reaching the tipping point is illustrated by the ongoing crisis of the WTO Appellate Body, a crucial element of the WTO dispute settlement system tasked with deciding appeals against panel reports in disputes between WTO members. The US, critical of the Appellate Body's work and citing allegations of "judicial overreach" and flawed decisions, [13] took a decisive step by blocking the appointment of new members. Consequently, the Appellate Body ceased functioning in 2019 and its activities have not resumed as of 2024. [14]

---

[12] *Reparation for injuries suffered in the service of the United Nations*, Advisory Opinion, 11 April 1949, ICJ Reports 1949, p. 174 ff., p. 178.

[13] US Trade Representative, Report on the Appellate Body of the World Trade Organization, February 2020, available at https://ustr.gov/sites/default/files/Report_on_the_Appellate_Body_of_the_World_Trade_Organization.pdf.

[14] See Chapter 4, Section 4.9.6.

2.3.2. The Role of International Organizations in International Economic Law

The significance of international organizations for IEL has grown exponentially over the last century. With the various State economies becoming ever more interconnected, the need for international cooperation in economic matters has increased in parallel. Today, the architecture of two key sectors of IEL (trade law and monetary and financial law) chiefly revolves around international organizations. International investment law is the one major sector of IEL where no multilateral organizations currently exist.

The need for strong international economic institutions became particularly evident with the outbreak of the Second World War. Economic instability was identified as one of the main root causes of the war. The mounting protectionism of the years of the Great Depression – a prolonged and severe economic crisis that started in 1929 – no doubt played a role in worsening international tensions, and the economic downturn and hyperinflation experienced by Germany in those years contributed to the rise of the Nazis. This created a widespread awareness that the future world order required some form of international control over the global economic system. New economic institutions should have ensured monetary stability, given financial aid to countries in economic trouble, ensured infrastructure development resources, and contributed to the progressive liberalization of international trade.

The Allied States designed the bulk of this new institutional system at a conference held in 1944 in Bretton Woods, in the US State of New Hampshire. The Bretton Woods Conference led to the foundation of the world's two most important financial institutions, the IMF and the World Bank (officially International Bank for Reconstruction and Development, IBRD), both headquartered in Washington, DC. The primary function of the IMF was originally to ensure monetary stability with a focus on exchange rates, but its role has evolved into monitoring global financial stability and preventing and mitigating financial crises. For its part, the key function of the World Bank is to lend money to States for the realization of specific public projects, for instance, the building of a dam or the creation of a new transport system. Four other financial institutions (each a separate international organization in its own right) have been created under the umbrella of the World Bank to perform functions not falling within the competencies of the IBRD: the International Development Association (IDA), which focuses on providing zero or low-interest loans to less-developed countries; the International Finance Corporation (IFC), which finances private-sector projects; the International Centre for Settlement of Investment Disputes

(ICSID), whose main function is to resolve disputes between foreign investors and host States; and the Multilateral Investment Guarantee Agency (MIGA), which provides insurance against political risk to facilitate foreign investments in developing countries. Together, these five sister institutions form the World Bank Group.[15] Several other international investment banks exist. A major one is the Asian Infrastructure Investment Bank (AIIB), headquartered in Beijing and having China as its main shareholder.

The Bretton Woods Conference also recommended the creation of an international organization to regulate and liberalize international trade, but this objective proved more difficult to achieve. In 1948, 52 States agreed on the text of the Havana Charter, the constituent treaty of a future International Trade Organization (ITO). However, the negotiations collapsed after the US Congress denied ratification of the Havana Charter, and the ITO was never created. A universal organization in the field of international trade only saw the light of day in 1995 with the birth of the WTO. In the half-century in between, the regulation of international trade occurred through an international treaty called the General Agreement on Tariffs and Trade (GATT 1947). The drafters of this treaty had expected its application to be provisional because the GATT was supposed to be integrated into the future ITO. Due to its provisional character, it is no wonder that the GATT initially did not have any supporting institutional or organizational structure. Yet, in an informal and quite unconventional fashion, some institutions did develop over time to support the application of the GATT, including a small secretariat and a permanent Council of the GATT Contracting Parties. Many argued that the GATT should therefore be conceptualized as a *de facto* international organization, albeit lacking a constituent instrument. Be that as it may, the GATT has now been brought under the umbrella of the WTO, and its institutions have dissolved into the WTO's much stronger institutional setting.[16]

Many other international organizations are exclusively or primarily concerned with economic regulation. The Organization for Economic Co-operation and Development (OECD), whose 38 member States include all main industrialized economies, is a forum to promote economic development and cooperation among members in international economic governance, facilitating the adoption of legal instruments or policy guidance. Various organizations aim to enhance economic integration among the participating States at the regional level. The European Union is the prime example of such an organization. In the economic field, the EU legal system revolves

[15] See Chapter 5, Section 5.4.

[16] See Chapter 4, Sections 4.2 and 4.5.1.

around the concept of a "single internal market", comprising the free movement of goods, people and capital and freedom of establishment (the so-called "four freedoms"). Other organizations pursuing regional or sub-regional economic integration include, among others: in South America, the Andean Community and the Southern Common Market (Mercosur); in Africa, the African Economic Community, the Economic Community of West African States (ECOWAS) and the Eastern African Community; in Asia, the Association of Southeast Asian Nations (ASEAN).

2.3.3. The United Nations and the Global Economy

Mention should also be made of the role of the UN in the global economy. As mentioned earlier, the functions of the UN cover an extremely broad range of issues, not limited to the economic field. At the same time, economic progress and development constitute an important pillar of the UN mandate. The UN General Assembly, where all UN Member States are represented on a "one State, one vote" basis, has established two subsidiary bodies playing fundamental roles in IEL. The UN Conference on Trade and Development (UNCTAD), established in 1964, serves as a crucial forum for cooperation in finance, trade and investment matters. Within UNCTAD, developing countries articulate their positions mainly through an inter-governmental group called Group of 77 (G-77), which, despite its name, currently includes around 134 members. Another subsidiary body of the UN General Assembly is the UN Commission on International Trade Law (UNCITRAL), tasked with contributing to the development of the legal framework concerning international trade at both the national and international levels. Among other things, UNCITRAL plays a remarkable role in developing international "soft law" instruments in economic matters, as we will see later in the chapter.[17]

The UN Economic and Social Council (ECOSOC), one of the principal organs of the UN, is a political body composed of 54 States elected by the UN General Assembly for a 3-year term. ECOSOC serves as a discussion forum in the context of economic cooperation, grants "consultative status" to NGOs (which, as we will see, allows them to participate in some UN deliberative processes[18]) and coordinates the activities of the Specialized Agencies of the UN. Contrary to what this term might suggest, the Specialized Agencies are veritable international organizations distinct from the

---

[17] See Section 2.12.

[18] Section 2.5 below.

UN. They have their own constituent treaties and organs, and their members do not necessarily fully coincide with the UN's. These organizations are associated with the UN by virtue of international treaties they have concluded with the UN. These "Relationship Agreements", negotiated by ECOSOC, grant the UN the power of coordination over the activities of the Specialized Agencies. We encountered some Specialized Agencies during the preceding discussion: the IMF and the five members of the World Bank Group. Other examples whose activities are to some extent relevant to economic regulation include the World Intellectual Property Organization (WIPO), the UN Industrial Development Organization (UNIDO), and the Food and Agriculture Organization (FAO). Also relevant is the International Labour Organization (ILO), an entity much older than the UN itself, having been founded in 1919, but that became a Specialized Agency in 1946. The ILO promotes the improvement of working conditions through the formulation of international labor standards. Governments, employers and workers enjoy equal representation within the ILO.

The role of the UN Security Council also deserves some comment. The Security Council is the UN organ tasked with the maintenance of international peace and security. Among its 15 member States, five permanent members (the "P5") – China, France, Russia, the United Kingdom and the United States – hold the power to unilaterally veto any decision of the Council to which they are opposed (with the only exception of purely procedural decisions). Even though the regulation of the international economy is by no means the central task of the Security Council, its resolutions may still have a significant impact on global economic relations. Under Chapter VII of the UN Charter, when it determines "*the existence of any threat to the peace, breach of the peace, or act of aggression*",[19] the Security Council may adopt, among other measures, "*measures not involving the use of armed force*",[20] which typically consist in economic sanctions.

These coercive measures, binding for all UN member States, come in various types. The first type is a comprehensive embargo, prohibiting trade, investment and/or transportation with a target State. An example is provided by the sanctions adopted in 1966 against the State of Rhodesia (current Zimbabwe), which was governed by a white racist regime. Another type is an arms embargo, which prohibits the sale and shipment of arms, ammunition, and military materials, as was the case with Somalia during the civil war (the embargo was lifted in December 2023). In more recent times, the practice of the Security Council has evolved towards the use of

[19] Article 39 UN Charter.

[20] Article 41 UN Charter.

so-called "smart sanctions", which do not target a State as a whole but specific groups or individuals, for example freezing their funds and assets. After the September 11 attacks, members of Al-Qaeda received targeted sanctions, and the same has been true for ISIL (Da'esh) in more recent times.

Finally, it should be highlighted that not all economic sanctions are adopted or endorsed by the Security Council. Especially when the Council is paralyzed by vetoes, individual States or other international organizations sometimes adopt economic sanctions regimes against States or individuals. For example, after the start of Russia's war against Ukraine, Russia has been targeted by sweeping economic sanctions imposed by the US, the European Union and other Western States. These sanctions have been adopted on a unilateral basis. Since Russia holds the veto power, it is impossible for the UN Security Council to take any coercive action in the context of the Ukraine war.

2.4. Private Corporations

Private corporations play a crucial role in international finance, trade and investment. Particularly, multinational or transnational enterprises – which are established and operate in more than one country, usually through corporate structures called "subsidiaries" – stand out as some of the most powerful and influential economic players globally. Their annual revenues can surpass the GDPs of small or even medium-sized countries.

At the beginning of the previous section, we observed that international organizations and private corporations share some basic legal characteristics as juridical persons or "secondary" legal subjects. However, it is essential to avoid any confusion between them. The key difference is that international organizations are established according to international law, while corporations are founded on the basis of national corporate laws. Only States and other international organizations can be parties to international organizations, whereas corporations can be owned by private individuals, other corporations or, as discussed earlier with regard to SOEs, States and other public entities. Mixed private-public ownership of corporations is also common.

2.4.1. The Status of Private Entities in International Law

Despite their significant role in the global economy, corporations were traditionally not considered subjects of IEL. This perspective stemmed from the "orthodox" view (now largely outdated, as will be seen) that private entities, including both individuals and corporations, could not hold international rights or obligations but could only be subjects of national law. To understand this view, we must consider the historical context of the so-called "classical" international law in the 1800s and early 1900s. At that time, international law had, for the most part, a purely "inter-State" content, and the legal position of individuals largely fell outside of its scope. States were believed to possess nearly absolute sovereignty (*domaine réservé*) within their territories and on any private subjects located therein.

It is important to note that there already existed rules of international law that provided benefits to private individuals. The most notable example was the legal regime concerning the treatment of aliens, which constrained the discretion of States in relation to foreign subjects located in their territories by preventing, for example, arbitrary takings of foreigners' assets or expropriation without compensation (note that, during that time, States had the freedom to treat their nationals and their economic assets as they pleased). As we will explore later,[21] this set of rules – still in force today as norms of customary international law[22] – laid the foundation for what would later be known as international investment law. However, although they benefited individuals, these rules were usually conceptualized in purely "inter-State" terms rather than granting rights to private subjects. An individual did not have any "right" under international law to be free from mistreatment from a foreign State's authorities; only the State of nationality of the individual had the right to request that its citizens were not mistreated. Similarly, a State did not have any international obligation toward foreign individuals but was only obligated to other States not to mistreat their nationals. Therefore, one may say that individuals could only derive an "indirect" benefit from international norms. This mindset was also reflected in the structure of international claims for violations of rules on the treatment of aliens. If a State violated those rules, only the State of nationality of the injured alien could initiate an international claim against the violator, according to a mechanism called "diplomatic protection".[23]

The issue of whether private entities should be considered subjects of international law remains a topic of discussion. Some legal experts answer this question in the negative or the affirmative, while others, arguably the majority, adopt more nuanced views. It is probably true that many disagreements stem from different understandings of the concept of international legal personality. As we mentioned in this chapter's introductory sec-

[21] See Chapter 3, Section 3.1.

[22] See Section 2.8 below.

[23] See Chapter 3, Section 3.7.

tion, when we assert that States and international organizations are subjects of international law, we refer to two distinct aspects: first, that international law grants them rights and obligations, and second, that they can create rules of international law through their actions, for example by concluding international treaties. Private entities do not possess this latter power. Neither individuals nor corporations can directly establish rules of international law, whether by concluding treaties or by any other means. From this perspective, the divide between "traditional" subjects of international law (States and international organizations) and other entities remains as clear as ever.

However, matters differ when considering the other aspect of international legal personality: the capacity to possess rights and obligations. It is now beyond discussion that private entities can be conferred rights and duties under international law. This is broadly related to the historical evolution experienced by international law after the Second World War. With the progressive erosion of the absolute *domaine réservé* of States, international law has shifted from a purely inter-State legal order to one concerned with all aspects of the human experience. Many rules of international law now look "inside" the State and are directed at safeguarding private individuals from the once-absolute State power. This process is sometimes described as the "humanization" of international law. In international human rights law, for instance, individuals are granted basic human rights; entitlement to these rights is not contingent on national law. Individuals may also have obligations under international law, with a relevant example being the rules of international criminal law that prohibit international crimes and provide mechanisms for punishing violators (for instance, the International Criminal Court). While these aspects may not be directly related to the economy, they underscore a general point that applies to all branches of international law, including IEL: there exists no theoretical or structural obstacle to the conferral of rights and obligations directly upon private entities under international law.

Whether or not this occurs in practice will depend on how concrete legal rules are formulated and the subjects to which they are addressed. Most norms of international law do not designate individuals as right or duty-bearers but only address States or other entities. For instance, norms presupposing territorial control, citizenship or possession of an army can only be addressed to States or other territorial entities. As far as IEL is concerned, international trade law is a prime example of a legal framework primarily based on inter-State rules. Although international obligations relating to trade directly impact private parties engaged in cross-border trade, these obligations are construed as conferring rights and obligations upon States exclusively. The WTO dispute settlement system, which is the mechanism established within the WTO to resolve international trade disputes, only addresses disputes between WTO members and cannot be resorted to by private parties. According to the courts of key WTO members – including the US, the EU, Japan and China – WTO obligations lack direct effect and cannot be relied upon by private parties in judicial proceedings before national courts.[24] In this sense, international rules addressed at private entities may still be considered "exceptional". But this does not call their subjectivity into question. To make a parallel with national law, comparatively few rules directly address minors or limited liability companies, but this does not negate their status as subjects of national law.

2.4.2. The International Legal Regime on Private Corporations: Corporate Rights

The preceding discussion also sheds light on the legal position of corporations in contemporary international law. Similar to what was seen above about individuals, many rules of international law directly address the status of corporations. In particular, juridical persons, including corporations, have reaped the benefits of the so-called "humanization" of international law, receiving substantive or procedural rights under several international legal frameworks.

The key examples can be drawn from the area of international investment law. States routinely enter into international investment agreements, i.e. treaties aimed at the reciprocal promotion and protection of investments. Most of these treaties only involve two States and are therefore referred to as "bilateral investment treaties" (BITs). Through BITs, States commonly grant special rights to investors from the other contracting State investing in their territory. These rights include a set of legal provisions – referred to as "standards of treatment" – which essentially impose constraints on the actions the State where the investment took place (known as "host State") can take regarding the assets of foreign investors. Additionally, investors are typically granted procedural rights, that is, legal remedies in cases where they believe their rights have been violated. The main remedy BITs grant foreign investors is investment arbitration, a distinctive form of legal proceedings addressing disputes between a foreign investor and the host State.[25] All this marks a significant difference between investment

---

[24] See, for example, European Court of Justice, Case C-280/93, *Germany v. Council of the European Union*, Judgment of 5 October 1994, paras. 103-12.

[25] See Chapter 3, Sections 3.5-3.13.

treaties and the aforementioned "classical" rules governing the treatment of foreign citizens. As was seen earlier, those rules failed (and still do, to the extent they still exist in contemporary international law) to confer rights directly upon individuals and were to be conceptualized in purely inter-State terms.

It should also be noted that international investment law confers certain rights not just upon corporations but also upon individual shareholders. It is generally admitted that shareholders can initiate legal claims for losses resulting from a decrease in the company's overall value. If a State breaches a company's rights under international investment law, shareholders may incur damages "by reflection" if the harm also reduces the value of their individual shares (so-called "reflective losses").

Corporations are granted rights not only by international investment law but also by other international legal frameworks. Notably, they are among the entities eligible to bring claims before the European Court of Human Rights (ECtHR) against the States parties to the European Convention on Human Rights (ECHR). Corporations can indeed qualify as "victims" of ECHR violations under Article 34 ECHR, which regulates individual applications to the Court (that is, applications by private parties against State parties). Corporate rights under the ECHR include the right to property: Article 1 of Protocol 1 to the ECHR states that "*[e]very natural* or legal *person is entitled to the peaceful enjoyment of his possessions*", thus making express reference to juridical persons. But that is not the only ECHR right that corporations can invoke. Other undisputed examples are the right to a fair trial under Article 6 ECHR, which also protects from arbitrary limitations on the right to defend one's rights in court, or the freedom of expression under Article 10.

2.4.3. The Problem of Corporate Duties under International Law

A matter of greater contention is whether companies may also be deemed to bear obligations under international law.

There is a prevailing consensus today that it would be highly desirable to subject private companies to international legal constraints, and this is for several compelling reasons. As previously highlighted, corporations are powerful actors in the world economy, sometimes surpassing the power of many States. They make significant contributions – in terms of occupation, tax revenue, and overall development – to the economies of the countries where they operate. However, their negligent, reckless or malicious conduct can result in substantial harm to the environment, human rights or the overall State economies. Picture, for instance, a corporation devastating a pristine forest for economic gain, jeopardizing the livelihood of indigenous tribes living therein; running an offshore oil platform with scant regard for basic safety measures, resulting in massive oil spills in the sea; or knowingly outsourcing production to impoverished areas where child labor is prevalent. In all such cases, national laws may prove insufficient to rein in corporate behaviors. Some types of corporate malpractice may be prohibited in certain countries but not in others, and some countries might be unable, or perhaps unwilling, to exert meaningful control over powerful corporations operating within their borders. In fact, corporations have been able to exploit the weaknesses of the existing patchwork of national legal systems to their advantage, evading national regulation. It is a bit like taxes: the existence of tax havens has not only attracted corporate revenue, but it has also allowed corporations to circumvent the tax laws of other countries. Establishing a common international legal framework would result in the same fundamental rules applying to corporate behavior irrespective of national laws, and the uniformity of the legal framework would facilitate implementation.

So what renders this point contentious? As we have seen before, there is little doubt that, in theory, it might be possible for international law to impose obligations on corporations: once it is acknowledged that individuals may have duties, as evident in the field of international criminal law, then there is arguably no barrier preventing the same with juridical persons. However, there is ongoing debate on whether and to what extent existing rules of international law address private corporations by establishing binding obligations for them. The key challenge arises from the structure and content of potentially relevant international laws. International human rights obligations, for instance, are primarily designed to address States, as they derive their key historical rationale from the necessity to safeguard private individuals from the arbitrariness of public authorities. If a State commits itself to an international treaty stipulating certain human rights, those obligations are only binding for the contracting State itself and do not extend to other subjects. The same argument holds for international environmental law obligations, labor standards, and most other international legal rules: in principle, all these legal frameworks regulate State, not private, behavior. For this reason, it is conceptually difficult to extend to corporations sets of international obligations created with States as their primary addressees.

So far, attempts to regulate transnational corporate activities internationally have failed to produce any binding set of rules. While several international acts have been adopted, particularly within the framework of international organizations, specifically addressing the conduct of multinational corporations and their impact on human rights, these acts consistently fall under the "soft law" category.[26] In essence, they only offer non-binding guidelines, standards, or codes of conduct. Take, for instance, the "Global Compact", a UN initiative that corporations can subscribe to in order to showcase their commitment to a responsible approach to business in human rights, labor practices, environmental protection and anti-corruption.

In 2011, the UN Human Rights Council (a subsidiary organ of the UN General Assembly comprising 47 elected States) endorsed the UN Guiding Principles on Business and Human Rights (UNGPs), furnishing guidelines for both States and businesses on how to prevent, address and remedy breaches of human rights. The text of the UNGPs highlights the lack of binding international obligations on corporations: the State "duty" to protect human rights is juxtaposed to a corporate "responsibility" to respect them, and the language employed is predominantly hortatory (Principle 11 dictates that "Business enterprises *should* respect human rights"). Another pertinent soft law instrument is the OECD Guidelines for Multinational Enterprises on Responsible Business Conduct, initially adopted in 1976 and subject to periodic revision (most recently in 2023). Over 50 countries have expressed their adherence to these Guidelines. An intriguing feature of the OECD system lies in the establishment of a non-judicial and non-binding mechanism to address individual grievances against corporations. This is done through offices known as National Contact Points, established by all adhering countries at the national level.

The prevalence of soft law regulation in this field, as opposed to binding rules, does not depend on structural limitations of international law but rather on the inability of the international community to agree on more detailed rules concerning the international behavior of corporations. Negotiations for drafting a binding international treaty on business and human rights are currently progressing slowly within an open-ended intergovernmental working group established by the UN Human Rights Council in 2014. If adopted, the instrument is anticipated to impose obligations on enterprises, such as the requirement to conduct human rights due diligence during their business. But the 9th negotiation session, held in October 2023, encountered substantial disagreement among participating States and was adjourned without significant progress.

Nonetheless, it appears that international law is evolving on the matter of corporate obligations. In 2016, an ICSID investment tribunal addressing

[26] Section 2.12 below.

a dispute between a Spanish investor and Argentina allowed the respondent State to file a counterclaim alleging that the investor had violated human rights.[27] The claimant, who held shares in the concessionaire providing water and sewer services in Buenos Aires, complained of damages suffered as a consequence of emergency measures adopted by Argentina to address its financial crisis. Argentina, in turn, argued that the concessionaire's inadequate investment in the concession resulted in infringements of the human right to water and sanitation. While the counterclaim failed on its merits, it is remarkable that the tribunal rejected the view put forward by the investor that human rights obligations are only binding on States and not on non-State actors. The *Urbaser* precedent has been followed in subsequent investment cases.[28]

While this development is significant, it does not negate the importance of more comprehensive international regulation. The *Urbaser* jurisprudence is limited to a particular sector of international law and only concerns counterclaims. This means that the State must already have been sued by an investor to invoke human rights or environmental obligations against the private party.

2.5. Non-Governmental Organizations

Non-governmental organizations (NGOs) constitute another category of actors in IEL that warrants attention. This term encompasses private entities not affiliated with or controlled by governments dedicated to pursuing public interests at the domestic or international levels. These entities are established in accordance with national law, of which they are subjects, and are typically, but not necessarily, non-profit organizations. In fact, according to the definition provided by the OECD, they "*may include profit-making organisations, foundations, educational institutions, churches and other religious groups and missions, medical organisations and hospitals, unions and professional organisations, co-operatives and cultural groups, as well as voluntary agencies*".[29] Well-known NGOs include the International Committee of the Red Cross, the International Olympic Committee, and the Fédération Internationale de Football Association (FIFA).

---

[27] *Urbaser v. Argentina*, ICSID Case No. ARB/07/26, Award, 8 December 2016.

[28] *David Aven v. Costa Rica*, Case No. UNCT/15/3, Final Award, 18 September 2018, with regard to environmental law obligations. See further Chapter 3, Section 3.10.

[29] OECD, *Voluntary aid for development: the role of non-governmental organisations*, 1988, p. 14.

NGOs may undertake a variety of roles in IEL. First of all, as representatives of the interests and views of civil society, they are frequently consulted in the course of international lawmaking processes or other deliberative proceedings. Notably, NGOs may have a role in UN deliberations through the ECOSOC. Article 71 of the UN Charter stipulates that the ECOSOC "*may make suitable arrangements for consultation with non-governmental organizations which are concerned with matters within its competence*". As of 2024, almost 6500 NGOs have been granted consultative status within the ECOSOC, with "general consultative status" reserved for approximately 138 large international NGOs whose activities overlap with all the areas of ECOSOC's interest. NGOs with consultative status can engage in international conferences convened by the UN and in the meetings of these conferences' preparatory bodies.

Another way in which NGOs may express the views of civil society or specific public interests internationally is by submitting *amicus curiae* briefs or other information to international courts and tribunals. For example, the WTO Appellate Body has the authority to accept unsolicited briefs from NGOs in trade disputes before it. These briefs may address issues such as the environmental or human rights impact of the measures under scrutiny.

Several prominent NGOs operate specifically in the economic domain. A notable example is the Swiss-based World Economic Forum (WEF). The WEF is renowned for organizing meetings with and among world leaders, economists, academics and other stakeholders to discuss key issues and challenges in the global economy. The most famous of these gatherings is the annual event held in Davos, Switzerland. Another influential NGO in IEL is the International Chamber of Commerce (ICC), which is headquartered in Paris but has worldwide ramifications. The ICC represents the interests of entrepreneurs by promoting free trade and investment. The ICC International Court of Arbitration stands as the world's leading arbitral institution in international commercial arbitration (that is, arbitration between private businesses), but it also occasionally administers international investment arbitrations.

2.6. An Overview of the Sources of International Law

As clarified at the start of this chapter, legal sources are commonly defined as acts or facts that can give rise to legal obligations. Mirroring our approach to the subjects of IEL, an examination of the sources of IEL needs to be contextualized within the broader framework of the sources of international law.

A typical starting point for the analysis of the sources of international law is furnished by the Statute of the International Court of Justice (ICJ) – an organ of the UN and the most important permanent court in international law, whose key function is to resolve inter-State disputes. The Statute, annexed to the UN Charter of which "*forms an integral part*",[30] regulates the functioning of the Court. Article 38(1) of the Statute, in particular, contains a list of legal sources that the Court applies in its rulings. It provides as follows:

> "*The Court, whose function is to decide in accordance with international law such disputes as are submitted to it, shall apply:*
> *a. international conventions, whether general or particular, establishing rules expressly recognized by the contesting states;*
> *b. international custom, as evidence of a general practice accepted as law;*
> *c. the general principles of law recognized by civilized nations;*
> *d. [...] judicial decisions and the teachings of the most highly qualified publicists of the various nations, as subsidiary means for the determination of rules of law*".

We refer to this provision because it constitutes a convenient starting point for the analysis of international legal sources. Notably, the first two letters refer to the two main sources of international law: international treaties (letter a) and customary international law (letter b). This chapter will also explore the relevance of the other items on the list. While Article 38 only concerns the functioning of the ICJ, the sources listed therein are sources of international law as a whole and are thus relevant to any tribunal, not just the ICJ. For example, the ICSID Convention[31] provides, in Article 42(1), that an ICSID arbitral tribunal

> "*shall decide a dispute in accordance with such rules of law as may be agreed by the parties. In the absence of such agreement, the Tribunal shall apply the law of the Contracting State party to the dispute (including its rules on the conflict of laws)* and such rules of international law as may be applicable" (emphasis added).

As clarified in the Report of the Executive Directors on the ICSID Convention (a highly authoritative source on the interpretation of this treaty), "*the term 'international law' as used in this context should be understood*

[30] Article 92 UN Charter.

[31] See Chapter 3, Section 3.6.

in the sense given to it by Article 38(1) of the Statute of the International Court of Justice, allowance being made for the fact that Article 38 was designed to apply to inter-State disputes".[32]

Three clarifications are needed regarding the actual relevance of Article 38. First, it should be remembered that the sources of international law do *not* derive their bindingness from this provision: they exist independently of the ICJ Statute, and Article 38 confines itself to "photographing" the underlying situation.

Secondly, the list contained in Article 38 is not exhaustive, and international courts and tribunals, including the ICJ itself, commonly apply various other sources that are not included therein. The main reason is that the formulation of Article 38 is quite old, as it reproduces the same article contained in the Statute of the Permanent Court of International Justice, the predecessor of the ICJ in the times of the League of Nations. Therefore, Article 38 of the ICJ Statute does not reflect the evolution experienced by international law in the last century, which has significantly enriched the landscape of relevant international legal sources (as well as subjects, as we saw earlier). But the text of Article 38 leaves the door open to utilizing ulterior sources, insofar as it stresses that the Court decides disputes *in accordance with international law*. The same applies to the aforementioned Article 42(1) of the ICSID Convention.

Thirdly, the list of Article 38 does not reflect any hierarchy among the sources. One should not be led to think, for example, that the source under letter a) (treaties) prevails over the source over letter b) (custom) similar to the way, in national law, a constitution prevails over legislation. The interactions among the sources of international law, as will be seen below, are regulated by different principles, the foremost being the principle of *lex specialis*. The list of Article 38 roughly reflects the order of priority in which legal sources would be applied by a judge.

2.7. International Treaties

The first item in the list of Article 38 of the ICJ Statute is "international conventions", a synonym for international treaties. Treaties constitute by far the most important source of IEL and provide the backbone of most areas of international economic regulation.

This is a type of source that we already met in the course of the preceding chapter. There we saw that the concept of treaty is somewhat similar to

[32] Para. 40.

that of a contract in national law: it is, so to say, a "contract between States". A treaty is only obligatory upon its parties; other States, termed "third States", cannot derive any obligations from treaties they have not concluded. Moreover, as with contracts, participation in treaties is voluntary. For example, just like a contract concluded under threat of physical violence is invalid, a treaty is also invalid where a party has not expressed genuine consent (imagine a treaty concluded by threat or corruption). International organizations can also conclude international treaties with other organizations or both member and non-member States.

It is also important to keep in mind that not all agreements involving States or international organizations are legally binding. The practice of concluding non-legally binding international agreements, which are merely sources of political commitments, has gained significant prominence in contemporary international law, including IEL. Whether or not an agreement is a proper international treaty depends on the intention of the parties. In practice, however, it is not always easy to distinguish, because the intention may not be stated explicitly but result implicitly from the text or the overall circumstances of an agreement's conclusions. What is certain, however, is that the name is not decisive. For example, political agreements are often termed "memorandums of understanding" (MoUs), but a MoU may also qualify as a full-fledged treaty depending on the circumstances.[33]

2.7.1. The Relevance and Interplay of Treaties in International Economic Law

Generally speaking, treaties may be categorized into two broad categories: bilateral and multilateral. Bilateral treaties only have two parties, while multilateral treaties have three or more. Within the latter category, particularly important are regional treaties, which are only open to States from a certain area of the world, and universal treaties, which are in principle open to States from any region of the globe. All these types of treaties are crucial to the regulation of the world economy.

Universal treaties are pivotal to the global regulation of international trade, where they mostly fall under the umbrella of the World Trade Organization (WTO). The constituent treaties of the global financial institutions, like the World Bank or the International Monetary Fund, are also examples of universal treaties.

[33] See Chapter 5, Section 5.3.3.

Regional treaties hold paramount significance within the framework of continental and sub-continental economic integrations. Just like any international organization, also the regional economic integration organizations mentioned above in the chapter[34] are of course established pursuant to one or more international treaties. For example, the European Union has two main founding treaties: the Treaty on the Functioning of the European Union (TFEU, an amended version of the original 1957 Treaty of Rome that created the European Community) and the Treaty on European Union (TEU, the 1992 Treaty of Maastricht). Regional customs union or free trade areas may also come into without the creation of a corresponding international organization. An example was the 1994 North American Free Trade Agreement (NAFTA), which was subsequently replaced by the United States-Mexico-Canada Agreement (USMCA) in 2020. The term "mega-regionals" refers to agreements designed to integrate major trade markets situated in different geographical regions. The most prominent example is the Comprehensive and Progressive Agreement for a Trans-Pacific Partnership (CPTPP), concluded among a number of States bordering the Pacific Ocean. The CPTPP was concluded after the failure of negotiations for the Trans-Pacific Partnership (TPP), originally intended to include the United States, when the US declared its withdrawal in 2017. Another megaregional agreement, the Trans-Atlantic Trade and Investment Partnership (TTIP), has been under negotiation between the US and the EU, but the negotiations were temporarily halted and remain so as of 2024.

Finally, bilateral treaties are especially relevant in the field of investment protection. International investment law arises primarily from a myriad of international agreements concluded by States on the matter of the reciprocal promotion and protection of investments (so-called international investment agreements, or IIAs). The vast majority of such treaties have been concluded between two States only, hence the name Bilateral Investment Treaties (BITs). Over 2200 BITs are in force as of 2024.[35] Other common examples of bilateral economic treaties are double taxation treaties (DTTs), by which two countries agree not to tax the same income twice. Without DTTs, income earned in a country different from the country of residence would risk being taxed by both.

With such a high number of treaties in force and considering that the scope of treaties may be extremely wide-ranging, it should not be surprising that States may undertake conflicting treaty obligations in economic or

[34] Section 2.3.2.

[35] All data is available at https://investmentpolicy.unctad.org/. Over 370 treaties with investment provisions (TIPs) are also in force.

economy-related matters. Imagine, for instance, two States having committed to a reciprocal liberalization of trade and investment through a bilateral treaty. Sometime later, by the effect of economic sanctions adopted by the UN Security Council, which are binding under Article 41 of the UN Charter,[36] international trade with one of these two States is effectively prohibited. Should the other State live up to its obligations under the bilateral treaty or the UN Charter?

The matter of treaty conflicts is particularly complex, as there are no universal rules that can unambiguously resolve all instances of conflicts. However, treaties themselves frequently provide indications as to how these conflicts should be addressed. In our example the State will be required to prioritize the UN Security Council's sanctions regime, because Article 103 of the UN Charter provides that obligations under the Charter prevail over any other treaty in case of conflict. Another example of treaty provision managing possible conflicts with other treaties is Article XXIV of the General Agreement on Tariffs and Trade (GATT), allowing member States to create regional free trade areas in derogation of certain GATT obligations, most notably the Most-Favored Nation (MFN) clause of Article I GATT. The MFN clause requires, as a general rule, that any trade concession to one member State should automatically apply, if more favorable, to any other GATT member. However, treaties establishing regional free trade areas, such as the one created within the European Union, do not envisage extending privileges to other States, as doing so would defeat the very purpose of establishing a regional free trade area. The risk of conflict is defused by Article XXIV, which exonerates from extending free trade privileges to States outside the free trade area.[37] The rules of treaty interpretation, which will be discussed in the following section, also play a role in addressing treaty conflicts, particularly where the issue is not resolved by dedicated treaty provisions.

While it was said above that treaties are conceptually similar to contracts, it is important to mark the distinction between the two types of acts. All aspects of a contract's life – the rules concerning its conclusion, its interpretation, the consequences of its breach, its termination, etc. – are regulated by the applicable national law, not by international law. States and international organizations can also conclude contracts when they negotiate with private entities. In particular, State contracts concluded with foreign parties are widespread in international economic interactions, particularly in the fields of foreign direct investments, concessions,

[36] Section 2.3.3 above.

[37] See Chapter 4, Sections 4.5.4 and 4.11.3.

or trade in goods and services. These contracts are not international treaties and their violation is normally not a breach of international law. Nonetheless, the situation may be different where specific international rules require respect for a contract. A typical example is provided by so-called "umbrella clauses" which are often included in BITs.[38] Through these clauses, any commitments undertaken by the host State towards foreign investors, including contractual commitments, could be brought under the protective "umbrella" of the BIT. Consequently, investors could be able to complain about contract breaches as if they were BIT violations.

2.7.2. The Interpretation of International Economic Treaties

International law regulates all aspects of the life of treaties – what is needed for them to become binding, how their text should be interpreted, validity requirements, the consequences of their breach, how they may be terminated, etc. Many of the rules concerning treaties are collected in a fundamental instrument named Vienna Convention on the Law of Treaties (VCLT) of 1969. While itself an international treaty, the VCLT is commonly held to largely reflect customary international law[39] and is thus binding on all States regardless of participation in the VCLT itself.

A central aspect of the law of treaties is the rules on treaty interpretation, essentially methodological tools for ascertaining the meaning of treaty provisions. This issue may be particularly complex in economic matters, not just because treaty clauses are often worded in broad, vague or ambiguous ways, reflecting disagreements and difficult compromises among the States involved in the negotiations, but also, more simply, because the language employed in economic treaties is often highly technical.

The matter of treaty interpretation is regulated in Articles 31 to 33 of the VCLT. These principles are commonly applied to treaty interpretation in IEL. For example, the Dispute Settlement Understanding – an annex to the WTO Agreement regulating the settlement of inter-State trade disputes – expressly provides at Article 3.2 that the WTO dispute settlement system "*serves […] to clarify the existing provisions of those agreements in accordance with customary rules of interpretation of public international law*". This is an implied reference to the VCLT rules on treaty interpretation. The WTO Appellate Body has indeed clarified on multiple occasions that Arti-

---

[38] See Chapter 3, Section 3.3.6.

[39] Section 2.8.1 below.

cles 31, 32 and 33 of the VCLT belong to the "*customary rules of interpretation of public international law*".[40] Articles 31 to 33 of the VCLT are also commonly employed by investment tribunals to construe the meaning of BITs and other investment agreements.

The key provision in matters of treaty interpretation is Article 31(1) of the VCLT, which provides that "*a treaty shall be interpreted in good faith in accordance with the ordinary meaning to be given to the terms of the treaty in their context and in the light of its object and purpose*". The three criteria enshrined in this rule – literal, contextual and purposive interpretation – should always be employed jointly in interpretation, as the VCLT establishes no hierarchy between them. Article 31 also provides, at para. 3, that the interpreter shall take into account *a)* "*any subsequent agreement between the parties regarding the interpretation of the treaty […]*" and *b)* "*any subsequent practice in the application of the treaty which establishes the agreement of the parties regarding its interpretation*". This highlights that the States parties to a treaty may condition its interpretation (so-called "authentic interpretation"), if there exists an express or implied agreement among them as regards the meaning to be given to a treaty provision. Of paramount importance is the rule under Article 31(3)(c), according to which "*any relevant rules of international law applicable in the relations between the parties*" shall be taken into account (principle of "systemic integration"). This opens the door to coordination with other rules of IEL, both treaty and customary, that may be binding on the parties, thus serving as a tool to resolve conflicts between treaties by interpretive means. For example, this principle may be relevant whenever a State is a party to a multilateral trade agreement which overlaps to some extent with the BITs concluded by that State. The principle of systemic integration applies to the relationship between IEL and other areas of international law as well, including human rights obligations. The WTO Appellate Body has stated that the GATT "*is not to be read in clinical isolation from public international law*".[41]

The rule of treaty interpretation found in Article 32 of the VCLT also deserves attention. This provision allows reliance on "*supplementary means of interpretation, including the preparatory work of the treaty and the circumstances of its conclusion*", to confirm an interpretation reached through

---

[40] For example, *US – Gasoline*, Report of the Appellate Body, 29 April 1996, WT/DS2/AB/R, p. 17, with regard to Article 31(1); *US – Carbon Steel*, Report of the Appellate Body, 28 November 2002, WT/DS213/AB/R, paras. 61-62, with regard to Articles 31 and 32.

[41] *US – Gasoline*, 29 April 1996, WT/DS2/AB/R (note 40), p. 17.

Article 31 or in cases where Article 31 has led to inconclusive or obscure outcomes. The "preparatory work of the treaty" – to which Article 32 refers as the main example of "supplementary means" – is commonly termed *travaux préparatoires*. This term refers to the records of the treaty negotiations. Reliance on the *travaux* can be decisive, especially in the case of cryptic treaty terms.

For example, in the *Churchill Mining* case, the investment tribunal had to establish the meaning of Article 7(1) of the UK-Indonesia BIT, which provided that the State "shall assent" to requests of arbitration filed by investors of the other party. This wording was highly unusual for a BIT. In BITs, States normally provide their advance consent to future investment arbitrations, thus allowing foreign investors to commence arbitrations against them at will.[42] Article 7(1), however, did not clearly provide this unconditional consent. One of its possible readings was that it required consent from the State *after* the investor had initiated the dispute, thus leaving the State full discretion whether to assent or not. Because the application of Article 31 VCLT did not clarify the matter, the tribunal analyzed the *travaux préparatoires* of the BIT and concluded that the drafters of the treaty did not mean to introduce any uncommon requirements concerning consent. For this reason, the tribunal interpreted the words "shall consent" as "*functionally equivalent to 'hereby consents' or similar wording*".[43]

2.8. Customary International Law

Customary international law, the second source listed in Article 38 of the ICJ Statute, is more conceptually challenging than treaties. It refers to legal principles and rules which are unwritten and arise from the generalized practice of States. The concept of custom is not peculiar to international law. However, in national legal systems, customs have lost most of their relevance in favor of written law. In international law, by contrast, custom still represents one of the most important legal sources. This is due to many factors, one of them being that the lack of a centralized international lawmaker (a "world Parliament" of sorts) has made it impossible for written law to entirely replace unwritten law. Also, as will be seen below, customary law performs essential systemic roles in the international legal order.

---

[42] See Chapter 3, Section 3.7.

[43] *Churchill Mining Plc. v. Indonesia*, ICSID Case No. ARB/12/14 and 12/40, Decision on Jurisdiction, 24 February 2014, para. 230.

2.8.1. Elements and Basic Features of International Customs

The main legal feature of international custom is that it binds all States regardless of their express or tacit acceptance. For this reason, custom belongs to what is known as "general international law". The irrelevance of acceptance is highlighted by the fact that newborn States are bound by preexisting customs.

Article 38 describes customary law as "*evidence of a general practice accepted as law*". This definition gives us insights into how to ascertain the existence of a rule of customary international law. To this end, two elements are required: "general practice" and "acceptance as law" (*opinio juris*). A behavior, in other words, must be followed (that is, repeated over time) by the generality of States, and States must do so because they see this practice as required by law. This is crucial because not everything States do, however widespread, reflects a legal duty. For instance, when States grant each other economic aid, they frequently make sure to stress that they are doing so out of courtesy and not out of a sense of legal obligation. These declarations have the effect of preventing the formation of a customary rule requiring States to provide economic aid to other States in need. Generally speaking, relevant State practice for the formation of customary rules may arise from anything done by State organs, including executive statements, diplomatic correspondence, decisions of national courts, joint statements in a variety of political settings, resolutions adopted by States within the framework of international organizations, etc.

Considering the above, ascertaining the existence and exact content of rules of customary international law might seem like a hard task, which undoubtedly can be. However, this process is often facilitated by the existence of legal texts which largely reproduce in written form the content of relevant customary rules. The process of writing down unwritten legal rules is known as "codification" and is important primarily to enhance legal certainty. The UN Charter provides, at Article 13(1), that the UN General Assembly "*shall initiate studies and make recommendations for the purpose of [...] encouraging the progressive development of international law and its codification*". In order to exercise this task, the General Assembly has created a subsidiary organ called the International Law Commission (ILC), which is composed of experts in international law. After extensive surveys of existing State practice, the ILC drafts codification texts which are frequently transformed by the General Assembly into veritable treaties open to ratification by States. An example of codification treaty is the aforementioned 1969 VCLT, whose provisions are held to largely reflect the content of the customary rules on the law of treaties. Courts and tribunals commonly rely on codification texts as "shortcuts" for determining the content of customary international law. It should be noted that codification texts can, in turn, influence the content of custom, particularly when the existence or content of a customary rule are contentious. Indeed, codification can influence State behavior and bring uniformity to State practice, over time causing an evolution in customary international law. This is why Article 13 of the UN Charter mentions not only "codification" but also "progressive development" of customary law.

Many major rules of international law have a customary nature. Notable examples are the principle of territorial sovereignty, whereby every State has exclusive sovereignty over its territory; rules on the treatment of representatives of foreign States, which include the immunity of diplomatic agents; or the prohibition of serious breaches of fundamental human rights, such as genocide, war crimes and crimes against humanity.

Significant rules of customary law also exist in IEL, although this source has a lesser importance to this sector than international treaties. For example, it is well-established that, under customary international law, every State has the freedom to choose its political, economic and social system.[44] In the economic field, a State may opt for a market economy, a socialist economy or any other system it sees fit. This freedom derives from a basic principle of customary law, the principle of non-intervention in the internal affairs of other States, which is itself a corollary of the aforementioned principle of territorial sovereignty.

Other undisputed norms of customary law in the economic field are the rules on the treatment of foreign citizens, which have already been discussed to an extent earlier in the chapter.[45] These rules, which originated centuries ago and are still in force today, provide basic legal protections for the assets of foreign citizens, including their investments. It is provided, for example, that foreigners' assets can only be expropriated or nationalized in the presence of a public interest, and that the expropriating State must in any case pay compensation (even though there is some debate as to the amount of compensation that is required under customary law).

2.8.2. The Interplay between Treaties and Customs in International Economic Law

What happens when the content of a treaty conflicts with a rule of customary international law? Because, as mentioned in the Introduction, there is

[44] *Military and Paramilitary Activities in and against Nicaragua* (note 5), para. 258.

[45] Section 2.4.1 above.

no hierarchy between treaties and customs, conflicts do not result in invalidity, as is the case in national law for conflicts between the Constitution and legislation. Instead, they only require establishing which rule should take priority in application.

The most important criterion in this matter is the principle *lex specialis derogat generali*, according to which more specific rules are to be applied in lieu of more general rules. This rule implies that treaties, which establish a "special" regime only applicable to their own parties, will be applied instead of customary rules, which have a general character. The customary rule, of course, will continue applying among the States that are not parties to the treaty, as well as in the relations between parties and non-parties. Moreover, should the treaty cease to be in force for whatever reason, the customary rule will regain applicability for the former parties to the treaty. This shows that customary international law is primarily a "default" regime which applies in the lack of treaty rules.

In IEL, this relationship may be exemplified by observing the position of international law towards the States' choice of their own economic system. As mentioned earlier, customary law safeguards State freedom in this area. However, many international economic agreements guarantee or presuppose a market economy at least to some degree. These agreements, for instance, may put limitations on State monopolies, stipulating that trade in goods or services must be open to private entities. This implies that the State cannot be the only actor in the economy, thus derogating from the general freedom and effectively requiring States to open their markets to private actors. The main example of this is the system established within the European Union: EU Member States are required to be market economies. But the default regime of State freedom continues to apply in the absence of specific treaty derogations. For example, possession of a market economy is notably not required by the WTO. Romania, Poland and Hungary joined the GATT at a time when they were socialist States, between the 1960s and the 1970s. Special rules were put in place to address the distortions to international trade caused by the State's dominance over those countries' economies ("Anti-Dumping" rules), without however preventing participation in the WTO system. More recently, the accession of China in 2001 required introducing specific obligations ("WTO-plus obligations") and other WTO Members were allowed to treat China as a "non-market economy" (NME), which permitted differential treatment of Chinese goods. It is controversial whether, as China claims, NME status should have expired in 2016 pursuant to China's WTO Accession Protocol. Several WTO Members, including the EU, reject this interpretation and still consider China to retain NME status.

Two caveats are required as regards the relationship between treaties and custom. First, the principle according to which there is no hierarchy between the two sources finds an exception with respect to a limited number of customary rules, known as *ius cogens*, which admit no derogation by treaty in that they safeguard fundamental values of the international community. The prohibition of the use of force, the prohibition of genocide, slavery and torture, or the principle of self-determination of peoples provide universally accepted examples of *ius cogens*. Any treaty conflicting with these rules would be invalid and without legal effects. These limitations apply across the spectrum of international law, including IEL. For example, it would be a breach of *ius cogens* if two or more States concluded a treaty committing to use military force against another State to recover sums owed by that State to their own nationals. These instances of armed diplomatic protection[46] were commonplace in the past, at a time international law did not outlaw the use of force. An example is the Venezuelan crisis of 1902-1903, when the United Kingdom, Germany and Italy imposed a naval blockade on Venezuela to force it to repay its public debt and compensations owed to their nationals.

The second caveat relates to the role of custom in IEL. Providing default rules for cases where no treaty has been concluded is, of course, a much relevant function of customary rules, because many inter-State relations are not regulated by treaty. For instance, we saw earlier that there are over 2200 BITs in force. While this might look like a huge number, it is still significantly smaller than the number of possible pairings among the nearly 200 existing States. Thus, in the majority of inter-State bilateral relations, there will be no BIT to apply. Considering that other, non-bilateral treaties containing investment provisions are also limited in number, in many cases the customary rules on the treatment of foreign nationals will be the only international rules applicable in matters of foreign investments.

However, the principle of *lex specialis* does not capture the full importance of customary international law. This is because treaties are almost never self-sufficient. They often incorporate legal concepts borrowed from customary law; defining the content of such concepts will thus require looking into the underlying custom. For instance, it is commonplace for BITs to prohibit discrimination, without however clarifying in detail what a discriminatory treatment is. The corpus of general international law may be relied on to clarify, pursuant to the aforementioned principle of systemic integration.[47]

---

[46] On this concept see Section 2.4.1 above.

[47] Section 2.7.2.

2.9. General Principles

In international law, the expression "general principles" is commonly employed to refer to two different categories of sources: "general principles of law recognized by civilized nations", which is the third item (letter c) in the list of sources of Article 38(1) of the ICJ Statute; and "general principles of international law". Both types of principles, as will be seen, play important functions in IEL.

2.9.1. General Principles Common to Domestic Legal Systems

The formulation of Article 38(1)(c) – "*general principles of law recognized by civilized nations*" – is not crystal-clear and shows its age, as it is the result of a compromise reached in 1920 among different positions expressed by the drafters of the Statute of the PCIJ, the predecessor of the ICJ. The drafters were discussing ways for empowering the Court to decide cases even where no treaty or customary rules existed. Letter c) was intended to allow the Court to fill gaps by resorting to legal principles in use in the majority of national legal systems. A clearer and more modern nomenclature of this source can be found in the 1998 Rome Statute of the International Criminal Court, which defines it as "*general principles of law derived [...] from national laws of legal systems of the world*". Of course, it would be quite unrealistic to check out *all* of the world's national legal systems to search for a legal principle. What is required is a comparative analysis – that is, the principle should be employed in a diverse number of legal systems representing "the different regions of the world".[48] In judicial practice, all that is commonly required is that a legal principle exists in both common law and civil law legal systems. An example of such a principle is *res judicata*, which prevents from re-adjudicating a matter that has already been the object of a final decision by a court or tribunal.

General principles play an important role in IEL, particularly in cases where a certain matter has not received comprehensive regulation through treaties or custom. In these instances, the function of general principles might be nothing short of law-creation, as they may introduce new legal concepts – originating from domestic law – into international law.

For example, the WTO Appellate Body resorted to general principles in order to clarify the burden of proof in proceedings before it. It ruled that

---

[48] ILC, *General principles of law, Draft conclusions adopted on first reading*, 2023, Draft Conclusion 5(2).

"*it is a generally-accepted canon of evidence in civil law, common law and, in fact, most jurisdictions*" that the party asserting a claim or fact should provide evidence (*onus probandi incumbit ei qui dicit*).[49]

Another example, this time from the field of international investment law, can be drawn from the *Amco v. Indonesia* arbitration. Having established that Indonesia breached international law by revoking the investor's license without a public purpose, the tribunal had to determine the amount of damages owed to the investor. After an examination of select legal systems of both civil law and common law, the tribunal concluded that the "*full compensation of prejudice, by awarding to the injured party the* damnum emergens *and* lucrum cessans *is a principle common to the main systems of municipal law, and therefore, a general principle of law which may be considered as a source of international law*". In other words, it held that compensation must cover both the actual losses and the loss of foreseeable profits.

2.9.2. General Principles of International Law

In international law, the expression "general principles of law" is used to refer to another category of principles as well: the "general principles of international law" or, according to the language employed by the ILC, "general principles of law formed within the international legal system".[50] These principles differ from those analyzed in the previous section because they are not derived from national legal systems but from international law itself.

The key to understanding this source is the concept of inductive reasoning. In logic, "induction" involves making generalizations based on specific instances; in law, deriving a general principle out of a set of specific rules or norms. While the principle may not be expressed, it nonetheless underpins the whole legal framework and constitutes its logical basis. The relevance of such principles is twofold. Not only do they perform a function similar to the general principles of law derived from domestic legal systems (the function of "filling gaps" in international law, where there is no applicable treaty or custom), but they also help interpret and apply international obligations in the correct way, possibly allowing to evolve, update or rectify their meaning and scope in the light of their underlying rationale.

---

[49] *US – Wool Shirts and Blouses*, Report of the Appellate Body, 25 April 1997, WT/DS33/AB/R, p. 14.

[50] ILC, *General principles of law, Draft conclusions adopted on first reading*, 2023 (note 48), Draft Conclusion 7.

For example, many norms of international law incorporate the concept of good faith. We saw earlier that the general rule of treaty interpretation under Article 31 of the VCLT provides, among other things, that "*a treaty shall be interpreted in good faith [...]*". The VCLT also provides, in Article 26, that treaties "*must be performed [...] in good faith*". From these and other norms, one may derive that good faith is a general principle of international law that governs the application and interpretation of all international obligations. Furthermore, it is also possible that a general principle develops within one specific international law sector because it underpins that sector's rules only. It has been argued, for example, that the Fair and Equitable Treatment (FET) standard[51] constitutes a general principle specific to international investment law.[52]

The status of certain general principles may be controversial. This is understandable because there is a subjective element to inductive reasoning: different people may read the same practice differently. For example, commentators have differing views on the concept of abuse of rights, the idea that States should not use their rights under international law for purposes different from those for which the rights were created. While some consider this principle a corollary of the general principle of good faith,[53] others deny any role to it in international law.[54] Nonetheless, this principle seems to have acquired extensive acceptance in IEL. Notably, the WTO Appellate Body has opined that "*the principle of good faith [...], at once a general principle of law and a general principle of international law, controls the exercise of rights by states. One application of this general principle [is] [...] widely known as the doctrine of* abus de droit".[55]

Investment tribunals have also referred to this principle, particularly in the context of abuses of procedural rights. One example is the *Philipp Morris v. Australia* case. This case represented Philipp Morris' attempt to sue Australia over its enactment of tobacco control legislation (so-called "plain-packaging" requirement). Philipp Morris claimed that its brand had lost much of its economic value in Australia and considered the legislation tantamount to an expropriation of its intellectual property rights. Philipp

[51] On which see Chapter 3, Section 3.3.2.

[52] F.M. Palombino, *Fair and Equitable Treatment and the Fabric of General Principles*, Asser Press, 2018.

[53] Bin Cheng, *General Principles of Law as Applied by International Courts and Tribunals*, Stevens & Sons, 1953, p. 121.

[54] J. Paulsson, *The Unruly Notion of Abuse of Rights*, CUP, 2020.

[55] *US – Shrimp*, Report of the Appellate Body, 12 October 1998, WT/DS58/AB/R, para. 158.

Morris had initially invested in Australia through a Swiss subsidiary, but the lack of a BIT between Switzerland and Australia meant that it was impossible to have recourse to arbitration. To overcome this hurdle, Philipp Morris proceeded to a corporate restructuring, bringing its Australian branch under the ownership of a Hong Kong subsidiary, and launched arbitration based on the Hong Kong-Australia BIT. The tribunal declined jurisdiction[56] by holding that "*the initiation of a treaty-based investor-State arbitration constitutes an abuse of rights […] when an investor has changed its corporate structure to gain the protection of an investment treaty at a point in time when a specific dispute was foreseeable*".[57]

2.10. Decisions of Courts and Tribunals

The fourth and last letter in the list of Article 38(1) refers to two types of "subsidiary means for the determination of rules of law": judicial decisions and "*the most highly qualified*" legal scholarship. The expression "subsidiary means" indicates that these two items cannot be used as the only authority to decide a case. They can only help uncover the content of "primary" sources such as treaties or customs. For example, if a court or a highly renowned expert of IEL has argued that a certain customary rule exists, courts may rely on this in subsequent cases to corroborate the existence of that rule.

This requires some clarification. Whenever an international court or tribunal renders a judgment over a dispute, that judgment is legally binding for the parties to the dispute. In this respect, the judgment is not a subsidiary source for them but it directly produces legal obligations under international law. For example, Article 94 of the UN Charter provides that "*[e]ach Member of the United Nations undertakes to comply with the decision of the International Court of Justice in any case to which it is a party*". The ICSID Convention provides in Article 53 that ICSID awards (the final decisions of the arbitral tribunal) shall be binding on the parties. The same applies to any award rendered in investment arbitrations before non-ICSID tribunals.[58] Dispute settlement within the WTO also results in binding outcomes for the parties once the reports of the panels or the Appellate Body are adopted by the Dispute Settlement Body.

---

[56] On this notion see Chapter 3, Section 3.8.

[57] *Philipp Morris Asia Ltd. v. Australia*, PCA Case No. 2012-12, 17 December 2015, para. 554.

[58] See Chapter 3, Section 3.11.

The expression "subsidiary means" refers instead to the effects of judicial decisions outside of the specific dispute in which they were rendered – that is, their effects on non-parties to the dispute or the parties to the dispute in different cases. Notably, Article 59 of the ICJ Statute clearly stipulates that "*[t]he decision of the Court has no binding force except between the parties and in respect of that particular case*". This provision highlights that, in international law, judicial precedent has no binding force. This means that courts or tribunals are not obligated to follow legal interpretations given in previous rulings by themselves or other courts. A similar obligation, known in Latin as *stare decisis*, is, in principle, typical of legal systems of common law (but even there it comes with significant exceptions).

However, judicial precedents' role is more central to international law than would appear from Article 38. It is important to keep in mind that, while there is no legal obligation to follow precedents, there is no prohibition to do so either. In practice, references to the body of case law developed by courts and tribunals are pivotal to international legal reasoning. International courts and tribunals commonly refer to judicial precedents – both "internal" (a court's own precedents) and "external" (precedents of other judicial bodies). For instance, whenever an ICJ judgment ascertains the existence of a rule of customary international law, the Court will likely cite that judgment in future cases to justify applying that rule ("internal" precedent). In its turn, ICJ jurisprudence is frequently cited by other international courts and tribunals, too, which tend to defer to the Court's highly authoritative interpretation of international norms ("external" precedent). This should not be surprising because a legal framework where precedents are systematically ignored or disregarded may be seen as unpredictable and incoherent.

The practice of international investment tribunals proves particularly instructive in this regard. Because investment tribunals are created to decide over specific disputes, there is no hierarchy among them and no overarching investment court that can ensure consistency in their interpretations of the law. Against this backdrop, investment tribunals have sometimes attracted criticism for delivering conflicting decisions on similar matters. For example, various ICSID tribunals expressed differing views on whether a serious economic crisis experienced by Argentina constituted a "state of necessity" that allowed derogation from foreign investors' rights under international law.[59] Tribunals have also disagreed on whether MFN

---

[59] Compare *CMS Gas Transmission Company v. Argentina*, ICSID Case No. ARB/01/8, Award, 12 May 2005, answering in the negative, with *LG&E v. Argentina*, ICSID Case No. ARB/02/1, Decision on Liability, 3 October 2006.

clauses in BITs only apply to substantive standards of treatment or also cover more favorable dispute settlement arrangements, including permitting recourse to arbitration where a BIT is silent on the matter.[60] In response to criticism, however, investment tribunals have grown more sympathetic toward precedents. For example, a 2020 award acknowledged that "*it is desirable, in general, to foster the development of a* jurisprudence constante *based on previous decisions, not only as a means of providing certain predictability to the parties but also as a response to an ongoing demand for more consistency within the international investment system [...]*".[61] It is now widely recognized that tribunals should at least consider previous cases on similar matters while remaining free to depart from them should valid reasons apply. This is sometimes described as the "taking into account" approach.

The WTO Appellate Body initially developed a comparable approach. In 1996, it affirmed that, even though "*they are not binding, except with respect to resolving the particular dispute between the parties to that dispute*", nonetheless "*[a]dopted panel reports [...] are often considered by subsequent panels. They create legitimate expectations among WTO Members, and, therefore, should be taken into account where they are relevant to any dispute*".[62] Later on, however, it seemingly increased the precedential value of its decisions by stating that "absent cogent reasons, an adjudicatory body will resolve the same legal question in the same way in a subsequent case".[63] This innovation, described as aiming to ensure "stability and predictability" in the resolution of trade disputes, attracted criticism for covertly introducing a doctrine of *stare decisis* into the WTO dispute settlement system.[64] The United States criticized this approach as "judicial overreach" and invoked it as one of the justifications for blocking the appointment of new Appellate Body members.[65]

---

[60] See Chapter 3, Section 3.3.4.

[61] *Lee Chin v. Dominican Republic*, ICSID Case No. UNCT/18/3, Partial Award on Jurisdiction, 15 July 2020, para. 80.

[62] *Japan – Alcoholic Beverages*, Report of the Appellate Body, 4 October 1996, WT/DS8/AB/R, WT/DS10/AB/R, WT/DS11/AB/R, p. 14.

[63] *United States – Stainless Steel*, Report of the Appellate Body, 30 April 2008, WT/DS344/AB/R, para. 160.

[64] For example, J. Miranda, M.S. Miranda, "Chronicle of a Crisis Foretold: How the WTO Appellate Body Drove Itself into a Corner", in *Journal of International Criminal Justice*, 2023, p. 435 ff.

[65] See Chapter 4, Section 4.9.6.

2.11. Acts of International Organizations

As already mentioned, Article 38 of the ICJ Statute does not contain a comprehensive list of the sources of international law. It is now important to briefly address an important category of legal sources not included therein, namely that of acts issued by international organizations.

The acts belonging to this category are extremely diverse in that their names, structures and legal effects vary widely between different organizations. Still, a common element is that they are all created by organs of international organizations in accordance with procedures normally established in the constituent treaties. Not all acts adopted by international organizations are legally binding in international law. Most of them, notably including UN General Assembly resolutions, fall within the "soft law" category.[66] However, the constituent treaties may empower organizations to adopt acts binding upon member States. In this case, the acts in question constitute veritable formal sources of international law. An example we have already discussed is the economic sanctions adopted by the UN Security Council under Article 41 of the UN Charter.[67]

The international organization possessing the most wide-ranging law-making powers, including in the economic field, is undoubtedly the European Union. According to the EU founding treaties, EU organs are empowered to adopt three main acts: regulations, directives, and decisions. A regulation, the most important and characteristic type of act, is binding for all member States and is directly applicable throughout the EU, not unlike legislation produced at the national level. "Directly applicable" denotes that regulations create rights and obligations for individuals and can be invoked before national courts. Therefore, after the adoption of a regulation, States need not take any other steps to implement it and are simply required to apply it. A directive, by contrast, typically requires Member States to achieve an objective within a certain time frame. In this case implementation is required, so that every State must adopt national legislation to give effect to the directive. Finally, while regulations and directives both provide general rules, a decision refers to specific situations and can be addressed at individual States or even at private individuals. For example, a decision can block the merger of two companies if required under EU competition law. These three acts are collectively known as "secondary law", the founding treaties being the "primary law" of the EU.

Despite their differences, all these EU acts are equally binding. The ap-

---

[66] See Section 2.12 below.

[67] Section 2.3.3.

plication of both primary and secondary EU law is governed by the fundamental principle of primacy (or supremacy) of EU law, according to which conflicts between EU law and the national laws of member States are always resolved in favor of EU law. Nor do the three types of secondary law differ in the procedures for their adoption, which always involve the same EU organs. Under normal circumstances, legislation is proposed by the EU Commission and adopted by the EU Parliament and the Council of the EU. The latter organ comprises ministers of the EU Member States, which may be competent by subject matter. Compliance with EU legislation on the part of States, private individuals and the EU institutions themselves is ensured by the Court of Justice of the EU, a court with sweeping powers. Among other things, the EU Court of Justice can issue binding preliminary rulings, upon request by the national courts of EU Member States, over the interpretation and validity of EU law.

Besides addressing economic matters internal to the EU, including anything related to the realization of the "single market", EU legislation is often concerned with international economic relations external to the EU. One example is Regulation (EU) 1219/2012 establishing transitional arrangements for bilateral investment agreements between EU and non-EU countries. This regulation aimed to manage the transition towards a system where BITs with non-EU countries would be negotiated by the EU and not by individual Member States. Other recent examples include EU Regulation 2019/452, which entered into force in October 2020, that has established a common regulatory framework (based on the introduction of national "screening" mechanisms) for the admission of extra-EU foreign direct investments into EU Member States; and Regulation (EU) 2023/2675, which has created a framework for countering forms of economic coercion by third countries directed at the Union or its member States.

2.12. Soft Law

In international economic relations, significant importance is attributed to what is commonly known as "soft law". Soft law operates beyond the traditional boundaries of the formal sources of international law. This term encompasses a diverse array of acts characterized by two basic features. First and foremost, these acts lack formal binding force and thus cannot be enforced through legal means – hence the term "soft", contrasting with "hard" international law such as treaties or custom. Second, despite their non-binding nature, these acts are relevant from a legal standpoint because they wield influence over the subjects and actors of international law, shaping their behavior in ways that, in practice, may closely resemble the impact of "hard law". Even the appearance of soft law acts mirrors that of traditional legal sources. Indeed, they are typically formulated as legal instruments, articulated into articles, paragraphs and commas and possibly including expressions of command. These instruments go by various names, such as guidelines, recommendations, understandings, or codes of conduct.

The relevance of soft law remains a perpetual subject of debate among international law scholars. Some contend that it is simply not "real" law or even deem it entirely undesirable,[68] while others argue that, despite being non-binding and unenforceable, soft law possesses normativity akin to hard law. This debate is influenced by the theoretical and ideological viewpoints of each scholar. What is certain, in any event, is that soft law significantly influences social behavior in practice, either because its addressees consider it as *de facto* binding or because they voluntarily choose to comply with it. Additionally, soft law acts are frequently cited and applied by judges and arbitrators, either as "self-standing" instruments or as aids in interpreting formal sources of law.

Explaining why this occurs is complex. As one commentator aptly put it, "*[a] number of reasons, better articulated by psychologists than by lawyers, account for this behaviour. They include mainly such considerations as a sense of respect for the authority of the 'soft lawmaker', social conformism, convenience, the search for predictability and certainty, the desire to belong to a group, and the fear of naming and shaming*".[69] Probably the main factor explaining the relevance of a certain soft law instrument is the prestige of the body that produced it: the higher its reputation, the more influential the instrument will be in international practice.

A good illustration of this process is found in the declarations of the UN General Assembly. Unlike the Security Council, the General Assembly generally lacks binding powers. However, its resolutions often exert a significant impact on State practice. States tend to align their conduct with the content of these resolutions, which can have profound implications for international "hard law". For example, the Universal Declaration of Human Rights (UDHR), adopted by the UN General Assembly in 1948, played a pivotal role in the birth of an entirely new sector of international law – international human rights law. Over time, the content of the UDHR was incorporated into binding treaties, and a large portion of it became part of

---

[68] J. Klabbers, "The Undesirability of Soft Law", in *Nordic Journal of International Law*, 1998, p. 381 ff.

[69] G. Kaufmann-Kohler, "Soft Law in International Arbitration: Codification and Normativity", in *Journal of International Dispute Settlement*, 2010, p. 283 ff., pp. 284-285.

customary international law. The UDHR is also frequently cited by courts and tribunals at both the national and international levels.

In IEL, soft law acts may primarily be issued by international organizations. As discussed in the preceding section, while some international organizations have the authority to adopt binding acts, most of their acts are not legally binding and should thus be classified as soft law. We discussed a few examples of soft law instruments in the previous chapter within the context of attempts to regulate the conduct of private businesses. Soft law in this area includes the UN Guiding Principles on Business and Human Rights (UNGPs) and the OECD Guidelines for Multinational Enterprises on Responsible Business Conduct.[70] Another example of soft law is the "Santiago Principles" adopted by the IMF's International Working Group of Sovereign Wealth Funds (IWG) in 2008, which collects guidelines and best practices for sovereign wealth funds (SWFs). Many SWFs have voluntarily adhered to the Santiago Principles, including, for example, China's China Investment Corporation, UAE's Abu Dhabi Investment Authority or Italy's Cassa Depositi e Prestiti (CDP Equity SpA).

The UN Commission on International Trade Law (UNCITRAL), a subsidiary body of the UN General Assembly, plays a crucial role in producing soft law in the economic sector. A notable example is the UNCITRAL Model Law on International Commercial Arbitration, intended to serve as a "blueprint" for national legislation on commercial arbitration (i.e., arbitration between private businesses). National lawmakers may choose to draw inspiration from or simply replicate the content of the Model Law.

Private parties, including professional or academic associations and NGOs, also contribute to the production of soft law. All arbitral institutions, including the International Chamber of Commerce (ICC),[71] have adopted their own rules regulating all procedural aspects of the arbitration.[72] Parties are free to choose any set of rules they deem suitable. In the alternative, parties may also opt for the UNCITRAL Arbitration Rules, which are especially popular in (both commercial and investment) *ad hoc* arbitrations. The ICC also publishes the widely used International Commercial Terms (Incoterms), which includes a glossary for interpreting common terms in the language of international trade and commerce and a set of rules from which the parties may choose to allocate costs between the seller and the buyer. Other examples of soft law instruments adopted by a private association include the Rules on the Taking of Evidence in International Arbitration and the Guide-

---

[70] See Section 2.4.3 above.

[71] Section 2.5 above.

[72] See Chapter 3, Section 3.6.2.

lines on Conflicts of Interest in International Arbitration, both approved by the International Bar Association (IBA). These instruments hold great importance in arbitral practice, as they frequently serve as guidelines for arbitrators in exercising their powers during arbitrations.

References

Bin Cheng (1953). *General Principles of Law as Applied by International Courts and Tribunals*, Stevens & Sons.

Cullet, P. (1999). "Differential Treatment in International Law: Towards a New Paradigm of Inter-state Relations", in *European Journal of International Law*, 1999, pp. 549-582.

International Law Commission (2001). *Articles on Responsibility of States for Internationally Wrongful Acts* (ARSIWA).

International Law Commission (2023). *General principles of law, Draft conclusions adopted on first reading.*

Kaufmann-Kohler, G. (2010). "Soft Law in International Arbitration: Codification and Normativity", in *Journal of International Dispute Settlement*, p. 283 ff.

Klabbers, J. (1998). "The Undesirability of Soft Law", in *Nordic Journal of International Law*, p. 381 ff.

Miranda, J., Miranda, M.S. (2023). "Chronicle of a Crisis Foretold: How the WTO Appellate Body Drove Itself into a Corner", in *Journal of International Criminal Justice*, p. 435 ff.

OECD (1988). *Voluntary aid for development: the role of non-governmental organisations.*

Palombino, F.M. (2018). *Fair and Equitable Treatment and the Fabric of General Principles*, Asser Press.

Paulsson, J. (2020). *The Unruly Notion of Abuse of Rights*, Cambridge University Press.

US Trade Representative (2020). *Report on the Appellate Body of the World Trade Organization*, available at https://ustr.gov/sites/default/files/Report_on_the_Appellate_Body_of_the_World_Trade_Organization.pdf.

Chapter 3
INTERNATIONAL INVESTMENT LAW

Giuliana Lampo and Caterina Milo *

ABSTRACT: *This Chapter examines, in Part I, the substantive law on the protection of foreign investments, first by briefly sketching the historical evolution of the normative framework on foreign investments' protection and then by analyzing the standards of treatment host States must abide by when dealing with foreign investors, as usually contained in investment treaties. In Part II, the Chapter outlines the main characteristics of the settlement of investment disputes. It illustrates the key notions of investor-State dispute settlement (ISDS), mainly focusing on investment arbitration within the framework of the International Centre for Settlement of Investment Disputes (ICSID). An overview of the main steps of arbitration is provided, as well as basic notions concerning the enforcement and annulment of awards. Finally, the chapter provides an overview of the recent developments concerning ISDS and the ongoing reform.*

KEYWORDS: *Foreign Investments – International Investment Agreements – Expropriation – Fair and Equitable Treatment – National Treatment – Most Favored Nation Treatment – Full Protection and Security – Umbrella Clauses – Investor-State Dispute Settlement – Arbitration – Applicable Law – Awards – ICSID.*

SUMMARY: PART I. Substantive Rules on the Protection of Foreign Investments. – 3.1. The Sources of International Investment Law: From Customary International Law to Investment Treaties. – 3.1.1. The Conclusion of Investment Treaties: The Case of European Union Member States. – 3.2. The Object of International Investment Law: The Notion of Investment. – 3.3. The Rules on the Treatment of Foreign Investments: The Main Standards of Treatment. – 3.3.1. Expropriation and Nationalization. – 3.3.2. Fair and Equitable Treatment. – 3.3.3. National Treatment. – 3.3.4. Most-Favored Nation Treatment. – 3.3.5. Full Protection and Security. – 3.3.6. Umbrella Clauses. – 3.4. Reconciling the Protection of Foreign Investments with Other Public Interests. – PART II. The Settlement of Investment Disputes. – 3.5. Introduction to the Settlement of Investment Disputes: Fundamental Notions. – 3.6. From Disputes between States to Investor-State Dispute Settlement. – 3.6.1. The International Centre for Settlement of Investment Disputes. – 3.6.2. Other Relevant Frameworks. – 3.7. Consent as the Basis of Investment Arbitration. – 3.8. Jurisdiction and Admissi-

* This Chapter is the result of the joint work of the two Authors. However, Giuliana Lampo drafted Part I, concerning the substantive rules on the protection of foreign investments (Sections from 3.1 to 3.4), while Caterina Milo drafted Part II, concerning the settlement of investment disputes (Sections from 3.5 to 3.13).

bility of Investment Arbitration Claims. – 3.8.1. The Scope of Jurisdiction: A Dispute Arising Out of an Investment Between the Investor and the Host State. – 3.8.1.1. Jurisdiction *Ratione Materiae*. – 3.8.1.2. Jurisdiction *Ratione Personae*. – 3.8.1.3. Jurisdiction *Ratione Loci*. – 3.8.1.4. Jurisdiction *Ratione Temporis*. – 3.9. The Laws Applicable to Investment Disputes. – 3.9.1. The Law Governing the Merits of the Dispute. – 3.9.2. The Law Governing the Arbitral Process and the Law of the Seat of Arbitration. – 3.10. The ICSID Procedure. – 3.10.1. Institution of a Claim. – 3.10.2. Constitution of the Tribunal. – 3.10.3. The Written and Oral Procedure. – 3.10.4. Conclusion of the Procedure. – 3.11. The Award. – 3.11.1. ICSID Awards. – 3.11.2. Non-ICSID Awards. – 3.12. Post-Award Remedies. – 3.12.1. ICSID Awards. – 3.12.2. Non-ICSID Awards. – 3.13. Conclusions: The Ongoing Debate on ISDS. – References.

Part I

Substantive Rules on the Protection of Foreign Investments

3.1. The Sources of International Investment Law: From Customary International Law to Investment Treaties

International investment law can be defined as the field of public international law regulating the relationship between a State in which an investment is carried out (so-called host State) and foreign investors.

Under general international law, States enjoy a great margin of discretion when deciding whether or not to admit foreign investments. Actually, from the perspective of customary international law, States are in no way obliged to admit foreign investments. Quite the contrary, what has been called the "economic dimension of territorial sovereignty" [1] confers States the right to decide whether or not and to what extent to open their economies. However, when States do decide to open them and attract and admit foreign investments, there are rules they must respect, and they must afford foreign investors a certain treatment.

The content of the rules on the treatment of foreign investments has varied greatly over time. Over the decades, international investment law has become a sub-field of international law with very precise and distinct features. Yet, international investment law emerged as an autonomous field of international law relatively recently.

The need for a normative framework regulating investments made by non-nationals can be said to have emerged only between the end of the XIX and the beginning of the XX century. However, for this framework to

[1] R. Dolzer, U. Kriebaum, C. Schreuer, *Principles of International Investment Law*^{3}, OUP, 2022, p. 132.

actually acquire its current characteristics, it took a long and complex process. The reason for this lies in the longstanding tension between developed and developing (mostly Latin American) countries, whose ideas on how to treat foreign investors were to a great extent antipodal.

As a consequence, for a long period of time, the normative framework on the treatment of aliens – and of investors, in particular – has been characterized by only a few very vague rules. The sum of these rules constituted the so-called international minimum standard. Actually, the international minimum standard concerned the status of aliens in general and applied to the issue of the taking of property as well as issues concerning other individual rights of the foreigner.

This is very well evidenced by the fact that what is considered to be the leading case on the concept of international minimum standard originated by a claim presented against Mexico for the failure of the latter to properly investigate the death of a United States national. The widow and the daughter, also United States nationals, brought a claim for compensation before a Mixed Claims Commission, which rendered its decision in 1926. In particular, the Commission held that:

> *"The treatment of an alien, in order to constitute an international delinquency, should amount to an outrage, to bad faith, to wilful neglect of duty, or to an insufficiency of governmental action so far short of international standards that every reasonable and impartial man would readily recognize its insufficiency".*[2]

The existence of rules on the treatment of aliens of a customary nature was also confirmed by both the Permanent Court of International Justice (PCIJ)[3] and the International Court of Justice (ICJ).[4] However, as mentioned, these rules were very vague, and the consequence was a state of uncertainty that lasted several decades. This uncertainty was also fueled by historical events such as the Russian Revolution of 1917 and the nationalizations and expropriations deriving therefrom, for which Russia did not pay any compensation and which only once led to a dispute between the State and the investor.[5] Further impulse to the formation of rules on the

---

[2] *Neer v. Mexico*, 15 October 1926, Reports of International Arbitral Awards, IV, p. 60 ff., pp. 61-62.

[3] PCIJ, *Certain German Interests in Polish Upper Silesia*, Judgment (Merits), 25 May 1926, PCIJ Series A. No. 7, p. 4 ff., p. 22.

[4] ICJ, *Elettronica Sicula S.p.A. (ELSI) (United States of America v. Italy)*, Judgment, 20 July 1989, ICJ Reports 1989, p. 15 ff., p. 66, para. 111.

[5] *Lena Goldfield v. Soviet Government*, Award of 2 September 1930 (original in

treatment of foreign investors was given by the expropriations made by Mexico of agrarian properties owned by United States citizens in the 1930s. These led to tensions between the two Governments, addressed by the then United States Secretary of State Cordell Hull in a now famous letter to his Mexican counterpart, invoking "*the universally recognized principle of compensation*" that ought to be "*adequate, effective and prompt*".[6]

On the contrary, Latin American countries had long espoused the so-called Calvo doctrine, named after Carlos Calvo, an Argentinian jurist and diplomat, according to which foreigners were not entitled to any right or privilege not accorded to nationals; therefore, the treatment of foreigners was to be deemed equivalent to that accorded to private property of nationals.

The opposing views of developing and developed States often clashed within the context of the United Nations General Assembly, in which, however, the former had the majority of votes. Thus, in 1962, Resolution no. 1803 was adopted, stating that in cases of nationalization or expropriation only an "*appropriate compensation*" was to be paid,[7] i.e. a compensation not necessarily reflecting the market value of the expropriated or nationalized goods. Again, in 1974, a series of resolutions advocating for a "New International Economic Order" were passed. In Resolution no. 3281 of 12 December 1974, it was clearly expressed the view that

> *"[e]ach State has the right: [...] c) To nationalize, expropriate or transfer ownership of foreign property, in which case appropriate compensation should be paid by the State adopting such measures, taking into account its relevant laws and regulations and all circumstances that the State considers pertinent. In any case where the question of compensation gives rise to a controversy, it shall be settled under the domestic law of the nationalizing State and by its tribunals, unless it is freely and mutually agreed by all States concerned that other peaceful means be sought on the basis of the sovereign equality of States and in accordance with the principle of free choice of means".*[8]

German, an English translation is published in A. Nussbaum, "Arbitration Between the Lena Goldfields Ltd. and the Soviet Government", in *Cornell Law Review*, 1950, p. 31 ff., p. 42 ff.

[6] Letter of Secretary of State Cordell Hull to the Mexican Secretary of State, 21 July 1938, Foreign Relations of the United States Diplomatic Papers, 1938, The American Republics, Volume V, 812.52/2939a.

[7] Permanent Sovereignty over Natural Resources, UNGA Res. 1803 (XVII) (14 December 1962), para. 4.

[8] Charter of Economic Rights and Duties of States, UNGA Res. 3281 (XXIX) (12 December 1974), Article 2(2)(c).

The state of uncertainty on the treatment to be accorded to foreign investments, however, could not last, as in the long run it proved detrimental to the economic development of most countries: "*[I]t became clear that, together with the end of the Soviet Union, the socialist view of property had collapsed and that the call for economic independence had brought a major financial crisis, rather than more welfare upon the people of Latin America*".[9] In 1992, guidelines on the treatment of foreign direct investments were adopted by the World Bank. In the foreword by the President of the World Bank Group it can be read that "*[f]or the first time, the world community found it appropriate [...] to ask the World Bank Group through the Development Committee to prepare universal standards for the legal treatment of foreign direct investment*".[10]

Thus, the fight on the content of customary rules on the treatment of foreign investors left the floor to new cooperation based on the will of capital-importing countries to attract foreign investments beneficial to their economic growth. This cooperation led to the conclusion of a great number of investment treaties, mostly bilateral, in which States agreed on the standards of treatment to be accorded to investors having the nationality of the other contracting party.

As a consequence, today's legal framework for the protection of foreign investments is mainly based on the so-called Bilateral Investment Treaties (BITs). Some notable exceptions are multilateral conventions such as the Energy Charter Treaty (ECT) or the now terminated North American Free Trade Agreement (NAFTA). There were, of course, efforts to establish a multilateral framework on the treatment of investments. For instance, provisions on foreign investments were included in the Havana Charter for an International Trade Organization of 1948. The Charter, however, was never ratified by the United States and, consequently, by the other countries and it never came into effect. The following year, the International Chamber of Commerce's Committees on Foreign Investments and on Foreign Establishments developed the International Code of Fair Treatment for Foreign Investments which, unfortunately, was never adopted. Again, in 1962, the Organization for Economic Cooperation and Development proposed the Draft Convention on the Protection of Foreign Property, later modified in 1967, which has never been open for signature. These and

---

[9] R. Dolzer, U. Kriebaum, C. Schreuer, *Principles of International Investment Law*[3] (note 1), p. 7.

[10] World Bank Group, "Guidelines on the Treatment of Foreign Direct Investment", in *Legal Framework for the Treatment of Foreign Investment*, vol. II, *Guidelines*, 1992, p. 3.

similar efforts never proved successful, and the treaties governing the relationship between host States and foreign investors remain, as mentioned, mainly bilateral.

Despite the fact that these treaties are only concluded between two States, they have pretty much uniform scope, content and structure, as they usually provide for a clause putting forth the requirements for a lawful expropriation and several other standards of treatment, such as: the national treatment, the most-favored nation treatment, the fair and equitable treatment and the full protection and security standard, all of which will be analyzed more in depth in the following Sections.

One of the main features of modern investment treaties, which greatly accounts for their success, is the possibility for investors to directly bring a claim for the violation of the standards contained in the treaty against the host State, through the so-called Investor-State Dispute Settlement (ISDS) mechanisms. This possibility, indeed, removed the need to resort to diplomatic protection (meaning the protection of the investor's home State, which could – but not had to – bring a claim against the host State) but also the need for investors to have to bring their claims before the domestic courts of the host State, perceived as biased in favor of the latter. [11]

The above is not to say that customary norms on the treatment of aliens no longer play any role in the promotion and protection of foreign investments. First of all, the rules contained in investment treaties must be interpreted: according to the rules on the interpretation of treaties enshrined in the Vienna Convention on the Law of Treaties of 1969 (VCLT), which in turn reflect customary international law, in interpreting a treaty "*[t]here shall be taken into account [...a]ny relevant rules of international law applicable in the relations between the parties*" (Article 31(3)(c)). Secondly, certain aspects of international investment law continue to be regulated by custom, such as issues of State responsibility or issues of nationality of investors. [12]

3.1.1. The Conclusion of Investment Treaties: The Case of European Union Member States

In 2009, the Lisbon Treaty entered into force. After that date, the Treaty on the Functioning of the European Union (EU) establishes, in its Article 207, that the common commercial policy of the Union now comprises the

---

[11] The resolution of disputes between investors and host States will be dealt with in the second part of this Chapter.

[12] On the issue of the interplay between treaties and custom, in general, see Chapter 2, Section 2.8.2.

subject of Foreign Direct Investment; also, under Article 3(1)(e) of the same Treaty, the common commercial policy is an exclusive competence of the EU. This means that, since 2009, Member States of the EU have lost their competence to autonomously conclude investment treaties.

However, several Member States of the EU had already concluded numerous International Investment Agreements (IIAs), both with third non-EU countries and with other EU Member States. To regulate the former – i.e., treaties concluded with third countries – the Union adopted Regulation 1219/2012 of the European Parliament and of the Council of 12 December 2012 establishing transitional arrangements for bilateral investment agreements between Member States and third countries. Under this Regulation,

> *"[b]y 8 February 2013 or within 30 days of the date of their accession to the Union, the Member States shall notify the Commission of all bilateral investment agreements with third countries signed before 1 December 2009 or before the date of their accession, whichever is later, that they either wish to maintain in force or permit to enter into force"* (Article 2).

However, the Regulation acknowledges that IIAs concluded by EU Members could contain provisions at odds with those regulating the internal market. Therefore, Article 3 provides that "*bilateral investment agreements notified pursuant to Article 2 of this Regulation may be maintained in force, or enter into force, [...] until a bilateral investment agreement between the Union and the same third country enters into force*". In addition, the Regulation imposes obligations on Member States to obtain authorization from the Commission to amend existing BITs with third countries and to conclude new ones (Articles 7-11).

Thus, the agreements concluded by EU Member States with third countries must be notified to the EU Commission and can only be maintained in force *as long as the Union itself decides to conclude an investment agreement with said third country*; the amendment of one of such agreements and the conclusion of a new one are subject to the authorization by the EU Commission.

The situation has been slightly more complicated regarding intra-EU BITs, meaning BITs concluded between two EU Member States, usually at a time when one of them was not an EU Member yet. Indeed, intra-EU BITs, for the most part, are treaties concluded by Western European States and Eastern European States prior to 2004 and 2007, when the latter joined the EU. In the 2018 decision rendered in the *Achmea* case,[13] the

[13] Case C-284/16, *Slovak Republic v. Achmea BV*, Judgment of 6 March 2018.

Court of Justice of the EU ruled that the BIT concluded between the Netherlands and Slovakia was incompatible with the autonomy and full effect of EU law, as it allowed an investor national of an EU Member State to sue another Member State before an arbitral tribunal that was not part of the judiciary of an EU Member State.[14]

Just two years later, on 5 May 2020, 23 of the 27 EU Member States actually signed the Agreement for the Termination of Bilateral Investment Treaties between the Member States of the European Union. Therefore, all intra-EU BITs were terminated through a multilateral agreement between the EU Member States concerned.

As of today, the only investment agreement in force between some EU Member States remains the ECT, a multilateral treaty entered into force in 1998 concerning the promotion of international cooperation in the energy sector. Some Member States of the Union are parties to this agreement, whose intra-EU application has also been declared by the Court of Justice of the EU to be incompatible with the EU legal order.[15] However, this agreement has also been the subject of much criticism, due to the fact that it affords wide protection to investors in the fossil fuel sector, thus posing obstacles to the adoption of environment-friendly policies. Thus, a reform process was launched, the outcome of which, nevertheless, left the States and the EU disappointed. Therefore, the European Parliament adopted, in 2022, a Resolution in which it called the Commission and Member States to prepare a coordinated exit from the Treaty, seen as an obstacle in the pursuit of environment-friendly policies. On 7 July 2023, the European Commission consequently issued a proposal for the coordinated exit from the ECT of the EU itself, EU Member States and Euratom. The EU and numerous Member States have actually withdrawn from the ECT, in some cases before the Commission proposal, such as: Italy, France, Germany, Poland, Spain, the Netherlands, Slovenia, Luxembourg, Denmark and Portugal. Eventually, the Energy Charter Conference (an inter-governmental organization composed of all parties to the Treaty) adopted the decisions on the modernization of the ECT on 3 December 2024. The amendments will enter into force on the ninetieth day after at least three-fourths of the contracting parties have deposited their instruments of ratification; however, they will be provisionally applicable as of 3 September 2025, with the possibility for each party to opt out of the provisional application by 3 March 2025.

[14] On the functioning of investor-State arbitration established on the basis of an investment treaty see Section 3.7 of this Chapter.

[15] Case C-741/19, *Republic of Moldova v. Komstroy LLC*, Judgment of 2 September 2021.

3.2. The Object of International Investment Law: The Notion of Investment

It is to a certain extent intuitive that international investment law is the field of public international law regulating the treatment of foreign investments. However, it is certainly more surprising that there exists no agreed-upon definition of what actually constitutes an investment. Several and partially different definitions of the term "investment" can be found in national legislation as well as in treaties. For example, under Article 1(k) of the Cuban Foreign Investment Act, a foreign investment is "*capital input by foreign investors in any of the modalities established in this Act which involves, during the authorized term, the undertaking of risks in business, the expectations to obtain profits and a contribution to the development of the country*". As for treaties, one could mention the BIT between Bahrain and Brazil, concluded in 2022, under whose Article 1(a), "*the term 'investment' means every kind of asset owned or controlled, directly or indirectly, by an investor*", followed by a detailed non-exhaustive list of assets constituting an investment, such as: an enterprise and a branch of an enterprise, shares, stocks or other forms of equity participation in an enterprise, derivative instruments, rights under contracts, claims to money and intellectual property rights.

However, an interpretative problem arises: how are non-listed investments to be identified? Are there some intrinsic features of an investment that must be present irrespective of the applicable definition? In other terms, is there an "objective" definition of the concept of "investment"? This problem is of great practical importance. Indeed, according to Article 25 of the Convention establishing the International Centre for Settlement of Investment Disputes (ICSID), the most important Centre for the administration of investment disputes,[16] for a tribunal to have jurisdiction over a dispute, the latter must arise "*directly out of an investment*". Still, the Convention does not define the term, due to a disagreement between capital-exporting and capital-importing countries. Actually, in the Report of the Executive Directors of the World Bank Group on the Convention, it is stated that "*[n]o attempt was made to define the term 'investment' given the essential requirement of consent by the parties, and the mechanism through which Contracting States can make known in advance, if they so desire, the classes of disputes which they would or would not consider submitting to the Centre*".[17]

---

[16] Which will be dealt with in Section 3.6.1.

[17] Report of the Executive Directors on the Convention on the Settlement of Investment Disputes between States and Nationals of Other States, para. 27.

Having this in mind, it has been maintained by several scholars and by arbitral case law that the term investment in Article 25 of the ICSID Convention has an intrinsic meaning that parties cannot dispose of by way of an agreement, be it an investment contract or a treaty. This would mean that for an ICSID tribunal to have jurisdiction, both the definition contained in the Convention and the one contained in the agreement must be satisfied. To put it differently, under this approach, States could restrict the scope of the definition contained in the ICSID Convention but could not enlarge it. As stated by the Tribunal in the case *CSOB v. Slovakia*

> *"an agreement of the parties describing their transaction as an investment is not, as such, conclusive in resolving the question whether the dispute involves an investment under Article 25(1) of the Convention. The concept of an investment as spelled out in that provision is objective in nature in that the parties may agree on a more precise or restrictive definition of their acceptance of the Centre's jurisdiction, but they may not choose to submit disputes to the Centre that are not related to an investment. A two-fold test must therefore be applied in determining whether this Tribunal has the competence to consider the merits of the claim: whether the dispute arises out of an investment within the meaning of the Convention and, if so, whether the dispute relates to an investment as defined in the Parties' consent to ICSID arbitration, in their reference to the BIT and the pertinent definitions contained in Article 1 of the BIT".* [18]

To say that the term investment has an intrinsic meaning, however, is not sufficient, as this meaning must be clarified. The most notorious attempt at defining the features of an investment is the case of *Salini Costruttori v. Morocco*, [19] concerning a contract for the construction of a highway, which Morocco argued was not an investment. The Tribunal, applying an objective approach, reasoned that "*it would be inaccurate to consider that the requirement that a dispute be 'in direct relation to an investment' is diluted by the consent of the Contracting Parties. To the contrary, [...] the investment requirement must be respected as an objective condition of the jurisdiction of the Centre*". [20] The Tribunal then identified the features of an investment, and namely: *i*) a substantial commitment by the investor; *ii*) a

[18] *Ceskoslovenska Obchodni Banka, A.S. v. The Slovak Republic*, ICSID Case No. ARB/97/4, Decision of the Tribunal on Objections to Jurisdiction, 24 May 1999, para. 68.

[19] *Salini Costruttori S.p.A. and Italstrade S.p.A. v. Kingdom of Morocco (I)*, ICSID Case No. ARB/00/4, Decision on Jurisdiction, 31 July 2001 (original in French, English translation in 42 ILM 609 (2003)).

[20] *Ibid.*, para. 52.

certain duration of the performance; *iii)* the assumption of economic risk by the investor; and *iv)* a contribution to the development of the host State.[21] The so-called *Salini test* is the product of arbitral case law and, as such, is in no way binding on subsequent tribunals. Still, arbitral tribunals have usually applied these criteria to determine whether the economic operation under consideration actually constituted an investment,[22] sometimes adjusting and modifying the test a bit to adapt it to the circumstances of the specific case under consideration.

For instance, in the case of *Malaysian Historical Salvors v. Malaysia*, the Tribunal emphasized that

> *"[t]he classical* Salini *hallmarks are not a punch list of items which, if completely checked off, will automatically lead to a conclusion that there is an 'investment.' If any of these hallmarks are absent, the tribunal will hesitate (and probably decline) to make a finding of 'investment.' However, even if they are all present, a tribunal will still examine the nature and degree of their presence in order to determine whether, on a holistic assessment, it is satisfied that there is an ICSID 'investment'".*[23]

The Tribunal then proceeded to verify if a contract under which the Claimant had to locate and salvage a British vessel that sank off the coast of Malacca in 1817 constituted an investment. In doing so, it noted that "*the Contract is not a 'readily recognizable' 'investment'*".[24] Thus, the Tribunal considered the question of whether the economic operation contributed to the economic development of the host State to be of particular importance. In this regard, it stated that the requirement is satisfied when such contribution is significant.[25]

---

[21] *Ibid.* and ff.

[22] See, for instance: *Joy Mining Machinery Limited v. Arab Republic of Egypt*, ICSID Case No. ARB/03/11, Award, 6 August 2004, para. 53 ff.; *Bayindir Insaat Turizm Ticaret Ve Sanayi A.S. v. Islamic Republic of Pakistan*, ICSID Case No. ARB/03/29, Decision on Jurisdiction, 14 November 2005, para. 130 ff.; *Toto Costruzioni Generali S.p.A. v. The Republic of Lebanon*, ICSID Case No. ARB/07/12, Decision on Jurisdiction, 11 September 2009, para. 61 ff.; *Malicorp Limited v. The Arab Republic of Egypt*, ICSID Case No. ARB/08/18, Award, 7 February 2011, para. 106 ff.; *Flughafen Zürich A.G. and Gestión e Ingenería IDC S.A. v. Bolivarian Republic of Venezuela*, ICSID Case No. ARB/10/19, Award, 18 November 2014, para. 244 ff.

[23] *Malaysian Historical Salvors, SDN, BHD v. The Government of Malaysia*, ICSID Case No. ARB/05/10, Award on Jurisdiction, 17 May 2007, para. 106.

[24] *Ibid.*, para. 129.

[25] *Ibid.*, para. 131. See, however, the Decision on the Application for Annulment, 16 April 2009, paras. 56 ff.

More recently, and quite differently, the Tribunal in the case of *Mabco v. Kosovo* highlighted that the requirement of the contribution to the development of the host State has, since the *Salini* decision, "*fallen significantly out of favour*",[26] upholding this approach.

In contrast with this "objective" approach to the meaning of the term investment, other arbitral tribunals have considered sufficient that the definition of the relevant IIA was satisfied. One could mention, in this respect, the case of *Biwater Gauff v. Tanzania*, in which the Tribunal reasoned that, "*[g]iven that the [ICSID] Convention was not drafted with a strict, objective, definition of 'investment', it is doubtful that arbitral tribunals sitting in individual cases should impose one such definition which would be applicable in all cases and for all purposes*".[27] It then proceeded to apply "*a more flexible and pragmatic approach to the meaning of 'investment' […], which takes into account the features identified in* Salini*, but along with all the circumstances of the case, including the nature of the instrument containing the relevant consent to ICSID*".[28]

The idea that the term investment has an intrinsic and objective meaning, however, appears to be espoused by the majority of arbitral case law, to the point that it has also been recently applied by a non-ICSID Tribunal sitting in the case of *Komaksavia v. Moldova*, concerning a concession to operate the Chisinau airport.[29] In particular, the Claimant had acquired a 95% interest in the airport concessionaire from a Russian entity. The Tribunal considered that the economic operation clearly fell within the definition of an investment given by the relevant BIT (Cyprus-Moldova BIT); however, it went on to state that the notion of investment has an intrinsic and objective meaning which entails a "contribution *which is made in an attempt to earn a return* over a period of time*, a process that necessarily involves the possibility or risk of not earning a return*".[30]

In conclusion, it can reasonably be said that the objective approach seems to prevail in arbitral case law, with arbitral tribunals having designed a set of features an investment should typically have in addition to fulfilling the requirements set forth in the relevant IIA. At the same time, however, it should be considered that arbitral tribunals have also progressively shifted

---

[26] *Mabco Constructions v. Republic of Kosovo*, ICSID Case No. ARB/17/25, Decision on Jurisdiction, 30 October 2020, para. 296.

[27] *Biwater Gauff (Tanzania) Ltd. v. United Republic of Tanzania*, ICSID Case No. ARB/05/22, Award, 24 July 2008, para. 313.

[28] *Ibid.*, para. 316.

[29] *Komaksavia Airport Invest Ltd. v. Republic of Moldova*, SCC EA 2020/130, Award, 3 August 2022.

[30] *Ibid.*, para 151.

towards an approach under which the features of an investment are not to be considered in a rigid manner, i.e. considering that their lack automatically results in the tribunal not having jurisdiction. Rather, they are simply used as a useful tool in helping arbitrators understand the nature of the economic operation and can be adjusted considering the specific circumstances of each case.

3.3. The Rules on the Treatment of Foreign Investments: The Main Standards of Treatment

As discussed above, the legal framework on the treatment of foreign investments is today to be found mainly in treaties, mostly of a bilateral nature. Despite the fact that there exist more than 2800 BITs (of which more than 2200 are in force), it is safe to say that such treaties share common features, as they enshrine some obligations for host States; there are, indeed, standards of treatment often contained in almost all treaties with little exceptions. For these reasons, in the following Sections we will discuss the most frequently used provisions in IIAs, highlighting their scope, content and main features. However, it is always necessary to keep in mind that every treaty could be differently formulated and could contain a small variation in wording that makes it unique, and every treaty must be interpreted using the rules on the interpretation of treaties codified in the VCLT.[31]

Before analyzing the typical obligations of host States under investment treaties, it is also important to remember that, as already said, States enjoy a great margin of discretion in deciding whether or not to admit foreign investments into their territory and, from the perspective of general international law, States are in no way obliged to admit foreign investments.

Actually, many States have a mechanism in place for the screening of inward foreign investments, to ensure that the latter do not interfere with the country's essential needs. Usually, these screening mechanisms apply to investments in particularly sensitive sectors like communications, energy or defense and give the State the power to block economic operations or impose certain conditions for them to be acceptable.

For example, in 2019, the EU adopted Regulation 2019/452 establishing a common framework for the screening of foreign direct investments into the Union. The Regulation itself does not establish a common EU screening mechanism, but it sets forth common features for the different screening mechanisms adopted by EU Member States and provides the lat-

[31] See Chapter 2, Section 2.7.2.

ter with objective criteria according to which the screening of foreign investments should be carried out. Lastly, the Regulation is aimed at ensuring cooperation among Member States and between Member States and the European Commission on investments which are likely to affect security or public order.

The fact that States are free to decide whether or not to admit foreign investments into their territory does not necessarily entail, however, that no interference between international investment law and the power of States to adopt these screening regimes is possible. Actually, while from the standpoint of general international law there is no obligation to admit foreign investments, States may well assume obligations relating to the admission of investments in their IIAs.

Some IIAs are simply silent on the treatment to be accorded to investors prior to the establishment of an investment, sometimes going as far as explicitly providing that the admission of investments is regulated by domestic law. An example of this approach is the BIT between Switzerland and Trinidad and Tobago, whose Article 3(1) reads as follows: "*Each Contracting Party shall in its territory encourage and create favorable conditions for investments by Investors of the other Contracting Party and* admit such investments in accordance with its laws and regulations".[32] Another example could be the BIT concluded between China and Italy in 1985. Indeed, its Article 2 defines the investments covered by the treaty as "every kind of asset *accepted in accordance with the respective laws and regulations of either Contracting Party*".[33]

Quite the contrary, other IIAs could explicitly extend the standards of treatment they provide to the pre-establishment phase of an investment. For instance, Articles 3 and 4 of the 2012 United States Model BIT define the national treatment and the most-favored nation treatment obligations as applicable to the "*establishment,* acquisition*, expansion, management, conduct, operation, and sale or other disposition of investments*" (emphasis added). A similar wording is also adopted by the 2021 Canada Model BIT, Articles 5 and 6.

Apart from the fact that an IIA could explicitly address the pre-

[32] 26 October 2010, entered into force on 4 July 2012, emphasis added; see also the similarly worded Agreement Between the Islamic Republic of Pakistan and the Federal Republic of Germany on the Encouragement and Reciprocal Protection of Investments, 1 December 2009, not entered into force, Article 2(1); Agreement Between the Government of the Russian Federation and the Government of the Islamic Republic of Iran on Promotion and Reciprocal Protection of Investments, 23 December 2015, entered into force on 6 April 2017, Article 2.

[33] 28 January 1985, entered into force on 28 August 1987, emphasis added.

establishment phase of an investment, it must also be underlined that, as already discussed, the very definition of the term investment in international law is far from clear. As a consequence, and using the often very wide definitions given by IIAs, investors have sometimes tried to invoke the protection of investment treaties also in relation to pre-investment expenditures which can constitute a relevant part of the entire economic operation they carry out. For example, investors can spend substantial sums on feasibility studies or participation in tender proceedings. Although the majority of cases dealing with pre-investment expenditures resulted in arbitral tribunals declining their jurisdiction, there are still some cases in which these expenditures could be considered as falling within the protection of the relevant IIA.

In the case of *Nordzucker v. Poland*,[34] a dispute arose out of the Respondent State's implementation of a privatization program for its sugar industry. The Claimant alleged that Poland had breached several of the standards of treatment contained in the Germany-Poland BIT by retracting from the selling of two State-owned sugar producers. The Tribunal noted that, under Article 2(1) of the BIT, "*[i]nvestments that have been admitted in accordance with the respective law of one Contracting Party shall enjoy the protection of this Treaty. Each Contracting Party shall in any case accord investments fair and equitable treatment*".[35] Therefore, it interpreted the words "in any case" in the last sentence of this provision as requiring that fair and equitable treatment had to be also granted to investments not already admitted in accordance with the law of the host State and thus "in the making".[36] This example clearly evidences that an economic operation that has not yet undergone the host State's screening mechanism – and has thus not been admitted in accordance with the law of the host State – could already be deemed worthy of the protection granted by one of the IIAs the host State itself has ratified.

Thus, States are free, under general international law, to decide whether or not to admit foreign investments, and actually many States have in place regulations to make foreign investments undergo a screening process to ensure that they do not have negative effects in certain strategic and particularly sensitive sectors. However, States may well limit their freedom to decide on the admission of investments by assuming, in IIAs, specific obligations on admission. In the event a State has assumed such obligations, of course, the screening mechanism – if one exists – must comply with the latter.

---

[34] *Nordzucker AG v. Poland*, UNCITRAL, Partial Award of 10 December 2008.

[35] Now terminated.

[36] *Nordzucker AG v. Poland* (note 34), para. 176 ff.

3.3.1. Expropriation and Nationalization

One of the main features of IIAs is that they protect foreign investors against unlawful acts of expropriation and nationalization of their investment. The protection against such acts, actually, was the main purpose of the first IIAs, as expropriation and nationalization were considered to be the typical way in which a host State could infringe upon foreigners' property, to the point that some of the oldest BITs limit the scope of the dispute settlement clauses only to disputes over the amount and method of compensation for such acts.[37]

The term "expropriation" refers to the taking of the property of a foreign investor by the State, without the consent of the former; thus, expropriation refers to the deprivation of the ownership of an investment. The concept of nationalization, on the other hand, refers to the same kind of acts realized by the host State. However, nationalization normally describes a situation in which the deprivation of the ownership of an investment is the result of a wider policy of the host State aimed at eliminating or reducing the presence of foreign investments in an entire economic sector.

The concept of expropriation, however, is quite elusive. Indeed, expropriation may take many forms, and the practice of international tribunals has developed numerous notions.

Scholarship and arbitral tribunals are used to distinguishing between direct and indirect expropriation. The former refers to the transfer of the ownership title from the investor to the State, while indirect expropriation refers to all measures which, despite not explicitly depriving the investor of the title of ownership, have the same effect. Indeed, all IIAs, when fixing the criteria for an expropriation to be lawful, refer to both types of expropriation. An example is Article 13(1) of the ECT, as recently modified, according to which, unless certain requirements are met, "*Investments of Investors of a Contracting Party in the Area of any other Contracting Party shall not be the subject of direct or indirect expropriation*". In addition, paragraphs 2 and 3 clarify that "*[d]irect expropriation occurs when an Investment is nationalised or otherwise directly expropriated through formal transfer of title or outright seizure*", while "*[i]ndirect expropriation occurs when a measure or series of measures of a Contracting Party has an effect equivalent to direct expropriation, without formal transfer of title or outright seizure, in that it substantially deprives the Investor of the value of its Investment or of*

[37] For example, Article 10 of the BIT between Russia and Spain, or Article 10 of the China-Poland BIT.

the fundamental attributes of property in its Investment, including the right to use, enjoy or dispose of its Investment".

Actually, indirect expropriation is the prevalent type of expropriation, as through it host States may try to escape the application of the requirements for an expropriation to be lawful (and, in particular, the obligation to pay compensation to the expropriated investor).

For instance, in the case of *Quasar de Valores v. Russia*, the Claimants had argued that the Respondent State had expropriated their investment by applying a variety of different measures which constituted an abuse of executive and judicial power but were actually politically motivated. In particular, the Claimants had argued that the taxes imposed on the company in which they had invested were arbitrary and discriminatory and that the tax assessments imposed on the company were in fact a pretext to expropriate the latter's assets. The Tribunal reasoned that:

> "*All taxation of course has the effect of a taking of the taxpayer's money; but it is nonsense to say that it is therefore compensable. [...] But if the ostensible collection of taxes is determined to be part of a set of measures designed to effect a dispossession outside the normative constraints and practices of the taxing powers, those measures are expropriatory [...]. And it is then for the Tribunal to consider whether such expropriation has been properly compensated*".[38]

Ultimately, the Tribunal went on to find that Russian measures were indeed a pretext to expropriate the company of which the Claimants were shareholders.[39]

The termination of a contract can also constitute an expropriation. For example, in the case of *SPP v. Egypt*, an ICSID Tribunal found that Egypt had indeed expropriated the investment of the Claimant by terminating the contract for the development of a tourist site near the pyramids of Giza, and that thus the investor was entitled to receive compensation.[40]

The possibilities are many, as States can reach the effect of depriving the investors of their property in a myriad of different ways; however, it must be noted that it is required, for a measure to constitute an indirect expro-

---

[38] *Renta 4 S.V.S.A, Ahorro Corporación Emergentes F.I., Ahorro Corporación Eurofondo F.I., Rovime Inversiones SICAV S.A., Quasar de Valors SICAV S.A., Orgor de Valores SICAV S.A., GBI 9000 SICAV S.A. v. The Russian Federation*, SCC Case No. 24/2007, Award, 20 July 2020, para. 48.

[39] *Ibid.*, para. 177.

[40] *Southern Pacific Properties (Middle East) Limited v. Arab Republic of Egypt*, ICSID Case No. ARB/84/3, Award, 20 May 1992, paras. 160 ff.

priation, a certain degree of severity of the prejudice suffered by the investor, resulting in a "substantial loss of control or value".[41]

A different (but strictly related) issue concerns the object of expropriation, i.e. what can actually be expropriated. It is intuitive that the object of expropriation is property; however, to define property is an incredibly hard task, also in light of the numerous differences that exist among the definitions given by national jurisdictions. Usually, IIAs simply state that the protection against unlawful expropriation is accorded to investments. Thus, the question of what can be expropriated is intertwined with the problem of defining an investment, and everything that is an investment could be subject to expropriation.

Therefore, expropriation not only refers to movable and immovable property, but can also concern intangible rights, such as contractual rights,[42] claims to money,[43] and even rights arising from an arbitral award.[44] In the case of *Rockhopper v. Italy*, the Tribunal found that the State expropriated the Claimants' investment because it refused to grant a concession to exploit an offshore oilfield. Italy argued that since the concession had not been granted, the affected company had no extractive business in Italy "*that could be expropriated to begin with*".[45] However, the company had complied with all the requirements set forth by Italian legislation and, in particular, Italian authorities had approved its environmental impact assessment. Thus, under Italian legislation, all that was left to do was for the State to grant the concession, which had to happen within 15 days of the formal application. As a consequence, the Tribunal found that

> *"[a]s of that moment [...] the Claimants' right to be granted a production concession was taken away from it. Thereafter the Claimants had neither the right to be granted the production concession, much less the production concession itself. The Claimants went, in one fell swoop, from a posi-*

[41] United Nations Conference on Trade and Development (UNCTAD), *Taking of Property*, UN, 2000, 41.

[42] *Southern Pacific Properties (Middle East) Limited v. Arab Republic of Egypt* (note 40). *CME Czech Republic B.V. v. The Czech Republic*, UNCITRAL, Partial Award, 13 September 2001, para. 591 ff.

[43] *Daimler Financial Services AG v. Argentine Republic*, ICSID Case No. ARB/05/1, Award, 22 August 2012.

[44] *Saipem S.p.A. v. The People's Republic of Bangladesh*, ICSID Case No. ARB/05/07, Decision on Jurisdiction and Recommendation on Provisional Measures, 21 March 2007.

[45] *Rockhopper Italia S.p.A., Rockhopper Mediterranean Ltd, and Rockhopper Exploration Plc v. Italian Republic*, ICSID Case No. ARB/17/14, Final Award, 23 August 2022, para. 189.

tion where they had rights to a valuable production concession which would actually lead, under Italian law, to such production concession, to essentially nothing at all. No lengthy elaboration is required to arrive at this conclusion. There was, factually speaking, an immediate and complete deprivation of the Claimants' investment".[46]

Thus, investments – and not only physical property – are protected against unlawful expropriation, both direct and indirect. It is thus necessary to understand when an expropriation can be said to be lawful. IIAs, of course, set forth the requirements for an expropriation to be lawful, and it is therefore necessary to look at the exact wording of the treaty. However, usually, IIAs define as lawful an expropriation: *i*) made in the public interest; *ii*) non-discriminatory; *iii*) respecting due process; and *iv*) followed by compensation to the affected investor.

As for the first requirement, it can be said to be the least difficult one to fulfill, as arbitral tribunals give States a wide margin of discretion in assessing their own public interest. This is not to say that arbitral tribunals cannot review the determination made by the State of whether the expropriation fulfills a public purpose; however, tribunals tend to accept the assessment conducted by the State.

As regards the non-discrimination element, this mainly emerged as a requirement for a lawful expropriation to protect investors from discrimination based on nationality; however, today it is usually considered to be broader, also prohibiting religious, ethnic, racial and cultural discrimination.

The expropriation must also be carried out respecting due process. This means that it must be conducted in conformity with domestic law and procedure, granting an investor the possibility to challenge the expropriation before national authorities.

Lastly, the investor must be compensated. The debate on whether, under customary international law, the compensation must be "appropriate" or "prompt, adequate and effective" has already been mentioned. However, this debate is today largely irrelevant, due to the fact that IIAs usually spell out the type of compensation investors must be paid. Many IIAs adopt the Hull formula. Other IIAs are vaguer, simply referring to compensation or to just compensation or some other formula. However, the majority of IIAs use precise language to address the issue of the calculation of compensation. An example in this respect is, once again, the recently amended Article 13(1) of the ECT. According to this provision,

---

[46] *Ibid.*, para. 194.

> *"compensation shall amount to the fair market value of the Investment expropriated at the time immediately before the Expropriation took place or the Expropriation or impending Expropriation became known in such a way as to affect the value of the Investment, whichever is the earlier (hereinafter referred to as the 'Valuation Date'). Such fair market value shall at the request of the Investor be expressed in a Freely Convertible Currency on the basis of the market rate of exchange existing for that currency on the Valuation Date. Compensation shall also include interest at a commercial rate established on a market basis from the date of Expropriation until the date of payment".*

Another example is Article VI(2) of the Australia-Indonesia BIT:

> *"The compensation [...] shall be computed on the basis of the market value of the investment immediately before the expropriation or impending expropriation became public knowledge. Where that value cannot be readily ascertained, the compensation shall be determined in accordance with generally recognised principles of valuation and equitable principles taking into account the capital invested, depreciation, capital already repatriated, replacement value, currency exchange rate movements and other relevant factors".*

The language of IIAs, therefore, reduces the relevance of the problem of the uncertainty of customary international law on how compensation should be determined.

The last issue to address is the so-called power to regulate doctrine, or police powers doctrine. It has been said before that an expropriation is only lawful if it is made in the public interest. However, a trend has emerged in arbitral case law of considering that measures which are taken in the general public interest, are not discriminatory and are proportionate cannot constitute an expropriation and, accordingly, do not give rise to the State's obligation to compensate the investor. On the other side of the spectrum lies the so-called sole effect doctrine, according to which every taking of property is an expropriation, regardless of the State's intent. The sole effect doctrine has found the support of some tribunals in the past.[47] However, it is now quite established in the practice of arbitral tribunals that States have the right to adopt certain measures which infringe on investors' rights to pursue certain important policy objectives, in which case such actions cannot be considered to be expropriations and do not give rise to the obligation of the host State to compensate the investor.

---

[47] *Compañia del Desarrollo de Santa Elena S.A. v. Republic of Costa Rica*, ICSID Case No. ARB/96/1, Final Award, 17 February 2000.

This doctrine has emerged with a view to affording States a certain amount of discretion in regulating in the general interest and in accommodating the need to protect foreign investors with other, non-economic concerns.

One of the most known cases in which this doctrine was applied is *Philip Morris v. Uruguay*. The case concerned certain measures adopted by the Respondent State to tackle the issue of tobacco use in the country, including an obligation to increase the size of health warnings on cigarette packages, which, according to the investor, constituted an indirect expropriation. The Tribunal, however, ruled that:

> *"The Challenged Measures were taken by Uruguay with a view to protect public health in fulfilment of its national and international obligations. [...I]n the Tribunal's view the Challenged Measures were both adopted in good faith and were non-discriminatory. They were proportionate to the objective they meant to achieve, quite apart from their limited adverse impact on Abal's business. Contrary to the Claimants' contention, the Challenged Measures were not 'arbitrary and unnecessary' but rather were potentially 'effective means to protecting public health' [...]. In light of the foregoing, the Tribunal concludes that the Challenged Measures were a valid exercise by Uruguay of its police powers for the protection of public health. As such, they cannot constitute an expropriation of the Claimants' investment".*[48]

Numerous other cases have followed the same approach. For example, in the case *Marfin v. Cyprus*, the Tribunal considered measures adopted by the State to address the 2008 crisis of the banking sector could not be considered an expropriation, as they were taken by Cyprus to protect the "*safety and soundness of its banking sector, the interests of depositors and of taxpayers at large*" and were proportionate.[49]

The power to regulate doctrine is today recognized by a number of arbitral awards[50] and is also codified in some of the most recent IIAs.[51] Fur-

---

[48] *Philip Morris Brands Sàrl, Philip Morris Products S.A. and Abal Hermanos S.A. v. Oriental Republic of Uruguay*, ICSID Case No. ARB/10/7 (formerly *FTR Holding SA, Philip Morris Products S.A. and Abal Hermanos S.A. v. Oriental Republic of Uruguay*), Award, 8 July 2016, paras. 306-307.

[49] *Marfin Investment Group v. The Republic of Cyprus*, ICSID Case No. ARB/13/27, Award, 26 July 2008, para. 984.

[50] *Leopoldo Castillo Bozo v. Republic of Panama*, PCA 2019-40, Decision on Merits, 8 November 2022; *Casinos Austria International GmbH and Casinos Austria Aktiengesellschaft v. Argentine Republic*, ICSID Case No. ARB/14/32, Award, 5 November 2021; *Chemtura Corporation (formerly Crompton Corporation) v. Government of Canada*, PCA

thermore, the wide recognition of the doctrine has led it to be considered as a rule of customary international law,[52] meaning a rule that would apply even in the absence of a specific provision of an investment treaty spelling it out.

3.3.2. Fair and Equitable Treatment

The Fair and Equitable Treatment (FET) standard is ubiquitous in IIAs. Yet, it is a standard whose meaning still remains shrouded in ambiguity, as the expression "fair and equitable treatment" appears to be very vague. The difficulty in identifying the content of such standard is amplified by the variety of wordings in investment treaties.

Some BITs, for instance, have an autonomous clause enshrining the FET obligation. An example, in this respect, is Article 2(2) of the Italy-Albania BIT, according to which "*[e]ach Contracting Party will ensure a fair and equitable treatment to investments and investors of the other*". More often, however, FET is combined with other standards of treatment, such as the National Treatment or the Most Favored Nation treatment.[53] For example, under Article 3(1) of the Bangladesh-Denmark BIT, "*[e]ach Contracting Party shall in its territory accord to investments made by investors of the other Contracting Part fair and equitable treatment which in no case shall be less favourable than that accorded to its own investors or to investments of any third state, whichever is the more favourable from the point of view of the investor*".

Many FET clauses also refer to the obligation to accord such treatment

---

Case No. 2008-01, Award, 2 August 2010; *Saluka Investment B. V. v. The Czech Republic*, UNCITRAL, Partial Award, 17 March 2006; *Methanex Corporation v. United States of America*, NAFTA/UNCITRAL, Final Award of the Tribunal on the Jurisdiction and Merits, 3 August 2005; *Technicas Medioambientales Tecmed S.A. v. United Mexican States*, ICSID Case No. ARB(AF)/00/2, 29 May 2003; *Ronald S. Lauder v. The Czech Republic*, UNCITRAL, Final Award, 3 September 2001; *S.D. Myers, Inc. v. Government of Canada*, UNCITRAL, Partial Award, 13 November 2000.

[51] Article 23(1) of the Morocco-Nigeria BIT, not yet entered into force: "*In accordance with customary international law and other general principles of international law, the Host State has the right to take regulatory or other measures to ensure that development in its territory is consistent with the goals and principles of sustainable development, and with other legitimate social and economic policy objectives*". See also Article 5(5) of India's Model BIT, adopted in 2015: "*Non-discriminatory regulatory measures by a Party or measures or awards by judicial bodies of a Party that are designed and applied to protect legitimate public interest or public purpose objectives such as public health, safety and the environment shall not constitute expropriation under this Article*".

[52] See Chapter 2, Section 2.8.

[53] On both obligations see Sections 3.3.3. and 3.3.4 of this Chapter.

in accordance with customary international law or with the international minimum standard. An example of this can be found in Article 4(1) of the Australia-Paraguay BIT, under which "*[e]ach Party shall accord to investments of investors of the other Party treatment in accordance with the customary international law minimum standard of treatment of aliens, including fair and equitable treatment and full protection and security*".

This type of wording has sparked a heated debate among scholars and arbitral tribunals, which have expressed the most diverse views on the relationship between FET and the international minimum standard under customary international law. These views range from considering FET and the international minimum standard as equivalent, to considering FET broader and, in any case, a self-standing treaty clause to be interpreted according to Articles 31 ff. of the VCLT.

The majority of case law, however, is clear in considering FET broader than the international minimum standard, in the absence of treaty provisions clearly linking the two.[54]

Still, even if one accepts that the FET is broader than the international minimum standard, the problem of identifying its content remains. Ultimately, the content of this standard of treatment has been more or less precisely defined by the case law of arbitral tribunals, which have identified three main elements composing FET: *i)* the obligation to respect due process; *ii)* the protection of investors' legitimate expectations; and *iii)* proportionality.

As regards due process, this means that "*the adjudicator, be it a judge, tribunal member, or administrative authority, must give each party a fair opportunity to present its case and to marshal appropriate evidence, and then must assess the submissions and the evidence in a reasoned, even-handed, and unbiased decision*".[55]

The obligation to respect due process, although with some differences,[56] applies to all types of proceedings, be they civil, administrative or criminal proceedings. Indeed, "*a State may incur international responsibility*

---

[54] See *Orazul International España Holdings S.L. v. Argentine Republic*, ICSID Case No. ARB/19/25, Award, 14 December 2023, para. 613 ff.

[55] *Glencore International A.G. and C.I. Prodeco S.A. v. Republic of Colombia (I)*, ICSID Case No. ARB/16/6, Award, 27 August 2019, para. 1318.

[56] *Ibid.*, para. 1319: "*But the due process standard operates differently in different settings. In administrative proceedings [...] the decision-maker is often the investigator, the accuser, and the adjudicator, and a related officer (who may be the senior officer of the decision-maker) is often the one who rules on appeal. Due process does not require strict separation of these functions – provided that the final administrative decision is subject to full judicial review. The private individual must have an opportunity to have the case revisited, this time by an independent and impartial judge, with the guarantee of a formal adversarial procedure*".

for breaching its obligation under an investment treaty to accord fair and equitable treatment to a protected investor by a pattern of wrongful conduct during the course of a criminal investigation or prosecution, even where the investigation and prosecution are not themselves wrongful".[57] In the case of *Al Warraq v. Indonesia*, the investor argued that the conduct of the host State's authorities during a criminal investigation and subsequent criminal proceedings amounted to a violation of the FET.[58] The Tribunal actually found that Indonesia's actions – in particular, holding a criminal trial *in absentia* – did violate the FET.[59]

Typical elements of the obligation to accord due process, as recognized by arbitral case law, are the right of access to courts,[60] the conclusion of proceedings without undue delay,[61] the right to be heard,[62] and the independence and impartiality of the adjudicator.[63] Usually, the obligation to respect due process is not considered to include an obligation to apply the law correctly, and does not sanction an error in law. Sometimes arbitral tribunals have accepted that such an error could be considered a violation of an investment treaty, but a particularly high threshold applies: "*[T]he State can be held responsible for an unfair and inequitable treatment of a foreign indirect investor if and when the judiciary breached the standard by* fundamentally unfair proceedings and outrageously wrong, final and binding decisions".[64]

---

[57] *The Rompetrol Group N.V. v. Romania*, ICSID Case No. ARB/06/3, Award, 6 May 2013.

[58] *Hesham T. M. Al Warraq v. Republic of Indonesia*, UNCITRAL, Award, 15 December 2014, para. 391 ff.

[59] *Ibid.*, para. 556 ff.

[60] *Robert Azinian, Kenneth Davitian, & Ellen Baca v. The United Mexican States*, ICSID Case No. ARB (AF)/97/2, Award, 1 November 1999, para. 102; *Siemens A.G. v. The Argentine Republic*, ICSID Case No. ARB/02/8, Award, 17 January 2007, para. 308.

[61] *Valores Mundiales, S.L. and Consorcio Andino S.L. v. Bolivarian Republic of Venezuela*, ICSID Case No. ARB/13/11, Award, 25 July 2017, para. 583. However, in assessing whether there has been an undue delay on the part of the State, particular attention must be given to the circumstances of each specific case: *Jan de Nul N.V. and Dredging International N.V. v. Arab Republic of Egypt*, ICSID Case No. ARB/04/13, Award, 6 November 2008, para. 204.

[62] *Metalclad Corporation v. The United Mexican States*, ICSID Case No. ARB (AF)/97/1, Award, 30 August 2000, para. 91; *Middle East Cement Shipping and Handling Co. S.A. v. Arab Republic of Egypt*, ICSID Case No. ARB/99/6, Award, 12 April 2002, para. 147.

[63] *Vannessa Ventures Ltd. v. Bolivarian Republic of Venezuela*, ICSID Case No. ARB (AF)04/6, Award, 16 January 2013, para. 228.

[64] *Mr. Franck Charles Arif v. Republic of Moldova*, ICSID Case No. ARB/11/23, Award, 8 April 2013, para. 445 (emphasis added).

As mentioned, the FET obligation also comprises an obligation to respect investors' legitimate expectations and their reliance on the conduct of the State. Legitimate expectations can first derive from a contract. Not every breach of contract, however, is a violation of the FET; for the latter to occur, it is usually required something more than the mere breach by the State, like an abuse of sovereign power to escape the contract.[65] Also, legitimate expectations can derive from a unilateral promise by the State[66] or from its legislation. In the latter case, the expectations can be considered legitimate to the extent the investor is relying on a normative framework by which the State sought to *induce* the investment. In the words of an arbitral Tribunal:

> *"[T]he expectations of the Claimants with respect to their investment [...] did not suddenly and surprisingly come into their minds the way Athena sprang from the head of Zeus. [The host State] through its laws, the treaties it signed, its government statements, and especially the elaborate legal framework which it designed and enacted, deliberately and actively sought to create those expectations in the Claimants".*[67]

This does not mean, however, that the State can never modify its normative framework, as this would be too heavy of a burden. This is where proportionality as a FET element comes into play. Proportionality involves a balancing activity of investors' expectations and the State's power to regulate the investment, since

> *"it is inconceivable that any State would accept that, because it has entered into BITs, it can no longer modify pieces of legislation which might have a negative impact on foreign investors, in order to deal with modified economic conditions and must guarantee absolute legal stability. [...] In other words, fair and equitable treatment is a standard entailing reasonableness and proportionality. It ensures basically that the foreign investor is not unjustly treated, with due regard to all*

[65] *Impregilo S.p.A. v. Islamic Republic of Pakistan*, ICSID Case No. ARB/03/3, Decision on Jurisdiction, 22 April 2005, para. 260; *Toto Costruzioni Generali S.p.A. v. The Republic of Lebanon*, ICSID Case No. ARB/07/12, Award, 7 June 2012, paras. 161-162.

[66] *Crystallex International Corporation v. Venezuela*, ICSID Case No. ARB(AF)/11/2, Award, April 2016, para. 547; *Metalclad Corporation v. The United Mexican States*, ICSID Case No. ARB(AF)/97/1, Award, 30 August 2000, para. 89.

[67] *Suez, Sociedad General de Aguas de Barcelona, S.A. and Vivendi Universal, S.A.* and *AGW Group v. Argentine Republic*, ICSID Case No. ARB/03/19, Decision on Liability, 30 July 2010, para. 227.

> *surrounding circumstances. FET is a means to guarantee justice to foreign investors".* [68]

On the other hand, proportionality means that whenever a State adopts a measure affecting an investment, the measure must be proportionate, meaning that: besides being aimed at pursuing a relevant public objective, it must be suitable to reach the goal the State adopts it for and it must be necessary, in the sense that it must be the least intrusive possible in the investors' rights.

3.3.3. National Treatment

Most IIAs contain an obligation to accord foreign investments and/or investors a treatment not less favorable than the one accorded to domestic investors (National Treatment or NT obligation). This obligation, together with the Most-Favoured Nation (MFN) obligation, i.e. the obligation to accord investments and/or investors a treatment not less favourable than the one accorded to nationals of a third State, which will be discussed later, is part of a more general obligation of non-discrimination that can be found in most fields of international economic law. For instance, the NT obligation can be found in most agreements of the World Trade Organization (WTO). [69]

In the words of an arbitral Tribunal,

> "National treatment *and* Most-Favoured-Nation treatment *are treaty clauses that have the same substantive effect as the international treatment standard: foreigners should be afforded treatment no less favourable than the one granted to local citizens. [...] In other words, all the requirements, be they national treatment, most favoured-nation-treatment or non-discrimination at large, will in effect bar discrimination against foreign national investing in the country concerned".* [70]

---

[68] *El Paso Energy International Company v. Argentine Republic*, ICSID Case No. ARB/03/15, Award, 31 October 2011, paras. 367 and 373.

[69] See Article III of the General Agreement on Tariffs and Trade (GATT), Article XVII:1 of the General Agreement on Trade in Services (GATS) and Article III of the Agreement on Trade Related Aspects of Intellectual Property Rights (TRIPS).

[70] *Parkerings-Compagniet AS v. Republic of Lithuania*, ICSID Case No. ARB/05/8, Award, 11 September 2007, para. 367. See also *Archer Daniels Midland Company and Tate & Lyle Ingredients Americas, Inc. v. The United Mexican States*, ICSID Case No. ARB (AF)/04/5, Award, 21 November 2007, para. 193. This is also the reason why the

Thus, the NT obligation can be found in almost all IIAs since the early times of their conclusion, with very small textual variations, and it is often mentioned together with the MFN obligation.[71] Contrary to the latter, however, the NT obligation is less frequently invoked and, most importantly, such invocations are less frequently successful.

Still, an obligation such as the NT (and the MFN) is fundamental in a treaty regime on the protection of foreign investments, as it is commonly accepted that it is not part of customary international law:

> *"As to the question of whether a rule of customary international law prohibits a State, in the absence of a treaty obligation, from differentiating in its treatment of nationals and aliens, international law is clear. In the absence of a contrary rule of international law binding on the States parties, whether of conventional or customary origin, a State may differentiate in its treatment of nationals and aliens"*.[72]

For an arbitral tribunal to find that a State has breached the NT obligation, however, it is not at all necessary that the party alleging the violation proves that the State actually had a discriminatory intent. What is important is the effect of the State's conduct, since to require an investor to prove the intent behind the State's measures would be too onerous:

> *"More generally, requiring a foreign investor to prove that discrimination is based on his nationality could be an insurmountable burden to the Claimant, as that information may only be available to the government. It would be virtually impossible for any claimant to meet the burden of demonstrating that a government's motivation for discrimination is nationality rather than some other reason"*.[73]

---

case law on these obligations is used interchangeably: see *Parkerings-Compagniet AS v. Republic of Lithuania*, para. 366.

[71] An example is Article 3(1) of the Afghanistan-Germany BIT, according to which: "*Neither Contracting State shall subject investments in its territory owned or controlled by investors of the other Contracting State to treatment less favourable than it accords to investments of its own investors or to investments of investors of any third State*".

[72] *Methanex Corporation v. United States of America*, UNCITRAL, Final Award of the Tribunal on Jurisdiction and the Merits, 3 August 2005, Part. IV, Chapter C, para. 25.

[73] *Marvin Roy Feldman Karpa v. United Mexican States*, ICSID Case No. ARB (AF)/99/1, Award, 16 December 2002, para. 183. See also *Consortium RFCC v. Royaume du Maroc*, ICSID Case No. ARB/00/6, Award, 22 December 2003, para. 74; *Occidental Exploration and Production Company v. The Republic of Ecuador*, LCIA Case No.

What is actually necessary to reach the conclusion that a State has breached the NT obligation is that another, domestic investor has been accorded a more favorable treatment, without this treatment being justified by other circumstances. The NT, indeed, is a "relative" standard and not an "absolute" one, meaning that it is a standard involving a comparison between the situation of different subjects.

Thus, an arbitral tribunal needs to ascertain: *i*) who the term of comparison is; *ii*) whether the latter has been granted a more favorable treatment; and *iii*) whether this different treatment is justified by a specific policy objective by the State.[74]

For a domestic investor to be a suitable term of comparison, such an investor must be in similar or "like" circumstances to the one claiming the violation of the NT obligation. What actually constitutes similar or "like" circumstances is not always very clear; generally, the case law of arbitral tribunals has focused on whether the two investors operate in the same business or economic sector and whether there exists a competitive relationship between the two.[75]

However, arbitral case law has also stressed the importance of keeping the "likeness" test flexible, as the determination of whether two investors are in similar circumstances involves an assessment which is heavily fact-dependent: "*It goes without saying that the meaning of the term ['like circumstances'] will vary according to the facts of a given case. By their very nature, 'circumstances' are context dependent and have no unalterable meaning across the spectrum of fact situations*".[76]

Therefore, it could well be that two or more investors are considered

---

UN3467, Final Award, 1 July 2004, para. 177; *Parkerings-Compagniet AS v. Republic of Lithuania* (note 70), para. 368.

[74] *Archer Daniels Midland Company and Tate & Lyle Ingredients Americas, Inc. v. The United Mexican States* (note 70), para. 196; *Bayindir Insaat Turizm Ticaret Ve Sanayi A.S. v. Islamic Republic of Pakistan* (I), ICSID Case No. ARB/03/29, Award, 27 August 2009, para. 399; *Grand River Enterprises Six Nations, Ltd., et al. v. United States of America*, UNCITRAL, Award, 12 January 2011, para. 163. This is true even if the necessity of a comparison with a subject in similar or "like" circumstances is not prescribed by the relevant IIA, as it is "*inherent in an evaluation of discrimination*": *Total S.A. v. The Argentine Republic*, ICSID Case No. ARB/04/01, Decision on Liability, 27 December 2010, para. 213.

[75] *S.D. Myers, Inc. v. Government of Canada*, UNCITRAL, Partial Award, 13 November 2000, paras. 250-251; *Pope & Talbot Inc. v. The Government of Canada*, UNCITRAL, Award on the Merits of Phase 2, 10 April 2001, para. 78; *Archer Daniels Midland Company and Tate & Lyle Ingredients Americas, Inc. v. The United Mexican States* (note 70), paras. 198-199.

[76] *Pope & Talbot Inc. v. The Government of Canada* (note 75), para. 75.

to be in similar circumstances without operating in the same business sector. An emblematic example in this respect is the case of *Occidental Exploration and Production Company v. Ecuador*,[77] which concerned a resolution by Ecuadorian authorities to deny the Claimant its request for Value-Added Tax ("VAT") reimbursement. The investor contended that this course of action violated, *inter alia*, the NT obligation, as other companies continued to benefit from the VAT refund. Before finding that a breach of the NT obligation had actually occurred, the Tribunal reasoned that

> *"in the context of this particular claim the Claimant is right and its arguments are convincing. In fact, 'in like situations' cannot be interpreted in the narrow sense advanced by Ecuador as the purpose of national treatment is to protect investors as compared to local producers, and this cannot be done by addressing exclusively the sector in which that particular activity is undertaken"*.[78]

3.3.4. Most-Favored Nation Treatment

MFN treatment is "*treatment accorded by the granting State to the beneficiary State, or to the persons or things in a determined relationship with that State, not less favourable than treatment extended by the granting State to a third State or to persons or things in the same relationship with that third State*".[79] Thus, through an MFN clause, each State party to an IIA undertakes to accord investors or investments of the other parties a treatment no less favorable than the treatment it accords to any third investor or investment.

The MFN obligation is an essential feature of trade agreements; for example, an MFN obligation is today included in most WTO agreements, like the GATT,[80] the GATS,[81] and the TRIPS agreement.[82] When applied in international investment law, however, this obligation poses unique chal-

---

[77] *Occidental Exploration and Production Company v. The Republic of Ecuador* (note 73).

[78] *Ibid.*, para. 173.

[79] International Law Commission (ILC), *Draft Articles on Most-Favoured-Nation Clauses*, 1978, Article 5.

[80] Article I:1.

[81] Article II:1.

[82] Article IV. For an analysis of the MFN obligation in the context of the WTO system see Chapter 4, Section 4.10.1.

lenges, due to the structure of this field of international law. Indeed, the high number of IIAs, mostly of a bilateral nature, coupled with the fact that every treaty can contain a slightly differently formulated MFN clause, can give rise to a myriad of different obligations, depending on the wording of the treaty containing the clause and the treaty used as a comparison. It is not by chance that the MFN treatment standard has been defined as one of the most inconsistently applied standards in international investment law.[83]

Yet, the MFN obligation is an essential feature of IIAs and, together with the NT obligation, constitutes an application of the principle of non-discrimination in international investment law.

The ILC has identified six main types of MFN obligations contained in IIAs.[84] The first type is the one in which the obligation simply relates to treatment no less favorable than that accorded to others. An example was the now-terminated BIT between Austria and the Czech Republic, whose Article 3(1) read that "*[e]ach Contracting Party shall accord investors of the other Contracting Party treatment no less favourable than that accorded to its own investors or investors of a third State and their investments*".

The second type is the one where the clause explicitly states that it applies to *all treatment* or to all matters governed by the treaty, like in the Spain-Argentina BIT, whose Article 4(2) establishes that "*[i]n all matters governed by this Agreement, such treatment shall be no less favourable than that accorded by each Party to investments made in its territory by investors of a third country*".

The third type of MFN obligation is the one in which the MFN treatment is linked to specific aspects of the investment like the "management" or "use" or "disposal". An instance is the BIT between Serbia and Algeria: its Article 3(2) provides that "*[e]ach Contracting Party shall in its territory accord investors of the other Contracting Party, as regards their management, maintenance, use, enjoyment or disposal of their investments, treatment equally favourable that it accords to its own investors or to investors of any third State, whichever is more favourable*".

The fourth type of obligation is the one where the MFN obligation is linked to other specific obligations contained in the investment agreement, like the FET. An example of this kind of MFN clause is Article 3(1) of the Denmark-Egypt BIT, according to which: "*Each contracting Party shall in its territory accord to investments made by investors of the*

---

[83] A.Y. Vastardis, "Most Favoured Nation Treatment", in D. Schneiderman and G. Van Harten (eds.), *Rethinking Investment Law. Perspectives and Prospects*, OUP, 2023, p. 38.

[84] ILC, *Final Report of the Study Group on Most-Favoured-Nation Clauses*, 2015, UN Doc. A/CN.4/L.852, para. 59 ff. On the ILC see Chapter 2, Section 2.8.1.

other Contracting Party fair and equitable treatment which in no case shall be less favourable than that accorded to its own investors or to investors of any third state, whichever is the more favourable from the point of view of the investor".

The fifth type specifies that the MFN treatment must be accorded to investors and/or investments in similar or like circumstances, like in the Canada-China BIT, under whose Article 5(1) "*[e]ach Contracting Party shall accord to investors of the other Contracting Party treatment no less favourable than that it accords, in like circumstances, to investors of a non-Contracting Party with respect to the establishment, acquisition, expansion, management, conduct, operation and sale or other disposition of investments in its territory*".

The sixth type limits the scope of the MFN treatment obligation to the territory of each State. An example is Article 3(1) of the Georgia-Japan BIT: "*Each Contracting Party shall in its Territory accord to investors of the other Contracting Party and to their investments treatment no less favourable than the treatment it accords in like circumstances to investors of a non-Contracting Party and to their investments with respect to investment activities*".

From what has been just said, it is clear that the first complexity in interpreting and applying an MFN clause is the variety of MFN obligations actually contained in IIAs, considering also that an MFN clause can very well fall under more than one of the types listed above. It is thus no surprise that MFN clauses have been used for a variety of purposes. First of all, the clause has been used by investors to claim that another specific investor had been put in a more favorable position, which constituted a violation of the treaty enshrining the MFN obligation.

An emblematic case in this respect is represented by *Parkerings v. Lithuania.*[85] The dispute arose out of an agreement concluded between the city of Vilnius and the Egapris Consortium to build and operate a multi-storey car park (MSCP) in the city. Due to impairments in the performance of such an agreement, such as the adoption by Lithuania of legislation limiting the power of local authorities to negotiate with private companies and the fact that several government agencies objected that the proposed parking system was to be developed within an area designed as a World Heritage Site by the United Nations Educational, Scientific and Cultural Organization (UNESCO), the agreement was terminated by the city of Vilnius, which caused the investor to bring a claim before an arbitral tribunal. Before the Tribunal, Parkerings claimed, *inter alia*, that it was treated in a less favorable manner compared to another investor, Pinus Proprius, with

[85] *Parkerings-Compagniet AS v. Republic of Lithuania* (note 70).

which the city of Vilnius had contracted to develop a parking system in a similar area.

In ruling on this claim, the Tribunal specifies that an MFN obligation only arises when investors are in like circumstances, meaning that they have to be in the same economic or business sector.[86] In addition, the Tribunal clarified that no violation of the MFN obligation can be said to have occurred if the State has a legitimate reason to treat investors differently.[87] The Tribunal ultimately found that this was the case, because even if the investors had been treated differently, there was a legitimate reason to do so:

> *"[T]he fact that [Parkering's] project [...] extended significantly more into the Old Town as defined by the UNESCO, is decisive. [...] The historical and archaeological preservation and environmental protection could be and in this case were a justification for the refusal of the project. The potential negative impact of the [Parkering's] project in the Old Town was increased by its considerable size and its proximity with the culturally sensitive area of the Cathedral. Consequently, [Parkering's] MSCP [...] was not similar with the MSCP constructed by Pinus Proprius".*[88]

In other – and arguably more complex – cases, the MFN clause has been used to try and import into the treaty containing such clause (so-called basic treaty) a better treatment allegedly contained in treaties concluded between the host State and third States.

Actually, in several cases arbitral tribunals have allowed investors to benefit from a treatment that was not enshrined in the basic treaty, by virtue of the operation of an MFN clause, which "imported" such treatment from another IIA. For example, this was what happened in the case of *Bayindir v. Pakistan*,[89] arising out of the Pakistan-Turkey BIT, which does not contain a FET obligation. The Claimant sought to import such obligation from other BITs concluded by the Respondent State. In this respect, noting that a reference to the FET could be found in the preamble of the basic treaty, the Tribunal reasoned that: "*The Tribunal is [...] not persuaded that this [...] rules out the possibility of importing an FET obligation through the MFN clause expressly included in the Treaty. The fact that the States parties to the Treaty clearly contemplated the importance of the FET rather suggests the contrary. Indeed, even though it does not establish an op-*

---

[86] *Ibid.*, paras. 369-371.

[87] *Ibid.*, para. 371.

[88] *Ibid.*, para. 392.

[89] *Bayindir Insaat Turizm Ticaret Ve Sanayi A.S. v. Islamic Republic of Pakistan (I)* (note 74).

erative obligation, the preamble is relevant for the interpretation of the MFN clause in its context and in the light of the Treaty's object and purpose pursuant to Article 31(1) of the VCLT".[90] Eventually, the Tribunal imported the FET obligation from the BIT concluded between Pakistan and Switzerland,[91] although it ultimately reached the conclusion that no FET breach had occurred.

As already mentioned, however, the MFN treatment obligation is very inconsistently applied. Therefore, with different outcomes, it has been invoked by investors for a lot of different ends, such as to import a more favorably formulated standard of treatment than the one contained in the basic treaty[92] or to neutralize the operation of exceptions to obligations contained in the basic treaty, exceptions not contained in other treaties.[93]

However, the most controversial use of the MFN clause is its application to provisions on the settlement of disputes between host States and foreign investors. It has already been said that one of the main features of modern investment treaties is the possibility for investors to directly bring a claim for the violation of the standards contained in the treaty against the host State. This possibility is afforded through a specific clause on ISDS in the treaty itself and, as noted, is one of the main reasons for the success of IIAs. This is why investors have often tried to import better dispute settlement clauses via the MFN clause. However, arbitral tribunals and scholarship are split and the issue of whether the MFN treatment can apply to dispute settlement provisions. While some argued that MFN treatment can be used to import the State's consent to another dispute resolution mechanism, others maintained that this would not be possible. The debate started as early as 2000, when the Tribunal in the case of *Maffezini v. Spain* ruled that the MFN clause in the Spain-Argentina BIT could be applied to import a more favorable dispute settlement provision, and precisely that contained in the Chile-Spain BIT; the latter, indeed, unlike the one in the Spain-Argentina BIT, i.e. the basic treaty, did not contain the requirement for the investor to pursue local remedies before Spanish courts for eighteen months before resorting to arbitration.[94]

---

[90] *Ibid.*, para. 155.

[91] *Ibid.*, paras. 161-167.

[92] *Chemtura Corporation (formerly Crompton Corporation) v. Government of Canada*, PCA Case No. 2008-01, Claimant's Memorial, 28 June 2008, para. 450 ff.

[93] *CMS Gas Transmission Company v. The Republic of Argentina*, ICSID Case No. ARB/01/8, Award, Award, 12 May 2005, para. 343. The argument was rejected by the Tribunal: see para. 377.

[94] *Emilio Agustín Maffezini v. The Kingdom of Spain*, ICSID Case No. ARB/97/7, Decision of the Tribunal on Objections to Jurisdiction, 25 January 2000, para. 38 ff.

Just five years later, the Tribunal in *Plama v. Bulgaria* adopted a completely opposite approach, finding that the Claimant could not rely on dispute settlement provisions other than the one contained in the treaty from which the dispute had arisen. [95]

The latter position is, in our view, the most persuasive; this is because for a tribunal to decide on whether a certain most favorable treatment contained in another treaty can be accorded to an investor, it must first have jurisdiction over the claim for the violation of the MFN clause itself. This means that the treaty containing the MFN clause must be capable of autonomously grounding the jurisdiction of the arbitral tribunal. [96]

Still, the debate on whether MFN clauses can be applied to dispute settlement provisions has not been definitively settled. Suffice it to notice that, only in 2023, different tribunals decided the issue differently. For example, the Tribunal sitting in the case *AsiaPhos Limited v. China* believed that this was possible but only if there is a "*clear and unambiguous intention of both parties for the MFN clause to have this effect*". [97] On a different note, the Tribunal in the case of *Orazul v. Argentina* stated that MFN provisions can be applied to substantive and procedural issues alike. [98]

3.3.5. Full Protection and Security

Most modern BITs also include an obligation to accord investors and their investments full protection and security. Of course, as for all IIAs clauses, some textual variations may be found across different treaties: for instance, some simply refer to "*full protection and security*", [99] while others refer to "*full and constant protection and security*" [100] or to "*the most constant protection and security*". [101]

First and foremost, this obligation has been interpreted as an obligation

---

[95] *Plama Consortium Limited v. Republic of Bulgaria*, ICSID Case No. ARB/03/24, Decision on Jurisdiction, 8 February 2005, para. 183 ff.

[96] ICJ, *Anglo-Iranian Oil Co. Case (United Kingdom v. Iran)*, Judgment (Preliminary Objections), 22 July 1952, ICJ Reports 1952, p. 93 ff., in particular pp. 107-110.

[97] *AsiaPhos Limited and Norwest Chemicals Pte Ltd v. People's Republic of China*, ICSID Case No. ADM/21/1, Award, 16 February 2023, para. 211.

[98] *Orazul International España Holdings S.L. v. Argentine Republic*, ICSID Case No. ARB/19/25, Award, 14 December 2023, para. 391.

[99] See, for instance, Article 5(1) of the Japan-Bahrain BIT.

[100] Examples are: Article 3(1) of the Austria-Kyrgyzstan, Article 2(2) of the Azerbaijan-Syria BIT and Article 2(2) of the China-Korean Republic BIT.

[101] See Article 3(3) of the Japan-Russia BIT.

to protect the investment from physical damages. In this case, the obligation usually covers both the acts of a State and the acts of third parties.[102] With respect to the former, an emblematic example can be represented by the case of *Cengiz v. Libya*, in which the Tribunal found that the Respondent State had violated Article 2(2) of the Libya-Turkey BIT, containing an obligation on States to guarantee investments "full protection", through actions and omissions of the regular Libyan army and militias forming part of the insurrectional movement then controlled by the Libyan National Transition Council which had resulted in the destruction of the Claimant's construction sites.[103]

As regards the protection from actions of third parties, the breach by the State would mean that the latter did not act with due diligence, i.e. doing everything in its power to avoid and repress damages: in other words, "*[a] violation of the standard of full protection and security could arise in case of failure of the State to prevent the damage, to restore the previous situation or to punish the author of the injury. The injury could be committed either by the host State, or by its agencies or by an individual*".[104] A case of breach of the standard for actions of third parties is that of *AAPL v. Sri Lanka*, concerning the destruction of the Claimant's shrimp farm by the Tamil rebels.[105]

Another more recent case is *Ampal v Egypt*, arising out of the claim by the investors that the Respondent State had failed to protect their investment in a pipeline from attacks occurred during the Arab Spring.[106]

Besides the *physical* protection of the investment, it is very debated in scholarship and among arbitral tribunals whether the standard in question also entails an obligation to guarantee legal protection to the investment, such as the protection afforded through the provision of legal remedies against interference with the enjoyment of the investment itself.

In some cases, the debate is quickly resolved, as the relevant BIT provides for an answer, specifying the scope of application of the standard. For

[102] Although there have been arbitral tribunals implying that the standard only covers the actions of third parties and not of States: see *Oxus Gold v. Republic of Uzbekistan*, UNCITRAL, Award, 17 December 2015, para. 353.

[103] *Cengiz İnşaat Sanayi ve Ticaret A.S v. Libya*, ICC Case No. 21537/ZF/AYZ, Award, 7 November 2018, in particular para. 401 ff.

[104] *Parkerings-Compagniet AS v. Republic of Lithuania* (note 70), para. 355. For a similar statement, see also *Biwater Gauff (Tanzania) Ltd. v. United Republic of Tanzania* (note 27), para. 730.

[105] *Asian Agricultural Products Ltd. v. Republic of Sri Lanka*, ICSID Case No. ARB/87/3, Final Award, 27 June 1990.

[106] *Ampal-American Israel Corporation and others v. Arab Republic of Egypt*, ICSID Case No. ARB/12/11, Decision on Liability and Head of Loss, 21 February 2017.

example, Article 3(2) of the Netherlands-Nigeria BIT expressly states that "*each Contracting Party shall accord to [...] investments full physical security and protection*". Another example is Article 5(2)(b) of the USA-Rwanda BIT, according to which "*'full protection and security' requires each Party to provide the level of police protection required under customary international law*". On the contrary, other agreements expressly refer to legal protection. One could mention, in this regard, the BIT between Argentina and Germany, whose Article 4(1) refers to full legal protection and security. [107]

However, it is difficult to understand the precise scope of application of the standard when clarification is lacking in the text of the treaty. In the absence of such clarification, there have been different interpretations by arbitral tribunals.

A number of them have interpreted the standard as also entailing an obligation to guarantee legal protection. [108] This legal protection would require the State to create a secure and stable legal environment immune from unjustifiable and sudden changes and uncertainties.

As recognized by the very tribunals upholding the "legal dimension" of the full protection and security standard, this legal protection frequently overlaps with obligations owed by the State under the FET standard. This is also why other tribunals have considered that full protection and security only encompasses physical protection. For example, this has been the position upheld by the Tribunal in the *Crystallex v. Venezuela* case:

> *"The Tribunal is mindful that other investment tribunals have interpreted the 'full protection and security' standard more extensively so as to cover legal security and the protection of a stable legal framework. [...T]he Tribunal is of the view that the more 'traditional' interpretation better accords with the ordinary meaning of the terms. Furthermore, as rightly observed by a number of previous decisions, a more extensive reading of the 'full protection and security' standard would result in an overlap with other treaty standards, notably FET [...]. The Tribunal is thus unconvinced that it should depart from an interpretation of the 'full protection and security' standard limited to physical security".* [109]

---

[107] See *Siemens A.G. v. The Argentine Republic*, ICSID Case No. ARB/02/8, Award, 17 January 2007, para. 303.

[108] *Azurix Corp. v. The Argentine Republic*, ICSID Case No. ARB/01/12, Award, 14 July 2006, paras. 406-408; *Biwater Gauff (Tanzania) Ltd. v. United Republic of Tanzania* (note 27), para. 729; *Plama Consortium Limited v. Republic of Bulgaria* (note 95), Award, 27 August 2008, para. 180; *Marion Unglaube v. Republic of Costa Rica*, ICSID Case No. ARB/08/1, Award, 16 May 2012, para. 283.

[109] *Crystallex International Corporation v. Venezuela* (note 66), para. 634.

A similar view has also been adopted by the *Enron v. Argentina* Tribunal.[110]

Thus, arbitral tribunals seem split on the issue of whether the full protection and security standard only covers physical protection or also legal protection. The more "traditional" interpretation – that is, the interpretation more in line with the standard as developed in the customary international law on the treatment of aliens – is that the standard only encompasses physical protection. More and more tribunals, however, are recognizing the obligation to guarantee also legal protection for investments. This legal protection, however, should be guaranteed through conducts which in most cases are prescribed by other standards contained in IIAs, and mainly by the FET standard.

3.3.6. Umbrella Clauses

Some IIAs contain so-called umbrella clauses, i.e. clauses enshrining an obligation on the part of the host State to respect the commitments it enters into with respect to the investment. An example is Article 9 of the BIT between Austria and Namibia, under which "*[e]ach Contracting Party shall observe any obligation it may have entered into with regard to specific investments by investors of the other Contracting Party*". Another example is Article 10(3) of the Congo-Korea BIT, which reads that "*[e]ach Contracting Party shall observe any other obligation that may have entered into force with regard to investments in its territory by investors of the other Contracting Party*".

As for any other treaty clause, the wording may vary from one agreement to the other. However, all umbrella clauses oblige the State in some way to respect additional obligations it has assumed in relation to an investment covered by the treaty. Umbrella clauses are not as common as all the other standards of treatment already discussed; still, they are a very important feature of most investment agreements and have caused some interpretative problems. This is because umbrella clauses are capable of linking contractual commitments assumed by States to an international agreement. In other words, thanks to an umbrella clause, the breach of an obligation other than those enshrined in the treaty containing such a clause could entail a breach of the treaty itself.

---

[110] *Enron Corporation and Ponderosa Assets, L.P. v. Argentine Republic*, ICSID Case No. ARB/01/3 (also known as: *Enron Creditors Recovery Corp. and Ponderosa Assets, L.P. v. The Argentine Republic*), Award, 22 March 2007, para. 286.

According to some scholars, indeed, "*in the presence of an umbrella clause, a breach by the host country of an investment contract with the foreign investor constitutes a violation of the treaty and the investor can raise it in international arbitration*".[111] Some treaties, actually, specify that this is the case: according to Article 11(1) of the Austria-Kyrgyzstan BIT, for example, "*[e]ach Contracting Party shall observe any obligation it may have entered into with regard to specific investments by investors of the other Contracting Party. This means, inter alia, that the breach of a contract between the investor and the host State will amount to a violation of this treaty*".

Usually, however, these specifications are not contained in IIAs. This has led some scholars and arbitral tribunals to believe that umbrella clauses do not render any contractual breach a breach of the treaty containing the clause, as this would be too grave of a consequence for the host State. Indeed, by interpreting umbrella clauses in this way, all the actions of a State infringing on a contract will inevitably transform into an internationally wrongful act. Thus, something more than a mere contractual breach would be required to trigger the application of the umbrella clause.

This uncertainty surrounding the proper interpretation of umbrella clauses is well exemplified by the cases of *SGS v. Philippines* and *SGS v. Pakistan*. Both cases arose out of similar facts and in both cases the investors invoked the umbrella clauses contained in the Switzerland-Philippines BIT and the Switzerland-Pakistan BIT, respectively.

The *SGS v. Pakistan* Tribunal refused to accept the Claimant's thesis according to which the umbrella clause transforms purely contractual claims into BIT claims and reasoned as follows:

> *"[W]e do not preclude the possibility that under exceptional circumstances, a violation of certain provisions of a State contract with an investor of another State might constitute violation of a treaty provision [...] enjoining a Contracting Party constantly to guarantee the observance of contracts with investors of another Contracting Party. [...] The modes by which a Contracting Party may 'constantly guarantee the observance of' its contractual or statutory or administrative municipal law commitments with respect to investments are not necessarily exhausted by the instant transubstantiation of contract claims into BIT claims posited by the Claimant".*[112]

---

[111] R. Dolzer, U. Kriebaum and C. Schreuer, *Principles of International Investment Law*³ (note 1), p. 274.

[112] *SGS Société Générale de Surveillance S.A. v. Islamic Republic of Pakistan*, ICSID Case No. ARB/01/13, Decision of the Tribunal on Objections to Jurisdiction, 6 August 2003, para. 172.

Shortly after, the *SGS v. Philippines* Tribunal defined the reasoning of the previous Tribunal as "*unconvincing*"[113] and stated that

> *"it is a conceivable function of a provision such as [the umbrella clause] of the Swiss-Philippines BIT to provide assurances to foreign investors with regard to the performance of obligations assumed by the host State under its own law with regard to specific investments – in effect, to help secure the rule of law in relation to investment protection. In the Tribunal's view, this is the proper interpretation of [the umbrella clause]".*[114]

Some arbitral tribunals have adopted an approach which may be considered to stand in the middle of the two mentioned above, which requires that the breach of a contract is a breach of an umbrella clause if the host State acted abusing its governmental authority, with a view of distinguishing "the State as a merchant" from "the State as a sovereign".[115]

Still, the debate cannot be considered settled. A recent case dealing with the issue is *Gardabani v. Georgia*, concerning the generation and distribution of electricity by the Claimants in the host State's market. According to the Claimants, the host State, besides breaching the Netherlands-Georgia BIT, had also breached a contract also involving different parties than the Claimants; actually, a separate arbitration for the breach of the contract was initiated and concluded in favor of the investors. Against this background, the Tribunal found that Georgia had breached the umbrella clause contained in the Georgia-Netherlands BIT. In particular, the majority of arbitrators were not persuaded by the argument put forth by the Respondent that a breach of an umbrella clause can only occur when the State's actions involved the use and abuse of sovereign authority.[116]

This decision was harshly criticized by one of the arbitrators, Prof. Zachary Douglas, who appended a dissenting opinion in which he noted that, in general international law, the "*orthodox position [...] reflects a fault-based ground for liability for interference in a contractual relationship with a foreign national: the State has abused its sovereign power to deprive the for-*

[113] *SGS Société Générale de Surveillance S.A. v. Republic of the Philippines*, ICSID Case No. ARB/02/6, Decision of the Tribunal on Objections to Jurisdiction, 29 January 2004, para. 125.

[114] *Ibid.*, para. 126.

[115] The expression is from *Pan American Energy LLC and BP Argentina Exploration Company v. The Argentine Republic*, ICSID Case No. ARB/03/13, Decision on Preliminary Objections, 27 July 2006, para. 109.

[116] *Gardabani Holdings B.V. and Silk Road Holdings B.V. v. Georgia*, ICSID Case No. ARB/17/29, Award, 27 October 2022, para. 685 ff., in particular para. 692.

eign national of a benefit or to impose an additional burden that was not envisaged under the terms of the contract or its applicable law".[117]

The decisions discussed here evidence that the issue of the proper interpretation of umbrella clauses is still highly controversial, and arbitral tribunals seem to adopt both the restrictive and the wide approach in their case law.

3.4. Reconciling the Protection of Foreign Investments with Other Public Interests

For a very long time now, many States have been arguing that international investment law is an inherently unjust field of international law and that international investment arbitration is biased in favor of investors. Among the several reasons offered to support this position, it is often said that IIAs do not give States the possibility to adopt measures which, although infringing on investors' rights, are necessary to pursue certain policy objectives and are of public interest, such as the protection of public health or the environment, or the need to tackle climate change.

An emblematic example in this respect is the above-mentioned case of *Rockhopper v. Italy*, which has recently attracted the attention of scholars, and in which the refusal of the State to grant the investors a concession to exploit an offshore oilfield within its territorial waters was found to be in violation of the ECT. The decision has been regarded by many as evidence of the failure of the investment protection regime to protect other non-economic interests like the protection of the environment. Also, the already discussed attempt at reforming the ECT to address the climate crisis is an example of States' discontent with the current normative framework on foreign investments.

It is certainly true that IIAs mostly contain obligations for States, and not for investors. They usually do not impose on investors the obligation to respect the human rights of the population or, for instance, labor standards. Some recent agreements stand contrary to this general tendency, but they are few and often not (yet) in force. An example in this respect could be the Nigeria-Morocco BIT, under whose Article 18

> *"[i]vestments shall uphold human rights in the host state. Investors and investments shall act in accordance with core labour standards as required by the ILO Declaration on Fundamental Principles and Rights of Work,*

[117] *Ibid.*, Dissenting Opinion by Professor Zachary Douglas KC, para. 38.

> *1998. Investors and investments shall not manage or operate the investments in a manner that circumvents international environmental, labour and human rights obligations to which the host state and/or home state are Parties".* [118]

It is, however, an agreement which is not in force, despite having been signed by States in 2018.

Sometimes, IIAs – also older IIAs – contain clauses prescribing that measures adopted to pursue certain objectives cannot be considered as breaching the obligations contained in the treaty, even if they actually infringe upon investors' rights. These clauses are usually called "Non-Precluded Measures" (NPM) clauses. An example is Article XI of the USA-Argentina BIT, concluded in 1991 and entered into force in 1994: "*This Treaty shall not preclude the application by either Party of measures necessary for the maintenance of public order, the fulfillment of its obligations with respect to the maintenance or restoration of international peace or security, or the Protection of its own essential security interests*". In recent IIAs, the list of objectives falling into the application of the NPM clause is longer and more precise. Examples in this respect could be Article 13 of the Iran-Japan BIT and Article 9.8 of the China-Australia Free Trade Agreement, which mirror the exceptions contained in Articles XX and XXI of the GATT. [119]

It is important to note that these clauses do not give the State the possibility of autonomously assessing when a measure it has adopted is intended to pursue a protected objective, i.e. they are not so-called self-judging clauses. On the contrary, arbitral tribunals have the power to review the assessment made by the State. [120]

The main problem with NPM clauses, however, is that they can only be found in certain treaties, not in every investment agreement. This is the main reason why arbitral case law has developed concepts such as the power to regulate – for expropriation – and the principle of proportionality – for the FET standard – which have already been discussed, and whose main feature is that they can be applied *even if the relevant treaty does not*

---

[118] Paras. 2, 3 and 4.

[119] On which see Chapter 4, Sections 4.11.1 and 4.11.2.

[120] *CMS Gas Transmission Company v. The Republic of Argentina*, ICSID Case No. ARB/01/8, Award, 12 May 2005, para. 373; *Enron Corporation and Ponderosa Assets, L.P. v. Argentine Republic* (note 110), para. 339; *Sempra Energy International v. The Argentine Republic*, ICSID Case No. ARB/02/16, Award, 28 September 2007, para. 388; *Deutsche Telekom v. India*, PCA Case No. 2014-10, Interim Award, 13 December 2017, para. 231.

explicitly provide them (even if, as already seen, they are sometimes codified in treaties).[121]

Apart from the provisions contained in treaties allowing States to adopt certain measures and from instruments such as the power to regulate and the principle of proportionality, it is also important to stress that international investment law is a field of international law, as such embedded in a wider normative framework. Therefore, IIAs are to be interpreted taking into account fields of international law other than international investment law, such as international human rights or environmental law. Actually, this is dictated by Article 31(3)(c) of the VCLT, under which the interpretation of a treaty must be conducted taking into account "*any relevant rules of international law applicable in the relations between the parties*". As stated by the arbitral Tribunal in *Urbaser v. Argentina*,

> *"[t]he BIT cannot be interpreted and applied in a vacuum. The Tribunal must certainly be mindful of the BIT's special purpose as a Treaty promoting foreign investments, but it cannot do so without taking the relevant rules of international law into account. The BIT has to be construed in harmony with other rules of international law of which it forms part, including those relating to human rights".*[122]

This so-called "systemic" integration has been instrumental in reaching the conclusion that the proposition according to which investors cannot bear obligations under IIAs no longer reflects the reality, and that companies can and should be held accountable for human rights violations.[123]

Lastly, it is worth mentioning the possibility for States to justify their actions using circumstances precluding wrongfulness, which are norms of customary international law and can thus be applied to all internationally wrongful acts (apart from those breaching a *ius cogens* norm[124]). The difference between the above-mentioned mechanisms like NPM clauses, the power to regulate and circumstances precluding wrongfulness is the moment in which they operate: while the former render a certain conduct by the State not in violation of the relevant IIA, the latter operate at a later

[121] See *supra,* note 51.

[122] *Urbaser S.A. and Consorcio de Aguas Bilbao Bizkaia, Bilbao Biskaia Ur Partzuergoa v. The Argentine Republic*, ICSID Case No. ARB/07/26, Award, 8 December 2016, para. 1200.

[123] *Ibid.*, paras. 1193 ff. Yet, the Tribunal reached the conclusion that no obligation upon the investor could be said to exist in that case.

[124] On the concept of *ius cogens* norms see Chapter 2, Section 2.8.2.

moment in time, meaning that the conduct of the State does breach the treaty, but is nevertheless justified.

These circumstances precluding wrongfulness have been codified by the ILC in its Articles on the Responsibility of States for Internationally Wrongful Acts (ARSIWA). The two circumstances precluding wrongfulness which have sometimes been invoked by States in the context of ISDS proceedings are *force majeure* and state of necessity.

Force majeure, codified in Article 23 of the ARSIWA, is "*the occurrence of an irresistible force or of an unforeseen event, beyond the control of the State, making it materially impossible in the circumstances to perform the obligation*". In addition, according to the second paragraph of Article 23, *force majeure* cannot be invoked if its occurrence is due, either alone or in combination with other factors, to the conduct of the State invoking it or if the State has assumed the risk of that situation occurring.

In international investment arbitration, however, *force majeure* has seldom been invoked and only in cases arising from contracts; as a consequence, arbitral case law has never accepted a *force majeure* defense invoked by a State. [125]

It is certainly more frequent for States to invoke a state of necessity, which is codified by Article 25 of the ARSIWA, which would allow States to disregard an international obligation if this is the only way for them to safeguard an essential interest against a grave and imminent peril.

State of necessity has often been invoked in cases brought by investors against Argentina for the measures the latter has adopted to tackle the 2001 economic crisis. Indeed, Argentina argued that the economic crisis was a situation of necessity, forcing it to adopt certain measures – such as privatizations or debt-restructuring measures – even if they were detrimental to investors. Most tribunals, however, have rejected this defense, stating that Argentina could not invoke this circumstance because it had contributed to the situation of necessity, i.e. the occurrence of the economic crisis. In the words of the arbitral Tribunal in the case of *Impregilo v. Argentina*, "*a State's contribution to its necessity situation need not be specifically intended or planned – it can be the consequence,* inter alia, *of well-intended but ill-conceived policies*". [126] Similarly, the Tribunals in the cases of *Sempra* and *Enron v. Argentina* have concluded

[125] For a few examples of cases discussing *force majeure* see: *Autopista Concesionada de Venezuela, C.A. v. Bolivarian Republic of Venezuela*, ICSID Case No. ARB/00/5, Award of the Tribunal, 23 September 2003, paras. 106-129; *Enron Corporation and Ponderosa Assets, L.P. v. Argentine Republic* (note 110), paras. 214-218; *Sempra Energy International v. The Argentine Republic* (note 120), Award, paras. 243-246.

[126] *Impregilo S.p.A. v. Argentine Republic*, ICSID Case No. ARB/07/17, Award, 21 June 2011, para. 356.

that Argentina had, to a certain extent, contributed to the economic crisis it suffered and was thus precluded from invoking it as a defense.[127]

The only cases in which the defense of state of necessity was invoked successfully were *Continental Casualty*[128] and *LG&E v. Argentina.*[129]

In conclusion, attempts have been made at rendering international investment law a normative regime more receptive to States' non-economic interests and at finding a balance between the need to protect foreign investments and that of regulating in the public interest. These efforts have sometimes been embedded into IIAs: this is the case of NPM clauses, and also of the recent tendency to insert power to regulate clauses into investment treaties. In addition, systemic integration – i.e., the principle according to which treaties must be interpreted in light of the wider normative framework in which they are inserted – has been regarded as a useful tool for "opening" IIAs to other fields of international law. Lastly, States have sometimes invoked circumstances precluding wrongfulness generally applicable in international law to justify their actions infringing upon investors' rights, but the case law of arbitral tribunals shows that it is very difficult to invoke them successfully. Other mechanisms specific to international investment law, such as NPM clauses – when present in a treaty –, the power to regulate or the principle of proportionality, are more frequently used to address States' need to regulate in the public interest.

Part II

The Settlement of Investment Disputes

3.5. Introduction to the Settlement of Investment Disputes: Fundamental Notions

In order to be fully effective, the legal framework described in the previous sections requires an efficient system for settling disputes relating to alleged violations of international investment law. This system, which has evolved

[127] *Sempra Energy International v. The Argentine Republic* (note 120), paras. 353-354; *Enron Corporation and Ponderosa Assets, L.P. v. Argentine Republic* (note 110), paras. 311-312.

[128] *Continental Casualty Company v. The Argentine Republic*, ICSID Case No. ARB/03/9, Award, 5 September 2008, para. 160 ff.

[129] *LG&E Energy Corp., LG&E Capital Corp., and LG&E International, Inc. v. Argentine Republic*, ICSID Case No. ARB/02/1, Decision on Liability, 3 October 2006, para. 226 ff.

over time and is now highly detailed and complex, relies on some fundamental concepts of public international law that need to be clarified at the outset. These are the concepts of dispute, settlement of disputes, and arbitration.

In the *Mavrommatis* case, the Permanent Court of International Justice (PCIJ) – the antecedent of the International Court of Justice (ICJ) – defined a "dispute" as "*a disagreement on a point of law or fact, a conflict of legal views or of interests between two persons*".[130] Today, the definition still adheres to the broad phrasing employed by the PCIJ. However, it has been further refined by the practice of international courts and tribunals: the ICJ, for instance, has clarified that you can only have a dispute if the claim of one party is "*positively opposed by the other*".[131] Remarkably, a dispute is defined as a disagreement "between two persons". The PCIJ did not limit the notion of dispute to the relations between States. Accordingly, a dispute concerning alleged violations of international investment law may arise between two States, as well as between the host State and a foreign investor.

Another essential notion is the "settlement of disputes", to which the next sections are devoted. In inter-State disputes, this refers to the broader notion of the peaceful settlement of disputes, i.e. the array of means through which a dispute may be peacefully resolved, with the choice left to the parties.[132] All means of peaceful dispute settlement depend on consent since "*no State can, without its consent, be compelled to submit its disputes with other States either to mediation or to arbitration, or to any other kind of pacific settlement*".[133] This also applies to the settlement of investment disputes, with some peculiarities that will be outlined in Section 3.7.

It is important to note that not all dispute settlement means may lead to a binding outcome. For example, the solution reached through negotiation, mediation, and conciliation will not be binding. In inter-State disputes, these are the so-called diplomatic means of settlement. In the set-

[130] PCIJ, *The Mavrommatis Palestine Concessions*, Judgment, 30 August 1924, PCIJ Reports, Series A, No. 2, p. 11.

[131] ICJ, *South West Africa Cases (Ethiopia v. South Africa; Liberia v. South Africa)*, Preliminary Objections, Judgment, 21 December 1962, ICJ Reports 1962, p. 319 ff., p. 328.

[132] ICJ, *Fisheries Jurisdiction (Spain v. Canada)*, Jurisdiction of the Court, Judgment, 4 December 1998, ICJ Reports 1998, p. 432 ff., p. 456, para. 56, referring to Article 33 of the UN Charter.

[133] PCIJ, *Status of Eastern Carelia*, Advisory Opinion, 23 July 1923, PCIJ Reports, Series B, No. 5, p. 27.

tlement of investment disputes, they correspond to what is often called "alternative dispute resolution" (ADR) mechanisms, not resulting in a binding outcome. Reference to some of these mechanisms will be made in Section 3.6.

On the contrary, when parties resort to legal means of dispute settlement – arbitration and recourse to permanent courts and tribunals – they accept in advance that a third party will decide the matter of the dispute and that the procedure's outcome will be binding, *res judicata*. However, there is a difference between the two legal dispute settlement means: recourse to permanent courts and tribunals means that the dispute is brought before a standing, pre-constituted adjudicative body, such as the ICJ, while arbitration leaves to the parties the choice of the adjudicators handling their dispute. Except for future developments that will be seen in the last Section, the settlement of investment disputes cannot rely so far on a specialized international permanent court and it is widely addressed through arbitration. For this reason, in the following paragraphs, references to dispute settlement will often coincide with investment arbitration. Specifically, Sections 3.7-3.12 will outline the key aspects of investment arbitration.

Before proceeding further, a last fundamental distinction concerning arbitration should be added. This means of dispute settlement originates in the age-old practice of referring a dispute to a prominent figure – for example, the Pope or a foreign head of State. While arbitration has become more sophisticated over time, its critical element remains the choice of third parties, called arbitrators, to resolve a dispute. A distinction can be made based on whether the parties refer the dispute to an arbitral institution that administers the arbitration, overseeing the procedure and offering support to the tribunal constituted for the dispute, or they nominate the arbitrators and administer the arbitration themselves without asking for any outside help. The first kind of arbitration is commonly referred to as institutional or administered arbitration, and the second as *ad hoc* arbitration. While *ad hoc* arbitration is always possible, Sections 3.7-3.12 will primarily focus on investment arbitration administered by the many arbitral institutions, which will be introduced in Section 3.6.

3.6. From Disputes between States to Investor-State Dispute Settlement

As mentioned, investment disputes arise from alleged violations of international investment law. Such disputes will typically involve the host State and the foreign investors. However, as extensively discussed in Chapter 2 of this book, investors are not traditional subjects of international law.[134] In the past, they did not have access to methods of international dispute settlement, which were only open to States. This meant that, on the international stage, the resolution of investment disputes could only occur between States, involving the host State and the State of nationality of the investor.

Investment disputes between States took place within the framework of so-called diplomatic protection. This expression refers to cases where State A takes international action against State B, accusing State B of violating the rights of a national of State A. State A pursues the claim of its national as its own through means of peaceful dispute settlement or even countermeasures. In investment-related disputes, the investor's State of nationality takes action against the host State.

While this mechanism allows investment claims to be brought to arbitration on the international stage, diplomatic protection has several requirements and drawbacks. These issues emerged in the case law of the ICJ and, specifically, in the *Barcelona Traction*[135] and *Diallo*[136] cases and were ultimately outlined in the International Law Commission's *Draft Articles on Diplomatic Protection* of 2006.

First, the only State entitled to exercise diplomatic protection is the State of nationality of the investor (whether an individual or a corporation). In the case of corporations, identifying the State of nationality can be complex. Generally, it is "*the State under whose law the corporation was incorporated*".[137] However, when the link with the State of incorporation is weak (e.g. due to a lack of business activities in that State) and the "*seat of management and the financial control of the corporation are both located in another State, that State shall be regarded as the State of nationality*".[138] Second, the link of nationality must have existed "*continuously from the date of injury to the date of the official presentation of the claim*".[139] Finally, the State of nationality can act in diplomatic protection only when the investor has exhausted all domestic remedies in the host State. Besides, an obvious drawback of diplomatic protection is that investors are not in control of

[134] See Chapter 2, Section 2.4.

[135] ICJ, *Barcelona Traction, Light and Power Company, Limited*, Judgment, ICJ Reports 1970, p. 3 ff.

[136] ICJ, *Ahmadou Sadio Diallo (Republic of Guinea v. Democratic Republic of the Congo)*, Preliminary Objections, Judgment, ICJ Reports 2007, p. 582 ff.

[137] ILC, *Draft Articles on Diplomatic Protection*, 2006, UN Doc. A/61/10, Article 9.

[138] *Ibid.* See also *Barcelona Traction* (note 135), paras. 70-71.

[139] *Draft Articles* (note 137), Article 10.

their claims. It is the State of their nationality that, at its own discretion, chooses whether and how to grant diplomatic protection. This also means that the choice to protect the investor might be subjected to ulterior political considerations of the State, including safeguarding its international relations. Also, diplomatic protection has traditionally been criticized by some States – mainly Latin American countries – as a tool for interfering in their internal affairs.

On the international plane, another option to settle investment disputes was the negotiation of "lump-sum agreements", i.e. treaties by which a State A that carried out an expropriation or nationalization agreed to pay a fixed sum to State B, the State of nationality of the individuals whose property had been expropriated or nationalized. State B would then allocate the sum to its affected nationals, who were prohibited from bringing any private claims relating to the measures of State A. However, these agreements were entirely left to the will of the States involved and often led to insufficient compensation for the individuals.

To take matters into their own hands, investors had to forgo any hopes of settling their dispute internationally and resort instead to the domestic courts of the host State. This solution was not ideal since the domestic courts of the host State were not perceived as a safe forum for the discussion of investment disputes. The reasons for this mistrust included the fear that the domestic courts of the host State might not be independent of their government, an alleged lack of impartiality in cases concerning foreign investors, and a reluctance (or inability) to correctly apply international law, combined with a tendency to apply national law. These fears may or may not be well-founded, but it has been observed that even the perception of a lack of impartiality may dissuade an investor from entering a State. [140]

Another option available to investors was to sue the host State before the courts of their own State of nationality. However, this option also created problems. First, as a respondent, the host State would likely fear a lack of impartiality of the courts of the State of nationality. Second, the State of nationality's courts, as well as the courts of third States, may lack jurisdiction over disputes concerning investments that took place in the host State. Third, a severe downside of recourse to domestic courts for investment disputes arises from the application of State immunity – the rule of customary international law according to which a State may not be subject to the jurisdiction of the domestic courts of another State for acts carried out in the exercise of its sovereign powers (*acta iure imperii*). Host States may thus

[140] D. Collins, *An Introduction to International Investment Law*[2], CUP, 2023, p. 230.

be protected from lawsuits brought before the domestic courts of the State of nationality.

All the means of dispute settlement that have been described, including diplomatic protection, still exist today. However, they are only residual solutions that apply when no other dispute settlement mechanism is available. Notably, the rules on diplomatic protection do not apply "*to the extent that they are inconsistent with special rules of international law, such as treaty provisions for the protection of investments*".[141] Purely inter-State disputes relating to the violation of an investment treaty may, in theory, happen, but they are extremely rare and will be resolved through typical inter-State arbitration.

Today, the primary means of solution of investment disputes is investor-State dispute settlement (ISDS), which developed in the second half of the 20th century. ISDS is usually carried out at the initiative of the investors, who now have direct access to means of dispute settlement. At the same time, by opening up to ISDS, host States hope to attract more foreign investment and avoid inter-State disputes connected, e.g., to diplomatic protection.

ISDS means that investors may have access to several methods of dispute settlement, including conciliation, mediation and arbitration. The first two methods belong to what has been defined in the previous Section as ADR. Specifically, conciliation implies the institution, by the parties to a dispute, of an impartial commission that will examine the dispute and propose the terms of a settlement, which the parties may or may not decide to accept. Mediation involves the appointment of a third party – the mediator – who actively attempts to further the negotiations between the parties to a dispute, with the aim of either reaching a settlement or proposing a solution which again may or may not be accepted by the parties.

The most common means of dispute settlement is arbitration, which will be the focus of most of the following analysis. Indeed, investor-State arbitration represents a remedy that investors may resort to independently of domestic courts and of the will of their own State of nationality. Compared to domestic judicial proceedings, arbitration is faster – although more expensive – and carried out by experts in the field of investment law. Investment arbitration builds on a structure initially meant for private commercial disputes, but it has been extensively developed through many innovations in terms of international legal instruments and new influential actors, the foremost of which is the International Centre for Settlement of Investment Disputes (ICSID or the Centre).

---

[141] *Draft Articles* (note 137), Article 17.

3.6.1. The International Centre for Settlement of Investment Disputes

The second half of the 20th century saw the rapid development of ISDS, but the attempts made within the United Nations to promote a universal investment arbitration agreement never found much fortune due to the political tensions of decolonization and the Cold War. For this reason, the task of promoting foreign investment through the development of investment arbitration fell upon the World Bank, guided in this endeavor by Aron Broches, the World Bank's General counsel from 1959 to 1979. This was not completely new for the World Bank: in 1958, the President of the World Bank successfully presided over the negotiations concerning foreign shareholders' claims against Egypt for the nationalization of the Suez Canal Company. Building on this experience, a proposal – co-drafted by the President of the World Bank, Eugene Black – was presented to the Executive Directors of the World Bank in 1961 concerning the creation of a new institution providing conciliation and arbitration for investment disputes. Consultations between States ensued, all focused on a preliminary Draft Convention prepared by Broches. These works culminated in 1965 with the conclusion of the Convention on the Settlement of Investment Disputes between States and Nationals of Other States (ICSID Convention), which entered into force on 14 October 1966. The Convention set up ICSID, an international organization with its seat in Washington DC and part of the World Bank Group.[142] As of 2025, ICSID counts 158 Member States and 7 additional signatory States.

The Centre comprises two organs: the Administrative Council and the Secretariat. The Administrative Council consists of one representative of each Contracting State and the President of the World Bank is *ex officio* Chairman. The Council performs the functions outlined in Article 6 of the Convention, which include the adoption of the administrative and financial regulations of the Centre as well as the rules of procedure for the institution and conduct of conciliation and arbitration proceedings. The Secretariat includes a Secretary-General, one or more Deputy Secretaries-General – all elected by the Administrative Council – and staff. The Secretariat administrates conciliation and arbitration proceedings carried out under the ICSID Convention through various forms of support, including providing the necessary facilities for the tribunals, as well as arranging the hearings through the Secretaries nominated for each tribunal. Finally, ICSID maintains a Panel of Conciliators and a Panel of Arbitrators, con-

---

[142] See Chapter 2, Sections 2.2.2 and 2.3.2. See also Chapter 5, Section 5.4.

sisting of qualified persons designated by the Contracting States and by the Chairman of the Administrative Council. These individuals are available for selection for Tribunals, Committees, and Conciliation Commissions.

ICSID is entirely dedicated to investment dispute resolution, its purpose being "*to provide facilities for conciliation and arbitration of investment disputes between Contracting States and nationals of other Contracting States in accordance with the provisions of this Convention*".[143] By contrast, it does not itself carry out the settlement of the disputes. The Conciliation Commissions and Tribunals are composed on an *ad hoc* basis for each dispute. Moreover, membership in ICSID does not automatically mean consent to the jurisdiction of ICSID tribunals: no recourse to conciliation and arbitration can be made without an expression of consent in writing of the parties to the dispute. The means through which consent may be given will be explored in Section 3.7 below.

After a slow start, recourse to ICSID arbitration has seen extraordinary growth in the past 30 years. The success of ICSID is connected to the several advantages that it offers: it shields the host State against diplomatic protection (Article 27 ICSID Convention) and other forms of foreign or international litigation (Article 26 ICSID Convention) and offers investors a remedy independent of diplomatic protection and of domestic courts which will lead to an award enforceable in all the States parties to the Convention. The details of the arbitral procedure will be explored at length in the following Sections, but it should be already highlighted that ICSID offers a dispute settlement framework specifically designed for ISDS, comprehensive of rules of procedure, institutional facilities, and support, as well as the application of the ICSID Convention.

Finally, according to Article 25 of the ICSID Convention, "*[t]he jurisdiction of the Centre shall extend to any legal dispute arising directly out of an investment, between a Contracting State […] and a national of another Contracting State*". Nevertheless, when only one side is a party to the ICSID Convention or a national of a State party to the ICSID Convention, it is possible to make recourse to the ICSID Additional Facility Rules. These rules, adopted in 1978 by the Administrative Council of ICSID, offer arbitration and conciliation for some disputes outside of ICSID jurisdiction. There are, however, some key differences, deriving from the lack of application of the ICSID Convention, the main one being that

143 Article 1(2), Convention on the settlement of investment disputes between States and nationals of other States (ICSID Convention), 575 UNTS 159, entered into force 14 October 1966.

Additional Facility awards can be subject to domestic courts' review, although on the basis of limited grounds, not concerning the merits of the dispute.[144]

3.6.2. Other Relevant Frameworks

Investment arbitrations take place predominantly within the framework of ICSID or the ICSID Additional Facility. Nevertheless, many other frameworks are available to both investors and States. This set of frameworks and institutions is often referred to as "non-ICSID arbitration", although they may also provide ADR.

Non-ICSID arbitration commonly takes place under the procedural rules of the United Nations Commission on International Trade Law (UNCITRAL), a subsidiary body of the UN General Assembly tasked with the harmonization of international trade law.[145] UNCITRAL, unlike ICSID, does not offer an institutional setting for investment arbitration (e.g. facilities, support). Instead, it has produced rules for carrying out commercial and investment arbitration. The UNCITRAL Arbitration Rules are the most important instrument, adopted in 1976 and subsequently modified until the current 2021 version.[146] These procedural rules may be chosen by the parties as the relevant procedure for arbitral proceedings concerning a dispute between them. The Rules discipline the entire arbitral proceedings and can be adopted by any arbitral tribunal. Due to their thoroughness and flexible application, the Arbitration Rules have been widely adopted: as of July 2023, they were the second most used arbitration rules after those of ICSID.

UNCITRAL has further perfected its toolset for arbitration, also offering the UNCITRAL Expedited Arbitration Rules of 2021 and the UNCITRAL Rules on Transparency for Treaty-based Investor-State Arbitration of 2013. Moreover, UNCITRAL has perfected the Model Law on International Commercial Arbitration, adopted in 1985 and amended in 2006. While not binding, the Model Law may be adopted by States in regulating commercial arbitration in their national legal systems.

Other frameworks offer an efficient setting for investment arbitration. They are only occasionally equipped with specific rules and often apply the UNCITRAL Arbitration Rules or a slightly modified version of them. His-

[144] See Section 3.12.2 of this Chapter.

[145] See Chapter 2, Section 2.3.3.

[146] See Chapter 2, Section 2.12.

torically, one of the first institutions to carry out investor-State dispute settlement was the Iran-US Claims Tribunal. This tribunal, established in 1981 as a result of the hostage crisis that took place in 1979, had the mandate of resolving claims of nationals of Iran against the United States and of nationals of the United States against Iran arising out of the events of the 1979 crisis. The Tribunal faced many foreign investment-related queries during its operations, applying a slightly modified version of the UNCITRAL Arbitration Rules.

Another actor of ISDS is the Permanent Court of Arbitration (PCA), established in 1899 by the Hague Peace Conference. The PCA is not a traditional court; it is a forum for temporary tribunals, where different procedural rules and arbitrators may be agreed upon for each case. As part of its vast mandate, the PCA may also address disputes concerning foreign investment and often applies the UNCITRAL Arbitration Rules as well as the PCA's own Arbitration Rules and any other procedural rules decided upon by the parties.

Aside from these two institutions, many more have emerged as ISDS keeps rapidly proliferating. Some examples can be mentioned. One is the International Chamber of Commerce (ICC), a non-governmental organization founded in 1919. The ICC system was enriched over time by the ICC International Court of Arbitration, as well as by a number of mechanisms of ADR, offered by the ICC International Centre for ADR. The ICC Court is akin to the PCA insofar as it does not offer a traditional court but rather a forum for arbitral tribunals to be constituted and specific ICC Arbitration Rules, last updated in 2021. Other particularly active institutions are the London Court of International Arbitration (LCIA) and the Arbitration Institute of the Stockholm Chamber of Commerce (SCC), both of which offer arbitration and ADR and can apply their own rules or, upon request of the parties, the UNCITRAL ones. Finally, many other arbitral institutions for ISDS have emerged in Asia, such as the Shenzhen Court of International Arbitration, the Singapore International Arbitration Centre, the China International Economic and Trade Arbitration Commission, and the Hong Kong International Arbitration Centre.

3.7. Consent as the Basis of Investment Arbitration

As already outlined in the introduction, a distinctive feature of international dispute settlement and any type of arbitration is consent, which is thus the first element that must be analyzed. While investment arbitration adheres to the typical requirement of consent, it is peculiar in that consent must be expressed by a State (the host State) and an investor, unlike inter-

State arbitration, which only involves States. This regime is unique because it is open to an entity – the investor – which is not a traditional subject of international law [147] and could not traditionally claim a general right of access to international justice. The ways in which consent can be expressed are diverse, accommodating the peculiarities of the relationship between investors and States. The three possible ways of expressing consent include (i) an agreement between the investor and the host State, (ii) domestic legislation of the host State, and (iii) a treaty between the host State and the investor's State of nationality.

The most straightforward basis of consent is the first one: a direct agreement between the host State and the investor, stipulating that related disputes will be resolved through international arbitration, mediation or conciliation. Consent through a similar agreement may be provided after the materialization of a dispute, with the consent being specific only to a case, or before a dispute arises, covering all future disputes related to an investment. In the former case, consent may be recorded in a *compromis* between the parties. In the latter, the agreement may be included in an investment contract between the investor and the host State. The arbitration clauses included in investment contracts are often designed after the so-called "model clauses", i.e. contract language formulated by the relevant institutions, which may be adopted by States and investors while drafting their contracts. For example, the model clauses developed by ICSID recommend the following provision for expressing consent in respect of future disputes:

> *"The [Government]/[name of constituent subdivision or agency] of name of Contracting State […] and name of investor […] hereby consent to submit to the International Centre for Settlement of Investment Disputes […] any dispute arising out of or relating to this agreement for settlement by […] arbitration […] pursuant to the Convention on the Settlement of Investment Disputes between States and Nationals of Other States".* [148]

A second way of expressing consent to arbitration is through the domestic legislation of the host State. The leading case on the matter is *SPP v. Egypt*, [149] concerning an ICSID claim based upon Egypt's consent expressed in a national law. This case led to the diffusion of what has been

---

[147] See Chapter 2, Section 2.4.2.

[148] Clause 1, ICSID Model Clauses, available at http://icsidfiles.worldbank.org/icsid/icsid/staticfiles/model-clauses-en/7.htm#a.

[149] *Southern Pacific Properties (Middle East) Limited v. Arab Republic of Egypt*, ICSID Case No. ARB/84/3, Decision on Jurisdiction, 14 April 1988.

defined as "arbitration without privity" [150]: arbitration based on national laws and international treaties, irrespective of any prior contractual relationship between the investor and the host State. These instruments open investment arbitration to an infinitely wider number of parties, [151] including all cases where an investment contract is absent.

In arbitration without privity based on domestic legislation, the host State offers consent to arbitration with foreign investors in general terms in its own national legislation. This does not mean, however, that the basis of consent resides only in the State's legislation. The legislation is merely an offer to arbitrate, which needs to be perfected through acceptance by the investor and which can be withdrawn as long as it has not been accepted. In order to accept the offer to arbitrate, it is sufficient for an investor to make an application for instituting arbitral proceedings. By doing so, both parties to the arbitration (the State and the investor) will have expressed their consent, albeit at different moments in time. This highlights a further peculiarity of arbitration without privity: there may be a noticeable difference in the timing of the expressions of consent of the State and the investor. While the host State's expression of consent will usually occur before a dispute has arisen, the investor's acceptance and consent will be expressed after such event. [152]

A third way of expressing consent is through a treaty between the host State and the investor's State of nationality. This is another form of arbitration without privity, which found its first example in a case from 1990, *AAPL v. Sri Lanka*. [153] Today, this is the most common way of manifesting consent to investment arbitration, expressed through treaties, either bilateral or multilateral, offering arbitration to the nationals of the respective States. Most bilateral investment treaties (BITs) contain such clauses, with the BIT between Italy and Chad of 1969 being the first to provide in its Article 7 that

[150] J. Paulsson, "Arbitration Without Privity", in *ICSID Review - Foreign Investment Law Journal*, 1995, 10(2), p. 232 ff.

[151] J. Paulsson, "Arbitration Without Privity", in *Max Planck Encyclopedia of International Procedural Law*, 2019, para. 2.

[152] A.M. Steingruber, *Consent in International Arbitration*, OUP, 2012, p. 26.

[153] *Asian Agricultural Products Ltd. (AAPL) v. Republic of Sri Lanka*, ICSID Case No. ARB/87/3, Award, 27 June 1990. In this case the Tribunal found that claimant had become "entitled to institute the ICSID arbitration proceedings" (para. 3) on the basis of the relevant BIT since respondent had not replied to the claims submitted for more than three months.

> *"[a]ny investment dispute subject to this Agreement, which would be between a Contracting State [...] and physical or juridical person having the nationality of another State, shall be subject to the jurisdiction of the International Center for the Settlement of Investment Disputes, Washington under the Convention of 18 March 1965 [...]".*[154]

Many treaties include clauses such as the one just quoted, expressly conferring upon the investors that are nationals of the States parties to the treaty the right to resort to international arbitration. As with consent expressed in national legislation, treaties contain a mere offer to arbitrate, which must then be accepted by the investor, even just by instituting proceedings. Few exceptions to this general rule can be found. Notably, some treaties require specific approval of an investment for the foreign investor to benefit from the treaty provisions. Unlike national legislation, however, withdrawal by the State of the offer to arbitrate is not easy, as it would have to adhere to the rules for the termination of treaties outlined in the Vienna Convention on the Law of Treaties[155] (VCLT).

Consent can vary significantly depending on the wording of national laws, the treaty itself, and the interaction between the treaty's offer and the investor's acceptance. In cases of arbitration without privity, the State initially determines the breadth of its consent, specifying the scope of its offer. However, final consent is shaped by the agreement between the host State's offer and the investor's acceptance. The investor, by choosing to accept only certain parts of the State's offer, can further narrow the scope of consent. The interpretation of consent can thus be crucial because a dispute can be arbitrated only if both parties consent.[156]

Through all the means just outlined, parties can consent to purely *ad hoc* arbitration or refer to existing procedural frameworks. In any case, all forms of investment arbitration require consent. The ICSID Convention, for example, requires in Article 25 that the jurisdiction of the Centre extends to "*any legal dispute arising directly out of an investment, between a Contracting State [...] and a national of another Contracting State, which the parties to the dispute consent in writing to submit to the Centre*". Similarly,

---

[154] Article 7, Agreement Between the Republic of Chad and the Republic of Italy to Protect and Promote Investment Capital, 11 June 1969, entered into force 11 June 1969.

[155] Vienna Convention on the Law of Treaties, 1155 UNTS 331, entered into force 27 January 1980 (VCLT).

[156] See Section 3.3.4 of this Chapter for the debate on whether MFN clauses also apply to dispute settlement.

the UNCITRAL Model Law provides in Article 7 (option I) that the agreement to arbitrate shall be in writing.

The remaining paragraphs will predominantly focus on the most widely employed means of consent, i.e. investment treaties.

3.8. Jurisdiction and Admissibility of Investment Arbitration Claims

The first issue that emerges when a dispute is brought to arbitration is whether the tribunal has jurisdiction – i.e. "*the power to decide according to law (jus dicere) a dispute of a particular nature between specific parties*" [157] – and whether the claim is admissible. These requirements are necessary to begin arbitration. Even though investment arbitration tribunals frequently talk of jurisdiction or admissibility without much difference, these are different notions in international law and this distinction has important practical implications. For example, a tribunal can review *proprio motu* (i.e. on its own initiative) only its jurisdiction; the burden of proof is different for jurisdiction (on the claimant) and admissibility (on the respondent); and a final award can only be annulled for lack of jurisdiction, not of admissibility. [158] The implications for post-award remedies will be seen at the end of this Chapter, but suffice it to say that the distinction between jurisdiction and admissibility is as relevant to investment arbitration as it is complex.

The idea that jurisdiction and admissibility are distinct concepts has long been accepted by the ICJ, which mentions them separately in its Rules of Court and case law. [159] In short, an objection to admissibility means that the tribunal "*should rule the claim inadmissible on some ground other than its ultimate merits*", while an objection to jurisdiction "*is a plea that the tribunal itself is incompetent to give any ruling at all whether as to the merits or as to the admissibility of the claim*". [160]

In international investment arbitration the situation is different because there is usually no trace of the word "admissibility" in the constitutive instruments of the tribunals or the relevant treaties. For this reason, some arbitral tribunals have found that the distinction proposed by the ICJ does

[157] H. Thirlway, *The International Court of Justice*, OUP, 2016, p. 35.

[158] *Abaclat and Others v. Argentine Republic*, ICSID Case No. ARB/07/5, Decision on Jurisdiction and Admissibility, 4 August 2011, para. 247.

[159] ICJ, *Oil Platforms* (Islamic Republic of Iran v. United States of America), Judgment, 6 November 2003, ICJ Reports 2003, p. 161 ff., p. 177, para. 29.

[160] G. Fitzmaurice, *The Law and Practice of the International Court of Justice*, vol. II, *Jurisdiction*, OUP, 1986, pp. 438-439.

not apply to investment arbitration. As stated earlier, however, it is generally accepted that a distinction is necessary, and many attempts have been made by scholarship and jurisprudence to find an effective test to distinguish jurisdictional and admissibility claims. [161] Arguably, the most straightforward way of doing so is to look at whether a claim concerns the existence and scope of consent or conditions for instituting investment arbitration proceedings. [162] In the first case, it is a matter of jurisdiction, while in the second one of admissibility. Jurisdiction refers to the scope of the tribunal's authority as it emerges from the consent to arbitrate, while admissibility concerns the power of a tribunal to decide a specific claim at a given time.

Admissibility, therefore, does not depend on consent but rather on the conditions for instituting investment arbitration proceedings before a tribunal already possessing jurisdiction. These conditions are extremely varied. They include, for example, the requirement that parties attempt to reach an amicable settlement for a certain period and the prior exhaustion of domestic remedies, meaning that the investor must first bring its claim before the local remedies in the host State.

The so-called "fork in the road" clauses are another example. These treaty clauses provide that the investor may choose between bringing its claim to domestic courts or international arbitration. For example, the BIT between Italy and Lebanon provides that:

> *"the investor may submit the dispute, at his choice, for settlement to: a) The competent court of the Contracting Party in the territory of which the investment has been made; or b) The International Centre for Settlement of Investment Disputes [...] or c) An ad hoc arbitral tribunal [...] The choice made as per subparagraphs a, b, and c herein above is final".* [163]

---

[161] Another approach proposes to ascertain whether the objecting party is taking aim at the tribunal or at the claim (J. Paulsson, *Jurisdiction and Admissibility*, in G. Aksen et al. (eds.), *Global Reflections on International Law, Commerce and Dispute Resolution*, ICC Publishing, 2005, p. 601 ff.). The former leads to an objection to jurisdiction, while the latter to one of admissibility. However, this test leaves room for inconsistencies because it does not tell the tribunal how to distinguish objections targeting the tribunal from those targeting the claim.

[162] M. Hwang, L.S. Cheng, *The Chimera of Admissibility in International Arbitration*, in N. Kaplan, M. Moser (eds.), *Jurisdiction, Admissibility and Choice of Law in International Arbitration: Liber Amicorum Michael Pryles*, Kluwer Law International, 2018, p. 265 ff., p. 278.

[163] Article 7(2), Agreement Between the Italian Republic and the Lebanese Republic on the Promotion and Reciprocal Protection of Investments, 7 November 1997, entered into force 9 February 2000.

Once a claim is brought before domestic judges, access to arbitration is thus barred. This rule, however, applies only when the disputes are identical, meaning that there is "*identity of the parties, object and cause of action in the proceedings pending before both tribunals*".[164] For example, a claim concerning events subsequent to those giving rise to a claim before a domestic court is not barred and can be brought to international arbitration.

3.8.1. The Scope of Jurisdiction: A Dispute Arising Out of an Investment Between the Investor and the Host State

The arbitral tribunal itself verifies whether it has jurisdiction over a dispute. This exceptional power of tribunals to decide on their own jurisdiction derives from the doctrine of *Kompetenz-Kompetenz* or *compétence de la compétence* (literally, the competence to assess its own competence). It is one of the inherent elements of the international judicial function,[165] as it allows arbitration to effectively take place without the need for a superior body tasked with analyzing jurisdiction and without leaving the matter entirely at the discretion of the parties' objections. Tribunals thus can and should ascertain whether they have jurisdiction to entertain a dispute.

In practice, an arbitral tribunal exercising its *compétence de la competence* will look at the existence of consent and the scope of jurisdiction, i.e. at the limits of the expressed consent. The extent of jurisdiction can be divided into four categories: subject matter (*ratione materiae*), personal (*ratione personae*), territorial (*ratione loci*) and temporal (*ratione temporis*) jurisdiction. The first two elements are also outlined in Article 25(1) of the ICSID Convention, which states that the Centre – provided that the parties have consented in writing to it – shall have jurisdiction over "*any legal dispute arising directly out of an investment, between a Contracting State (or any constituent subdivision or agency of a Contracting State designated to the Centre by that State) and a national of another Contracting State*". Should any of the four elements of jurisdiction be missing, a claim would be immediately rejected on jurisdictional grounds.

3.8.1.1. Jurisdiction *Ratione Materiae*

Arbitral tribunals may decide on disputes arising out of an investment. The

---

[164] *S.A.R.L. Benvenuti & Bonfant v. People's Republic of the Congo*, ICSID Case No. ARB/77/2, Award, 8 August 1980, para. 1.14.

[165] ICJ, *Nottebohm Case*, Preliminary Objection, Judgment, 18 November 1953, ICJ Reports 1953, p. 111 ff., p. 119.

key element that defines the scope of jurisdiction is, thus, the existence of an investment. As already outlined, [166] the notion of investment is extremely complex, making jurisdiction *ratione materiae* often a matter of intense debate.

Less debated is the notion of "dispute", a jurisdictional requirement of any court or tribunal, already addressed in Section 3.5. This notion is extremely broad in public international law and so it remains in investment arbitration. Article 25 of the ICSID Convention refers to "any legal dispute", but the addition of "legal" does not add much. A dispute does not lose its legal character if it also has political elements or involves governmental actions. [167] This is in line with the original intentions behind the ICSID Convention: the Report of the Executive Directors on the Convention on the Settlement of Investment Disputes Between States and Nationals of Other States of 1965 states that the expression was used to indicate that "*while conflicts of rights are within the jurisdiction of the Centre, mere conflicts of interests are not*". [168] To this, some ICSID tribunals have added two methodological steps. Tribunals will determine whether (1) the claimant raised legal issues concerning a concrete situation and (2) the final decision might have practical consequences. [169]

Once these two elements are present, the scope of jurisdiction depends on the consent expressed, i.e. whether it covers the proposed dispute.

It is possible that an investment contract between the host State and a foreign investor stipulates that the domestic courts of the host State are competent to adjudicate disputes. At the same time, a BIT between the host State and the investor's State of nationality may provide for investment arbitration. Does consent to domestic courts' jurisdiction, expressed in a contract, exclude the jurisdiction of arbitral tribunals manifested in a treaty? In general, the answer is no. However, it is disputed whether the jurisdiction of the arbitral tribunal should be limited to treaty claims, i.e. concerning a breach of the relevant BIT, or should also encompass contract claims, i.e. breaches of the investment contract only. While tribunals often consider this distinction relevant to the ascertainment of jurisdiction, [170]

---

[166] See Section 3.2 of this Chapter.

[167] *Ceskoslovenska Obchodni Banka, a.s. v. The Slovak Republic* (note 18), para. 61.

[168] Report of the Executive Directors on the Convention on the Settlement of Investment Disputes Between States and Nationals of Other States of 1965, para. 26.

[169] *AES Corporation v. Argentine Republic*, ICSID Case No. ARB/02/17, Decision on Jurisdiction, 26 April 2005, para. 44.

[170] The first case to adopt this approach was *Compañía de Aguas del Aconquija S.A. (formerly Aguas del Aconquija) and Vivendi Universal S.A. (formerly Compagnie Gé-*

others have argued that a rigid division of claims is "*uneconomical and contrary to the goal of reaching final and comprehensive resolutions of disputes*".[171] In this latter perspective, therefore, an arbitral tribunal may have jurisdiction over the whole of the dispute.

3.8.1.2. Jurisdiction *Ratione Personae*

Relevant disputes are only those between a host State and an investor between whom consent has been expressed. This requirement creates no practical problems in cases where consent was expressed through direct agreement or reply to national legislation. When the basis of consent is an investment treaty, the host State must be a party to it and the investor must be a national of a State party to the same treaty.

Moreover, in the case of ICSID arbitration, Article 25 of the ICSID Convention specifies that the dispute must be "*between a Contracting State (or any constituent subdivision or agency of a Contracting State designated to the Centre by that State) and a national of another Contracting State*". To access ICSID arbitration, the investor cannot be a national of the host State and must be a national of a State party to the ICSID Convention. Should it fail to possess such a requirement, the dispute could still be brought to an Additional Facility tribunal, provided that the host State is a party to the ICSID Convention.[172]

Therefore, jurisdiction *ratione personae* depends on the nationality of the investor. This analysis will be straightforward when the investor is a natural person. However, in the majority of cases, the investor is a legal person (e.g. a corporation). Some of the issues connected to determining the nationality of investors have been outlined in Section 3.6 above, the key rule being that the investor has the nationality of "*the State under whose law the corporation was incorporated*".[173]

3.8.1.3. Jurisdiction *Ratione Loci*

The scope of jurisdiction is limited to investments made in the territory of the host State. This geographical limitation is not always expressed, but it applies nonetheless. For example, it is not mentioned in Article 25 of the ICSID Convention. At the same time, the Energy Charter Treaty – like

---

nérale des Eaux) v. Argentine Republic (I), ICSID Case No. ARB/97/3, Award, 21 November 2000.

[171] R. Dolzer, U. Kriebaum, C. Schreuer (note 1), p. 399.

[172] See Section 3.6.1 of this Chapter.

[173] *Draft Articles* (note 137), Article 9.

many IIAs – refers only to disputes "*between a Contracting Party and an Investor of another Contracting Party relating to an Investment of the latter in the Area [territory] of the former*".[174]

This element of jurisdiction is in line with the public international law notion that a State may not be accountable for events that took place outside of its territory and control. An interesting addition contained in the ICSID Convention is the extension of the territorial scope of the Convention (and of jurisdiction *ratione loci*) to "*all territories for whose international relations a Contracting State is responsible, except those which are excluded by such State by written notice*".[175] This means that disputes arising out of investments that took place in the territories "*for whose international relations a Contracting State is responsible*" can be brought before an ICSID tribunal against said contracting State. This extends the notion of relevant territory for the investment beyond the territory of the host State, but also the notion of relevant investors to those incorporated in the territories referred to in Article 70 of the ICSID Convention. For example, the mentioned *SPP v. Egypt* case concerned an investment of a Hong Kong corporation (SPP) in Egypt. Since, at the time, Hong Kong was "*a territory for whose international relations the United Kingdom, also a party to the Convention, [was] responsible*",[176] SPP could bring a case against Egypt as if it were a national of the United Kingdom, and thus the national of a party to the ICSID Convention.

3.8.1.4. Jurisdiction *Ratione Temporis*

The temporal jurisdiction of an arbitral tribunal hinges on the rule according to which the alleged breach of law must have taken place when the State was bound by the relevant obligations. The application of this rule can, however, lead to uncertainties when tribunals deal with investment treaties.

The basic rule is that States' obligations under a treaty do not cover events that took place before its entry into force.[177] Only disputes con-

---

[174] Article 26 ICSID Convention.

[175] Article 70 ICSID Convention.

[176] *Southern Pacific Properties (Middle East) Limited v. Arab Republic of Egypt*, ICSID Case No. ARB/84/3, Decision on Preliminary Objections to Jurisdiction, 27 November 1985, para. 46.

[177] This rule is enshrined in Article 28 VCLT, which provides that "[u]nless a different intention appears from the treaty or is otherwise established, its provisions do not bind a party in relation to any act or fact which took place or any situation which

cerning breaches that happened after the entry into force of the treaty can thus fall under the scope of jurisdiction of an arbitral tribunal. However, this does not mean that facts that took place before the entry into force of the treaty cannot be relevant. While a breach that happened before the entry into force is not under the jurisdiction of the relevant arbitral tribunal, facts or conduct taking place before such entry into force may be taken into consideration to determine whether a party subsequently breached an obligation.

Additionally, the application of the basic rule on jurisdiction *ratione temporis* may become complex when it comes to continuous acts, i.e. acts that came into existence before consent was expressed and continued afterward. The last words of Article 28 VCLT ("*any situation which...*") leave the door open to acts that began before the entry into force of the treaties but continued occurring once the treaty came into force. An example of such acts may be found in the *SGS v. Philippines* case,[178] where the tribunal had to analyze a question of jurisdiction over a failure to pay. The obligation to pay arose from a State contract that began before the entry into force of the treaty. However, the failure to pay constituted a continuous breach, still ongoing after the entry into force of the treaty. Thus, it fell under the jurisdiction of the tribunal.

3.9. The Laws Applicable to Investment Disputes

Another preliminary issue to be assessed at the beginning of an arbitration concerns the identification of the applicable law. This is a crucial step in any tribunal's analysis: a misidentification of the applicable law, whether substantive or procedural, may lead to a challenge to the final award and, possibly, hinder its enforcement.[179]

When discussing applicable laws, a preliminary distinction is in order between the *lex causae* (governing the merits of the dispute), the *lex arbitri* (the procedural law governing the arbitration), and the *lex loci arbitri* (the law of the seat of the arbitration).

---

ceased to exist before the date of the entry into force of the treaty with respect to that party".

[178] *SGS Société Générale de Surveillance S.A. v. Republic of the Philippines*, 29 January 2004 (note 113).

[179] See more in-depth details in Section 3.12 of this Chapter.

3.9.1. The Law Governing the Merits of the Dispute

The *lex causae*, the law governing the merits of the dispute, is the one presenting the most difficulties as multiple factors come into play.

First of all, the parties to a dispute (investors and States) can agree on the applicable laws. This possibility of choosing the applicable law is, for example, expressly provided for in Article 42 of the ICSID Convention, which states that *"[t]he Tribunal shall decide a dispute in accordance with such rules of law as may be agreed by the parties"*. Article 35 of the UNCITRAL Arbitration Rules similarly states that "*[t]he arbitral tribunal shall apply the rules of law designated by the parties as applicable to the substance of the dispute*". It is often the relevant contract or investment treaty which provides the choice of law. The chosen law may be public international law, with a complete exclusion of national law, as done by Article 26(6) of the Energy Charter Treaty: "*A tribunal established under paragraph (4) shall decide the issues in dispute in accordance with this Treaty and applicable rules and principles of international law*". Or the parties could choose a specific national law, as in the *CDC v. Seychelles* case, where the relevant contract provided: "*This Agreement and its performance shall be governed by and construed in all respects in accordance with the laws of England*".[180]

In the absence of such choice of law clauses, the matter becomes more complex since both international law and national laws are often relevant. Article 42(1) of the ICSID Convention, for example, provides that "*[i]n the absence of such agreement [i.e. the choice of the applicable law], the Tribunal shall apply the law of the Contracting State party to the dispute (including its rules on the conflict of laws) and such rules of international law as may be applicable*". In this case, the *lex causae* combines both international and national law.

A complex and still unresolved question is how arbitrators will manage the interaction between these different applicable laws. Traditionally, both laws were examined in parallel, without analyzing their relationship and often simply affirming that the contents of the two were harmonious. According to another approach, national law served as the primary source of the *lex causae* and international law had a "supplemental and corrective" role, filling any gaps in national law or ensuring that the application of national law did not lead to violations of international law. A more recent approach suggests applying both legal systems independently, without the obligation to prioritize national law. This last approach allows tribunals to address the

---

[180] *CDC Group plc v. Republic of Seychelles*, ICSID Case No. ARB/02/14, Award, 17 December 2003, para. 43.

different issues in a case through the appropriate legal framework, whether national or international. In the recent *Casinos Austria v. Argentina* case, for example, an ICSID tribunal faced with the challenge of multiple applicable laws has stated:

> *"A treaty claim, in other words, remains governed by treaty law. [...] [this] does not mean, however, that domestic law is wholly irrelevant for the determination of compliance with, or liability under, a BIT, including the BIT governing the present dispute. Domestic law will remain relevant in governing a variety of incidental questions, or preliminary matters, including questions for the determination of which a BIT may expressly refer to domestic law [...] or questions that must be assumed to be governed by domestic law for other reasons, for example because certain elements of a treaty can only be determined by recourse to domestic law".* [181]

3.9.2. The Law Governing the Arbitral Process and the Law of the Seat of Arbitration

The two remaining categories concern the proceedings themselves rather than the merits of the dispute. As mentioned, the *lex arbitri* governs the arbitral process and provides for its unfolding. The identification of this procedural law differs between ICSID and non-ICSID arbitration.

The *lex arbitri* in ICSID arbitration coincides with the ICSID Convention and, unless the parties agree otherwise, the ICSID Arbitration Rules. [182] Some argue that rules of public international law may also be added to this, while domestic legal systems play no meaningful role. For this reason, ICSID arbitration is defined as "delocalized" since it does not rely on national laws and the final awards cannot be challenged before domestic courts.

The *lex arbitri* in non-ICSID arbitration is more complicated to pinpoint. The parties may decide to adopt any specific set of rules different from the domestic laws of the seat of the arbitration – i.e. the place where arbitration is legally located. For example, the parties may choose to apply the UNCITRAL Arbitration Rules. However, this choice does not completely insulate non-ICSID proceedings from the application of national law. The chosen arbitration rules will usually only determine questions internal to the arbitration, i.e. the organization of hearings or the composition of arbitral tribunals. External matters – i.e. the role of supervision and

---

[181] *Casinos Austria v. Argentina* (note 50), paras. 314 and 316.

[182] Article 44 ICSID Convention.

support of the courts of the seat of arbitration – will be left to national law. Moreover, the *lex arbitri* may also be identified as the law of the seat of arbitration, the *lex loci arbitri*.

The law of the seat of arbitration – the *lex loci arbitri* – can thus have many roles. It may be identified with the *lex arbitri*, governing the arbitral proceedings. It may also coincide with the *lex causae* since, as already mentioned, parties may choose to apply national laws to the merits of the case. Outside of these two options, the *lex loci arbitri* will still play a role in the enforcement of arbitral awards, especially with its mandatory laws, i.e. laws from which no derogation is permitted. [183]

3.10. The ICSID Procedure

As seen in the previous Section, ICSID proceedings are entirely regulated by the ICSID Arbitration Rules and are not subjected to national law. On the contrary, non-ICSID proceedings are regulated by the Rules chosen by the parties (i.e. UNCITRAL Arbitration Rules) or even national law. For these reasons, this section will only give a brief overview of the ICSID procedure, as it is more clearly defined. Nevertheless, the main procedural steps are often similar for all kinds of investment arbitration.

3.10.1. Institution of a Claim

A party interested in starting arbitration ("claimant") should present a "request for arbitration" [184] to the Secretary General of ICSID. The request shall include information concerning the dispute, the parties and the consent to arbitration. A copy of it will be sent by the Secretary-General to the other party ("respondent"). Under Article 36(3) of the ICSID Convention, at this stage, the Secretary-General may refuse to register the request for arbitration on account of the dispute being "*manifestly outside the jurisdiction of the Centre*".

It should be noted that the ICSID Convention clearly provides that both investors and host States may be claimants in an arbitration. Article 36(1) provides that "*[a]ny Contracting State or any national of a Contracting State wishing to institute arbitration proceedings shall address a request to that effect in writing to the Secretary-General who shall send a copy of the request to the other party*". Nevertheless, almost all dispute resolution

---

[183] See Section 3.12 of this Chapter.

[184] Article 36 ICSID Convention.

clauses refer only to investors, with some even defining "claimant" as "*an investor of a Contracting Party that is a party to an investment dispute with the other Contracting Party*".[185] This privileged position of investors as claimants in investment arbitration is one of the reasons that has led many to point out an "asymmetry" of investment arbitration.

3.10.2. Constitution of the Tribunal

After a dispute is registered, the first procedural step is the constitution of the tribunal. This step may take some time since the appointment of arbitrators is often a matter of discussion between the parties. In investment arbitration, the rule is that of "equality of appointment", i.e. while the parties are free to choose the composition of the tribunal, they must be accorded equality in so doing. Article 37(2) of the ICSID Convention provides that the tribunal shall consist of one arbitrator or any uneven number. The Article continues by providing that if the parties do not agree on "*the number of arbitrators and the method of their appointment, the Tribunal shall consist of three arbitrators, one arbitrator appointed by each party and the third, who shall be the president of the Tribunal, appointed by agreement of the parties*".

The Convention and the Arbitration Rules set out the requirements necessary to be appointed arbitrator. For example, Article 38 of the Convention provides that the majority of arbitrators should not be nationals of the State party to the dispute or of the investor's State of nationality. Moreover, arbitrators shall be "*persons of high moral character and recognized competence in the fields of law, commerce, industry or finance*"[186] and shall offer guarantees of independence and impartiality.[187]

Once a tribunal has been constituted, its composition cannot be changed unless in cases of death, incapacitation, or resignment of an arbitrator.[188] Moreover, parties may propose the disqualification of an arbitrator due to, e.g., a lack of the qualities outlined in Article 14 of the Convention.[189]

---

[185] Article 1, Agreement between Japan and the State of Israel for the liberalization, promotion and protection of investments, 1 February 2017, entered into force 5 October 2017.

[186] Article 14 ICSID Convention.

[187] Rule 19 ICSID Arbitration Rules.

[188] Article 56 ICSID Convention.

[189] Articles 57-58 ICSID Convention.

3.10.3. The Written and Oral Procedure

Once the tribunal is constituted, parties meet during the "First Session", a first hearing often held remotely, which aims at clarifying preliminary matters such as the applicable rules of procedure and the procedural calendar. All this information comes together in "Procedural order no. 1".

After this, the procedure may continue through the regular sequence of written submissions and oral proceedings within the time limits for all procedural steps fixed by the tribunal. The first step of a regular procedure consists of the written submissions by the parties [190]: the claimant shall submit a memorial, followed by a counter-memorial of the respondent. To this, unless agreed otherwise by the parties, follow a reply by the claimant and a rejoinder by the respondent. It is during this time that documents and evidence are usually produced. Moreover, if a respondent wishes to introduce a counterclaim – a claim of the respondent against the claimant arising directly out of the subject matter of the main dispute – it must do so no later than in the counter-memorial. [191] After the written submissions, the tribunal shall hold one or more hearings [192] during which the parties' arguments are presented and witnesses and experts can be heard. [193]

A deviation from this standard procedure may happen if a party proposes bifurcation, i.e. that "*a question be addressed in a separate phase of the proceeding*". [194] The request for this special procedure, usually resorted to for jurisdictional issues, can be granted by the tribunal in light of a number of circumstances, such as whether "*(a) bifurcation would materially reduce the time and cost of the proceeding; (b) determination of the questions to be bifurcated would dispose of all or a substantial portion of the dispute; and (c) the questions to be addressed in separate phases of the proceeding are so intertwined as to make bifurcation impractical*". [195]

Other special procedures include the objection that a claim is manifestly without legal merit, [196] which leads to an accelerated arbitration, where parties have a short timeframe for submitting their observations and the analysis of the tribunal is inevitably cursory, and the request for provisional

[190] Rule 30 ICSID Arbitration Rules.

[191] Rule 48 ICSID Arbitration Rules.

[192] Rule 32 ICSID Arbitration Rules.

[193] Rules 38-39 ICSID Arbitration Rules.

[194] Rule 42 ICSID Arbitration Rules.

[195] Rule 42(4) ICSID Arbitration Rules.

[196] Rule 41 ICSID Arbitration Rules.

measures.[197] This latter may be presented in order to prevent actions that may cause harm to a party or the arbitral process, to maintain or restore the *status quo*, and to preserve evidence. These measures are generally considered binding[198] and are issued in light of their urgency and necessity. While, as mentioned, they are usually employed to secure evidence or ensure compliance with future awards, provisional measures are also used in extreme circumstances. For example, in *Bernhard von Pezold and Others v. Republic of Zimbabwe*, one of the claimants was informed that the Central Intelligence Organization of the respondent State had been instructed to kill him. The Tribunal granted the request for provisional measures, asking Respondent to "*take all necessary measures to protect the life and safety of the Claimants*".[199]

Finally, if one of the parties does not participate in the proceedings, the other may request that the tribunal render an award.[200] This means that the default of a party does not stop the proceedings, but its failure to appear cannot be considered an "*admission of the assertions made by the other party*".

3.10.4. Conclusion of the Procedure

Once the procedure is completed, the arbitral tribunal deliberates in private. These deliberations remain confidential[201] and lead to a final award, which normally rules over the merits of the dispute. The award may also not concern the merits if it decides on the jurisdictional issues and declines jurisdiction. Additionally, the award may embody the settlement of the parties. Indeed, the parties may agree to discontinue the proceedings under Rule 55. If, in discontinuing the proceedings, the parties agree on a settlement of the dispute before the issuance of an award, the tribunal shall issue an order on discontinuance at the request of the parties and may register the settlement in an Award.

---

[197] Rule 47 ICSID Arbitration Rules.

[198] *Emilio Agustín Maffezini v. The Kingdom of Spain*, ICSID Case No. ARB/97/7, Procedural Order No. 2 (Decision on Request for Provisional Measures), 28 October 1999.

[199] *Border Timbers Limited, Timber Products International (Private) Limited, and Hangani Development Co. (Private) Limited v. Republic of Zimbabwe*, ICSID Case No. ARB/10/25, Procedural Order No. 5 (Provisional Measures), 3 April 2013, para. 65.

[200] Rule 49 ICSID Arbitration Rules.

[201] Rule 34 ICSID Arbitration Rules.

3.11. The Award

The award is the final decision of the arbitral tribunal. Through it, the tribunal may offer a number of remedies to the disputes. Such remedies can take the form, under the law of State responsibility, of restitution, compensation or satisfaction. The first obliges the party responsible for a wrongful act to "*re-establish the situation which existed before the wrongful act was committed*".[202] The second implies that the responsible party shall compensate for the damage caused, covering "*any financially assessable damage including loss of profits*".[203] The third is applied to injury that cannot be repaired by restitution or compensation and can consist of "*an acknowledgement of the breach, an expression of regret, a formal apology*".[204] In investment arbitration, restitution and satisfaction are not as predominant as monetary compensation. The calculation of damages or compensation for expropriation is often a complex operation, requiring the participation of experts.

Aside from the remedy offered, the characteristics of awards vary according to the legal framework applicable to them. For the purpose of clarity, they may be split into ICSID awards and non-ICSID awards, according to the definition offered above.[205] This division will also be maintained for the next section on post-award remedies.

3.11.1. ICSID Awards

The awards produced by ICSID tribunals are peculiar insofar as they are entirely regulated by the ICSID Convention, in Chapter IV, Section 4, "The Award", at Articles 48-49. Sections 5 and 6 further expand the legal framework concerning awards, being respectively focused on "Interpretation, Revision and Annulment of the Award" and "Recognition and Enforcement of the Award".

Requirements for the validity of the award

Article 48 is the main reference point for the criteria that an ICSID award must meet in order to be valid. The first set of requirements deals with the formal aspects of the award.[206]

---

[202] ILC, *Articles on Responsibility of States for Internationally Wrongful Acts (ARSIWA)*, 2001, UN Doc. A/56/10, Article 35.

[203] *Ibid*, Article 36.

[204] *Ibid*, Article 37.

[205] See Sections 3.6.1 and 3.6.2 of this Chapter.

[206] See paras. 1 and 2 of Article 48 ICSID Convention.

First, an award (or any other decision) shall be decided by a tribunal through a majority vote. This rule applies to all decisions that a tribunal may have to take during the arbitral proceedings. In order for a tribunal to function, the presence of a majority of the members is required unless otherwise decided by the parties. Once a tribunal is correctly seated, a majority vote is necessary for a decision to pass. "Majority" here refers to an absolute majority, i.e. the number of votes in favor shall be more than half of the votes of all the members of the tribunal. According to the Arbitration Rules (both the 2006 and 2022 versions), abstentions count as negative votes. The need for a majority does not prevent arbitrators from adding a dissenting opinion or a declaration. They may, accordingly, vote in favor of a decision and simultaneously append a declaration explaining the reasons behind their doubts. This is possible since there are no requirements that the reasoning of all tribunal members be identical, only their vote.

Second, the award "*shall be in writing and shall be signed by the members of the Tribunal who voted for it*". These are typical requirements of international arbitration and are integrated by the Arbitration Rules. For example, Rule 59 of the 2022 Rules, "Contents of the Award", outlines all the information that should be included in an award, such as the names of the representatives of the parties or a brief summary of the proceedings.

Other requirements concern the content of the award. In particular, the award "*shall deal with every question submitted to the Tribunal, and shall state the reasons upon which it is based*".[207] This means that the award shall be exhaustive and reasoned. A "reasoned" award allows the reader to understand it on both facts and law. A lack of reasoning is grounds for annulment. Less clear is the first requirement of exhaustiveness. Broadly, it means that an award shall not leave questions submitted by the parties undecided. This is a consequence of the consensual nature of arbitration – the parties expressed their consent so that the tribunal could decide on the questions submitted to it – and of consideration of efficiency or procedural economy since the questions submitted should be finally decided by the award, without a need for additional decisions. It must be noted that the requirement of exhaustiveness refers to the questions submitted to the tribunal and not all the possible arguments of the parties. In connection to the requirement of exhaustiveness, paragraph 2 of Article 49 adds that, within 45 days after the award was rendered, a party may request the tribunal to decide a question "*which it had omitted to decide in the award*".

[207] *Ibid.*, para. 3.

Effects and enforcement of the award

Once a tribunal has issued an award, it shall not be published by ICSID without the consent of the parties.[208] Instead, it must be dispatched to the parties by the Secretary-General of ICSID. The date of the award is the one of dispatch to the parties.

Article 53(1) of the ICSID Convention stipulates that

> *"[t]he award shall be binding on the parties and shall not be subject to any appeal or to any other remedy except those provided for in this Convention. Each party shall abide by and comply with the terms of the award except to the extent that enforcement shall have been stayed pursuant to the relevant provisions of this Convention".*

Awards are binding for the parties to the specific case and only for them. This means that they cannot have effects on other actors and, moreover, that they are not binding for subsequent tribunals dealing with similar issues. Indeed, in international investment arbitration, there is no rule of *stare decisis*, i.e. the rule according to which tribunals are bound by precedent decisions. It should nevertheless be noted that tribunals and parties often refer to previous decisions in their arguments.

As a consequence of Article 53, ICSID awards are final and binding. This is one of the main traits of the ICSID regime, which is "self-contained". Indeed, awards cannot be challenged in the domestic courts of the Contracting States. The only available remedies are those provided in the Convention itself, which will be discussed in the next section.

Once an award has been issued, it shall be recognized as binding and enforced by the Contracting States "*as if it were a final judgment of a court in that State*". This provision, enshrined in Article 54 of the Convention, is a key element of the ICSID framework since it offers recognition and enforcement of the awards in all States Parties. Notably, the Article refers to "*[e]ach Contracting State*" and not only to the respondent State and the State of nationality of the investor in a specific case. This means that an ICSID award is fully enforceable in all State Parties to the Convention, the choice usually depending on the availability of assets of the losing party. Paragraph 3 of Article 54 adds that the execution of the award "*shall be governed by the laws concerning the execution of judgments in force in the State in whose territories such execution is sought*". This is probably a consequence of the consideration of ICSID awards as national judgments and only concerns procedural laws. The meaning of this last paragraph of Arti-

[208] Article 48(5) ICSID Convention.

cle 54 is clarified by Article 55, which adds that "*[n]othing in Article 54 shall be construed as derogating from the law in force in any Contracting State relating to immunity of that State or of any foreign State from execution*". In brief, while the Convention is self-contained for the entire arbitral process, execution is subject to the rules on State immunity from execution. As a consequence, certain State assets, protected by immunity from execution, will be exempted from the enforcement measures that derive from an award.

3.11.2. Non-ICSID Awards

While ICSID awards are only subject to the ICSID Convention, non-ICSID awards are subject to a multiplicity of legal instruments, such as the relevant institutional rules that may have been chosen, the law of the seat of arbitration and the United Nations Convention on the Recognition and Enforcement of Foreign Arbitral Awards (New York Convention),[209] a key text for non-ICSID arbitration that provides for uniform rules on recognition and enforcement of awards.

The requirements for the validity of the award are often similar to the ones provided in ICSID arbitration. According to the UNCITRAL Arbitration Rules, for example, the award, approved by a majority of the arbitrators, shall be in writing and signed by the arbitrators, and it shall state the reasons for the decision.[210] Moreover, tribunals have derived from Article 39 of the Arbitration Rules the requirements that the award be exhaustive, deciding on all questions submitted by the parties. Unlike ICSID arbitration, the date of the award is the one indicated in it.[211]

On the other hand, the recognition and enforcement of the award is particularly complex for non-ICSID awards due to the variety of legal tools that may be involved. Indeed, this process may be governed by national legislation or, in countries that are party to it, by the New York Convention. National legislation is oftentimes drafted according to the UNCITRAL Model Law,[212] which in turn resembles, in its key provisions, the New York Convention, which can thus be taken as an example.

An obligation parallel to that of Article 53 of the ICSID Convention can

[209] United Nations Convention on the Recognition and Enforcement of Foreign Arbitral Awards, 330 UNTS 3, entered into force 7 June 1959.

[210] Articles 33-34 UNCITRAL Arbitration Rules.

[211] Article 34 (4) UNCITRAL Arbitration Rules.

[212] See Chapter 2, Section 2.12.

be found in Article III of the New York Convention, providing that "*[e]ach Contracting State shall recognize arbitral awards as binding and enforce them in accordance with the rules of procedure of the territory where the award is relied upon, under the conditions laid down in the following articles*". Accordingly, recognition and enforcement are also granted to non-ICSID awards. However, a striking difference with ICSID arbitration emerges in the post-award remedies, outlined in Article V of the New York Convention and carried out through the review by domestic courts. These will be seen in detail in the next section.

3.12. Post-Award Remedies

Once an award has been issued, it is final and binding on the parties and international arbitration does not offer any appeal mechanism. Nevertheless, several post-award remedies are offered both in ICSID and non-ICSID arbitration.

3.12.1. ICSID Awards

The ICSID Convention shields ICSID awards from any dispute concerning their recognition and enforcement. A few exceptions are provided in the Convention itself. The Award can be subjected to rectification,[213] interpretation[214] and revision.[215] These three are usually carried out by the same tribunal that decided the main dispute. Additionally, ICSID Awards can be subjected to annulment, carried out by a specific *ad hoc* Committee.[216]

The first three remedies are straightforward. Rectification offers a remedy for omissions or minor technical errors. It can be activated by one of the parties within 45 days after the date on which the award was rendered and it must be carried out by the same tribunal that produced the award. This remedy is not meant to change the final decision but only to correct any minor mistakes.

Interpretation offers a way to solve disagreements between the parties concerning the meaning of an award. The request presented by a party is subjected to a number of requirements:

---

[213] Article 49(2) ICSID Convention.

[214] Article 50 ICSID Convention.

[215] Article 51 ICSID Convention.

[216] Article 52 ICSID Convention.

> *"(1) there must be a dispute between the parties over 'the meaning or scope' of the award; (2) the purpose of the application must be to obtain a true interpretation of the award, rather than to reopen the matter; and (3) the requested interpretation 'must have some practical relevance to the Award's implementation'".*[217]

Moreover, the request for interpretation should be submitted to the tribunal which rendered the award, if possible. This may not be possible, for example, when the request is presented a long time after the issuance of the award. In that case, a new tribunal may be constituted.

Finally, revision of the award may be requested by the parties if new, decisive facts are discovered. The application must be made within 90 days after the discovery of the facts and not later than three years after the award was issued. The new element must be a fact and not a law, and it must have been unknown to both the tribunal and the party requesting revision when the award was rendered. Finally, as for interpretation, the request should be submitted to the tribunal that produced the award, but only if possible.

Annulment of the award

More complex is the remedy enshrined in Article 52 of the ICSID Convention. Annulment is, indeed, the only general remedy available to the parties and is the only exception to the finality of the award. This implies that domestic courts can never annul ICSID awards and that annulments can only be carried out within the ICSID framework. This remedy, available exclusively for arbitral awards and not for other acts of tribunals, can be requested based on a series of reasons specifically listed in Article 52(1). The procedure must be initiated by one of the parties within 120 days from the date of adoption of the contested award and the annulment request is examined by an *ad hoc* Committee – composed of three members appointed by the Chairman of the Administrative Council – acting according to the procedural rules applicable in the main proceedings. The Committee can annul the award in whole or in part. Pending the decision, the enforcement of the award may be suspended (the so-called "stay of enforcement"), and if the annulment process concludes with annulment, the matter can be submitted to a new arbitral tribunal. In the annulment decision, the Committee has a certain discretion, often translated into a tendency to uphold

---

[217] *ATA Construction, Industrial and Trading Company v. Hashemite Kingdom of Jordan*, ICSID Case No. ARB/08/2, Decision on Interpretation and on the Request for Provisional Measures, 7 March 2011, para. 35.

the award considering the "*significance of the error relative to the legal rights of the parties*".

The grounds for annulment are outlined in Article 52 in a closed list, meaning that no other reasons can be added. Indeed, an annulment must not be confused with an appeal: it is not a second decision on the merits. It is only a gateway for complaints concerning the award or the process that led to it. More in detail, a party may complain:

> *"(a) that the Tribunal was not properly constituted; (b) that the Tribunal has manifestly exceeded its powers; (c) that there was corruption on the part of a member of the Tribunal; (d) that there has been a serious departure from a fundamental rule of procedure; or (e) that the award has failed to state the reasons on which it is based".*

Requests for annulment under letter (a) are rare since this letter concerns the respect of the ICSID rules on the tribunal's constitution, which are usually thoroughly checked during the proceedings. Frequent, on the other hand, is the reference to the ground in letter (b), which can be invoked whenever a tribunal goes beyond the consent of parties concerning jurisdiction or the applicable law. For example, in *Mr. Patrick Mitchell v. Democratic Republic of the Congo*, the ad *hoc* Committee annulled the award on the basis of manifest excess of power and failure to state reasons. The Committee found that the arbitral Tribunal that had decided the case exceeded its jurisdiction *ratione materiae* since it erroneously qualified as an investment something that was not. In particular, the Committee stated that "*the Arbitral Tribunal forced the concept of investment in the case at hand in order to affirm its jurisdiction*".[218]

Ground (c) is extremely specific – concerning the corruption of an arbitrator – and has rarely been invoked. The ground under letter (d), concerning the respect of fundamental procedural rules, is frequently invoked, but its wording complicates its application due to the vagueness of the terms "fundamental" and "serious departure". In brief, the violation must concern only fundamental due process principles and it must be "*such as to deprive a party of the benefit or protection which the rule was intended to provide*".[219] For example, in *Fraport AG Frankfurt Airport Services Worldwide*

---

[218] *Patrick Mitchell v. Democratic Republic of the Congo*, ICSID Case No. ARB/99/7, Decision on the Application for Annulment of the Award, 1 November 2006, para. 46.

[219] *Maritime International Nominees Establishment (MINE) v. Republic of Guinea*, ICSID Case No. ARB/84/4, Decision on Annulment, 22 December 1989, para. 5.05.

v. The Republic of the Philippines, the ad *hoc* Committee annulled the award on the basis of a serious departure from a fundamental norm of procedure. The arbitral Tribunal decided the case on the basis of documents sent by the Respondent after the proceedings were closed, depriving the Claimant of its right to respond to the submissions of the State and, thus, of its right to be heard.[220]

Finally, the ground under letter (e) is strictly connected to the requirements of the award outlined in Section 3.11, i.e. that the award "*shall state the reasons upon which it is based*".[221] If the missing reasons, however implicit, emerge from the rest of the award, the request for annulment will not be accepted.

3.12.2. Non-ICSID Awards

Post-award remedies for non-ICSID awards are more complex since they can be found either in the arbitration rules chosen by the parties or in the applicable national legislation. Correction or rectification, interpretation and revision are, to different degrees, offered by the most widely used rules of arbitration. For example, the UNCITRAL Arbitration Rules provide for them respectively in Article 37 (interpretation) and 38 (correction). Few rules expressly provide for a power of revision like the ICSID Convention does, but such power is oftentimes recognized to tribunals as part of their "inherent powers", i.e. the powers that are essential for carrying out the tribunals' functions. In general, these remedies work in similar ways for ICSID and non-ICSID awards.

Extremely different, on the other hand, are the general remedies offered for non-ICSID awards, i.e. setting aside (annulment) and refusal to enforce the award. These are carried out by domestic courts and not by *ad* hoc Committees and are regulated by national laws. Grounds for setting aside and non-enforcement provided by different national legal systems are usually similar to those outlined in the UNCITRAL Model Law in Articles 34 and 36 since 93 States have so far adopted the Model Law and States not adopting it often mirror its content. These rules are, in turn, modeled after Article V of the New York Convention, which can be used as a reference point. It must be stressed that, just like for ICSID awards, no review of the merits of the award is allowed.

---

[220] *Fraport AG Frankfurt Airport Services Worldwide v. Republic of the Philippines (I)*, ICSID Case No. ARB/03/25, Decision on Annulment, 23 December 2010, paras. 218-247.

[221] Article 48 ICSID Convention.

Article V provides that recognition and enforcement may be refused by national courts for a number of grounds, listed exhaustively in the Article. The first five are (a) the invalidity of the arbitration agreement; (b) violation of due process; (c) excess of authority by the arbitrator; (d) irregularity in the composition of the arbitral tribunal; (e) award not yet binding or already set aside. These grounds may be invoked by the losing party, and the invoking party has the burden of proof, i.e. must offer sufficient proof of their existence. The remaining two grounds concern (a) a subject matter not "capable of settlement by arbitration" under the law of the relevant country (non-arbitrability) and (b) contrariness to public policy. On these grounds, a court may refuse enforcement *ex officio*, i.e. on its own motion.

As mentioned, these grounds are also included in the UNCITRAL Model Law. For example, under Article 34 of the Model Law, the application for setting aside must necessarily be made within three months from the date of receipt of the award and a court may suspend the setting-aside proceedings in order to give the arbitral tribunal the opportunity and time needed to fix the possible reasons for setting aside.

In any case, like ICSID *ad hoc* Committees, national courts have a degree of discretion when deciding whether to set aside an award, even if they ascertained the existence of a breach that would call for setting aside since the grounds provided in Article V of the New York Convention and the UNCITRAL Model law are only permissive, but not mandatory.[222]

3.13. Conclusions: The Ongoing Debate on ISDS

The previous sections have outlined the key elements of ISDS and, specifically, of investor-State arbitration administered by ICSID. While investment arbitration is a widely used means of settlement of disputes between States and investors, the current system is far from perfect, with some States threatening to opt out of it.

Much criticism has been moved to ISDS over time, mainly based on the "asymmetry" of treaty-based investment arbitration – mostly initiated by investors and based on substantive provisions that primarily confer rights to investors – to the point of being accused of having a pro-investor bias. This, however, is not necessarily confirmed by the final awards, of which only a little over 50% are decided in favor of the investor.[223] Other criti-

---

[222] G.B. Born, *International Commercial Arbitration*[3], Kluwer Law International, 2021, p. 3435.

[223] Based on the ICSID caseload statistics of 2024, available at https://icsid.world

cism is specifically aimed at the way arbitration takes place, allegedly lacking in transparency and consistency, and at arbitrators, accused of lacking the necessary impartiality. This last criticism is mostly due to the phenomenon of the so-called "double-hatting", meaning that the same individual can take up different roles, as arbitrator or counsel, in different ISDS cases. This phenomenon, united with the closed nature of the circle of practitioners of investment arbitration, has led many to express doubts as to the ability of ISDS to prevent the highly probable conflicts of interest that may arise. Finally, in the past years, ISDS has also been criticized for its excessive costs and for a lack of attention to non-economic matters, such as the fight against climate change.[224]

For these reasons, a number of attempts at reform are currently being discussed in different *fora*, the most active of which is UNCITRAL's Working Group III, endowed with "*a broad mandate to work on the possible reform of investor-State dispute settlement*".[225] Working Group III has been working since 2017 on the reform of ISDS and has so far concluded that reform is desirable, starting to work on many fronts. While the reform process is slow and filled with obstacles, some elements have begun to delineate. In 2023, among other things, the Working Group discussed a Code of Conduct for Arbitrators aimed at tackling some of the perceived issues of investment arbitration, such as arbitrators' lack of impartiality and transparency. Interestingly, the Working Group also considered a Code of Conduct for Judges, to be implemented should a "standing mechanism" for the resolution of investment disputes come into existence. In 2024, the Working Group is focusing on three instruments: the "draft statute of a standing mechanism for the resolution of international investment disputes", but also the "draft provisions on procedural and cross-cutting issues" and the "multilateral instrument on ISDS reform".

It remains to be seen whether any of these attempts will soothe the legitimacy crisis that has characterized ISDS in the past years. It is undeniable that, while investment arbitration is still highly resorted to, States have started to denounce the ICSID Convention (e.g. Bolivia and Ecuador) and

---

bank.org/sites/default/files/publications/ENG_The_ICSID_Caseload_Statistics_Issue %202024.pdf.

[224] D.R. Boyd, *Paying Polluters: The Catastrophic Consequences of Investor-State Dispute Settlement for Climate and Environment Action and Human Rights – Report of the Special Rapporteur on the Issue of Human Rights Obligations Relating to the Enjoyment of a Safe, Clean, Healthy and Sustainable Environment*, 13 July 2023, UN Doc A/78/168.

[225] UNCITRAL, *Report of Working Group III (Investor-State Dispute Settlement Reform) on the work of its forty-ninth session (Wien, 23-27 September 2024)*, UN Doc A/CN.9/1194, p. 2.

many more have terminated their existing BITs (e.g. South Africa and India), with the European Union proposing to replace ISDS with an investment court system.[226] Certainly, the reform proposal is interesting since it proceeds on two apparently parallel tracks: on the one hand, it aims at "fixing" and perfecting the existing framework and, on the other, it hopes to propose a complete reform of ISDS, with the creation of a standing dispute resolution mechanism, akin to a court, which would substitute arbitration altogether.

References

Born, G.B. (2021). *International Commercial Arbitration*³, Kluwer Law International.

Collins, D. (2023). *An Introduction to International Investment Law*², CUP.

Dolzer, R., Kriebaum, U., Schreuer, C. (2022). *Principles of International Investment Law*³, OUP.

Douglas, Z. (2009). *The International Law of Investment Claims*, CUP.

Douglas, Z. Pauwelyn, J., Viñuales, J.E. (eds.) (2014). *The Foundations of International Investment Law Bringing Theory into Practice*, OUP.

Fitzmaurice, G. (1986). *The Law and Practice of the International Court of Justice*, vol. II, *Jurisdiction*, OUP.

Hwang, M., Cheng, L.S. (2018). "The Chimera of Admissibility in International Arbitration", in N. Kaplan, M. Moser (eds.), *Jurisdiction, Admissibility and Choice of Law in International Arbitration: Liber Amicorum Michael Pryles*, Kluwer Law International, pp. 265-288.

Kjos, H.G. (2013). *Applicable Law in Investor-State Arbitration: The Interplay between National and International Law*, OUP.

Kröll, S., Bjorklund, A.K., Ferrari, F. (eds.) (2023). *Cambridge Compendium of International Commercial and Investment Arbitration*, CUP.

Mauro, M.R. (2019). *Diritto internazionale dell'economia. Teoria e prassi delle relazioni economiche internazionali,* ESI.

McLachlan, C., Shore, L., Weiniger, M. (2017). *International Investment Arbitration. Substantive Principles*², OUP.

Muchlinski, P., Ortino, F., Schreuer C. (eds.) (2008). *The Oxford Handbook of International Investment Law*, OUP.

Nussbaum, A. (1950). "Arbitration Between the Lena Goldfields Ltd. and the Soviet Government", in *Cornell Law Review*, 36 (1), pp. 31-53.

[226] On the peculiarities of the European Union's position see Section 3.1.1 of this Chapter.

Palombino, F.M. (2018). *Fair and Equitable Treatment and the Fabric of General Principles*, Asser Press-Springer.

Paulsson, J. (1995). "Arbitration Without Privity", in *ICSID Review - Foreign Investment Law Journal*, 10 (2), pp. 232-257.

Paulsson, J. (2005). "Jurisdiction and Admissibility", in G. Aksen et al. (eds.), *Global Reflections on International Law, Commerce and Dispute Resolution*, ICC Publishing, pp. 601-617.

Paulsson, J. (2019). "Arbitration Without Privity", in *Max Planck Encyclopedia of International Procedural Law.*

Reinisch, A., Schreuer, C. (2020). *International Protection of Investments. The Substantive Standards*, CUP.

Report of the Executive Directors on the Convention on the Settlement of Investment Disputes between States and Nationals of Other States (1965). Available at: https://icsid.worldbank.org/sites/default/files/Report_Executive_Directors.pdf.

Schreuer, C.H. et al. (2022). *Schreuer's commentary on the ICSID convention: a commentary on the Convention on the settlement of investment disputes between states and nationals of other states*[3], CUP.

Sornarajah, M. (2021). *The International Law on Foreign Investment*[5], CUP.

Steingruber, A.M. (2012). *Consent in International Arbitration*, OUP.

Thirlway, H. (2016). *The International Court of Justice*, OUP.

United Nations Conference on Trade and Development (2000). *Taking of Property*, UN, New York.

Vastardis, A.Y. (2023). "Most Favoured Nation Treatment", in D. Schneiderman, G. Van Harten (eds.) (2023), *Rethinking Investment Law. Perspectives and Prospects*, OUP.

World Bank Group (1992). *Guidelines on the Treatment of Foreign Direct Investment. Legal Framework for the Treatment of Foreign Investment*, vol. II, *Guidelines*. Available at: https://documents1.worldbank.org/curated/fr/955221468766167766/pdf/Guidelines.pdf.

Chapter 4
THE LAW OF THE WORLD TRADE ORGANIZATION *

Donato Greco and Ester Ferriello

ABSTRACT: *This Chapter aims at providing an introduction to WTO from its historical foundation. It will focus on the normative framework and institutional structure of the Organization. In this context, it will be pointed out that the WTO should be read within the more general framework of public international law. It will specifically address the dispute settlement system, clarifying the nature and scope of its jurisdiction. In this regard, the analysis will focus on the main procedural rules and principles as well as existing mechanisms set up to ensure compliance with and enforcement of final decisions. The main substantive obligations, such as the most-favored-nation treatment and the national treatment, will be discussed. These obligations represent the legal means through which WTO law intends to ensure the multilateralization of international trade relations. The Chapter concludes by analyzing derogations of general scope, those related to the protection of national security interests and flexibilities based on regional integration or developing purposes.*

KEYWORDS: *International Trade – Multilateralization – Liberalization – WTO – Sources – Institutional Structure – Substantial Obligations – Dispute Settlement System – Regional Integration.*

SUMMARY: 4.1. Introduction. – 4.2. The Historical Origins of the WTO. – 4.3. Objective and Functions. – 4.4. Membership, Accession, and Withdrawal. – 4.5. Sources. – 4.5.1. The GATT 1994 and Other Multilateral Trade Agreements. – 4.5.2. The Single Undertaking Principle. – 4.5.3. Plurilateral Trade Agreements. – 4.5.4. Regional Trade Agreements. – 4.6. Interpretation of WTO Law and General International Law. – 4.6.1. The Application of General International Law Norms in the WTO System. – 4.7. The Legal Value of Judicial Precedents. – 4.8. Institutional Structure. – 4.9. The WTO Dispute Settlement System. – 4.9.1. The Dispute Settlement Body. – 4.9.2. Panels. – 4.9.3. The Appellate Body. – 4.9.4. Jurisdiction: Nature and Scope. – 4.9.5. Implementation and Enforcement. – 4.9.6. A Paralyzed System: Current Challenges and Future Perspectives. – 4.10. Substantial Obligations: The Multilateralization of International Trade. – 4.10.1. The Most-Favored-Nation Treatment. – 4.10.2. The National Treatment. – 4.10.2.1. ...for Internal Taxation on Like Products. –

---

* This Chapter is the result of the joint work of the two Authors. However, Sections 4.1-4.6.1, 4.8 and 4.10-4.10.2.3 are to be attributed to Donato Greco, whereas Sections 4.7, 4.9-4.9.6 and 4.11-4.11.4 to Ester Ferriello.

4.10.2.2. ...for Internal Taxation on Directly Competitive or Substitutable Products. – 4.10.2.3. ...for Internal Regulation. – 4.11. Derogations and Flexibilities. – 4.11.1. General Exceptions. – 4.11.2. Security Exceptions. – 4.11.3. Regional Integration. – 4.11.4. Enabling Clause. – References.

4.1. Introduction

International trade law is a branch of the international legal system governing trade among countries. Alongside international monetary law and international investment law, it falls within the scope of international economic law. As of today, it consists of bilateral, regional or multilateral agreements as well as non-written rules of general international law. While there are many examples of bilateral and regional arrangements, multilateral trade agreements are much more limited. To date, the 1994 Marrakesh Agreement establishing the World Trade Organization (WTO Agreement) constitutes the most prominent and broad multilateral trade regime existing worldwide. This Chapter deals with the law of the WTO.

The WTO, as we know it today, is an international organization that was set up by the WTO Agreement, concluded on 15 April 1994, and formally entered into force on 1 January 1995. The headquarters of the WTO is located in Geneva, based on a Headquarters Agreement concluded by the same Organization with the Swiss Confederation.

As an international organization, the WTO enjoys a legal personality under international law which is distinct from that of its Members. Symmetrically, WTO Members must accord the organization the legal capacity under their domestic law as may be necessary to exercise its functions. The WTO, its officials and the representatives of its Members enjoy privileges and immunities in similar terms as those stipulated in the 1947 United Nations Convention on the Privileges and Immunities of the Specialized Agencies.

4.2. The Historical Origins of the WTO

Although formally established in 1994, the WTO has a direct precedent in the General Agreement on Tariffs and Trade, which was concluded in 1947 (GATT 1947). After the Second World War and its atrocities, international cooperation gained momentum and States first realized the need to establish an international order that could foster economic development, welfare, and prosperity as indispensable conditions for maintaining enduring peaceful relations among nations.

It was at the Bretton Woods Conference in 1944 that the convening

States recognized the need to create an international organization with a general competence in international trade that could complement the International Monetary Fund (IMF) and the World Bank (WB). Eminent economists such as Harry White and John Maynard Keynes took part in the meeting and inspired the creation of an international regime that could facilitate trade and development among nations. However, on this occasion, States were unable to agree on the most appropriate course of action to take.

After an initial proposal by the United States (US) in December 1945, the United Nations Economic and Social Council adopted a resolution calling for States to set up an international trade organization. Between the spring and autumn of 1947, intense negotiation activities took place in parallel, with the aim of concluding, on the one hand, the Charter of the International Trade Organization (ITO Charter), which would have shaped the institutional framework for the new regime, and, on the other hand, the General Agreement on Tariffs and Trade, which would have provided the substantive obligations applicable in matters of international trade. Whereas negotiations led to a substantive agreement on the text of the GATT in October 1947, the establishment of the ITO proved to be a more complex topic.

In order not to wait for the end of the ITO Charter negotiations, to which the GATT 1947 was closely linked, with a very pragmatic approach the negotiating parties decided to overcome the existing uncertainties and conclude a Protocol of Provisional Application of the General Agreement on Tariffs and Trade (PPA) to ensure the immediate application of the GATT 1947 even before it formally entered into force. Through this Protocol, parties undertook to provisionally apply Parts I and III of the GATT 1947 starting from 1 January 1948. The PPA allowed the application of the GATT from 1947 until 1996, despite the fact that this agreement had never been formally adopted.

Turning to the institutional framework, the ITO Charter was adopted in Havana on 24 March 1948 but never came into effect: the conditions for the entry into force of the treaty, set forth in Article 103, were not fulfilled within the prescribed time limit. This failure led to an institutional gap, lacking an international organization that could administer and monitor compliance with the substantive obligations stemming from the GATT 1947. For this reason, starting in the 1950s, the contracting parties began to develop practices and procedures based on the few provisions of the GATT 1947 that outlined a minimum institutional framework. Over time, and thanks to solutions arranged on a case-by-case basis, the GATT 1947 was progressively transformed into a *de facto* international organization and operated in that capacity for almost half a century, from 1948 to 1996.

In this time frame, the GATT 1947 proved to be successful in lowering tariffs in trade in goods through the first five rounds of negotiations (Geneva 1947, Annecy 1949, Torquay 1951, Geneva 1956, and Dillon 1960-1961). Less significant results were instead achieved with regard to non-tariff barriers, on which attention has been focused since the Kennedy Round (1964-1967). The Tokyo Round (1973-1979) was more fruitful, but the impossibility of reaching a general agreement among the parties meant that the negotiations resulted in plurilateral rather than multilateral trade agreements, concluded between certain parties to GATT 1947 and thus binding only on them.

The 1980s showed that the new challenges of international trade needed a more advanced institutional and substantive framework than that designed by the GATT 1947. For this reason, in September 1986, in Punta del Este (Uruguay), the contracting parties decided to embark on a new round of negotiations: the Uruguay Round.

Setting up an international organization that could fill the gap left by previous attempts was not on the agenda. In February 1990, the then Italian Trade Minister, Renato Ruggiero, proposed the establishment of a new international trade organization. As a result, Canada, the EU, and Mexico put forward a joint proposal that formed the basis for the drafting of the Agreement Establishing the Multilateral Trade Organization.

At this stage, the US showed a relatively passive attitude, if not one of substantial yet undeclared opposition. However, when in 1993 it became clear that a broad consensus was catalyzing around the proposal, the US, under the Clinton Administration, changed its mind. From its perspective, after the fall of the Berlin Wall in 1989 and of the Soviet Union two years later, the weakening of its historic rival and the globalization prompted by technological development offered a propitious opportunity to conclude a multilateral trade agreement.

Within this framework, the Agreement Establishing the World Trade Organization was signed in Marrakesh on 15 April 1994 and formally entered into force on 1 January 1995. With this milestone, the WTO formally came into being, as an international organization *pleno iure*, unlike its predecessor.

The Marrakesh Agreement thus produced a twofold effect: on the one hand, it filled the gap affecting the previous institutional framework and, on the other hand, it greatly expanded international trade subjects covered by the new multilateral regime.

As will be seen in detail below (Section 4.5.1), although the GATT 1947 was terminated in 1996, several elements of the agreement have survived. First, its substantial obligations were incorporated by reference into the subsequent GATT 1994 and, therefore, are still in force today. Second, it is formally sanctioned in the new treaty that decisions and practices developed under the GATT 1947 can provide guidance in the application of the WTO Agreement.

Moreover, the dispute settlement system has been extensively re-evaluated by the WTO Agreement, which reformed its functioning, enabling it to become one of the most prolific and effective systems of international adjudication. Suffice here to mention that in the period from 1948 to 1994, the dispute settlement system under the GATT 1947 was able to issue 132 reports, whereas from 1995 to 31 December 2023, 621 disputes were brought before this forum. In 372 cases, a panel was established; in 290 cases, a panel report was issued; and in 192 cases, an appeal followed. In 80% of cases where a national measure was found to be unlawful in relation to one of the WTO obligations, the losing party subsequently removed or modified the measure at issue.

Since the Doha Round, launched in November 2001, and in the following decade, negotiating efforts have mainly focused on making the WTO a more responsive system to the needs of developing countries, in order to reconciling it with non-economic interests such as environmental protection and compliance with labor standards and to strike a new balance between intellectual property rights in the pharmaceutical sector with the human right to health and access to sanitary countermeasures.

However, since 2015, multilateralism has entered a crisis and, with it, some WTO institutions, in particular the dispute settlement system. This crisis was triggered by a combination of several factors. First, the loss of legitimacy of the institutions of global economic governance as a result of their inability to interpret the changing social needs and demands for protection coming from different areas of the world, particularly the Global South, in a complex and more fragmented international scenario. Secondly, and as a consequence, the emergence of widespread nationalist trends opposed to global institutions and more inclined to pursue protectionist economic policies. In the same context, since 2018, a trade war between the US and China over customs tariffs has opened up. The Trump Administration has imposed tariff barriers on numerous Chinese products, accusing China of unfair trade conduct, particularly in the intellectual property sector. US President Joe Biden kept the measures in place, extending them in some cases to new products. The Beijing Government, in turn, reacted with retaliation measures, blaming US policies as protectionist.

This general crisis has had a significant impact on the WTO system, which is based on an inherently multilateral international order. This development has led to a fragmentation of international trade law, which has developed, outside the WTO, into many regional trade agreements (Section 4.5.4), including the so-called "mega-regionals". The latter include the Canada-EU Comprehensive Economic and Trade Agreement (CETA), the Regional Comprehensive Economic Partnership (RCEP) between the Association of Southeast Asian Nations (ASEAN) Members and Australia, China, India, Japan, Korea, and New Zealand, as well as the Trans-Pacific Partnership (TPP) to which are parties North American States such as Canada, the US, and Mexico, Asian and Oceanic countries such as Brunei Darussalam, Japan, Malaysia, Singapore, Vietnam, Australia, and New Zealand, and South American States such as Peru and Chile.

4.3. Objectives and Functions

The WTO provides a common institutional framework for the conduct of trade relations among its Members in matters governed by the WTO Agreement and associated legal instruments.

As for its primary objectives, the Agreement is aimed at liberalizing international trade by reducing tariffs and other barriers to trade and eliminating discriminatory treatment in international trade relations. By doing so, the Organization also aims to raise standards of living, ensure full employment and a large and steadily growing volume of real income and effective demand, and expand the production of and trade in goods and services, while allowing for the optimal use of the world's resources.

This ambitious program of economic development should be pursued in accordance with the objective of sustainable development, seeking to protect and preserve the environment in a manner consistent with Members' differentiated needs, concerns, and levels of economic development. Here, the Marrakesh Agreement clearly echoes the 1992 Rio Conference on Environment and Development and its main outcomes regarding the principle of sustainable development.

To meet these general objectives, the WTO has been entrusted with specific tasks stipulated in Article III of the WTO Agreement. First, the Organization administers the multilateral and plurilateral trade agreements concluded under its auspices with a view to their effective implementation by all Members. Secondly, it provides a permanent forum for further negotiations in international trade matters to obtain additional concessions and further bring down trade barriers.

Thirdly, the WTO administers a dispute settlement system, which constitutes a key aspect of the effectiveness of the whole global trade system and its liberalization mission, as will be further discussed below (Section

4.9). However, this mechanism does not exhaust the set of liberalization strategies. To ensure the harmonization of national trade legislations and reduce barriers to trade or discriminatory treatment, the WTO, through the Trade Policy Review Mechanism (TPRM), exercises implementation and monitoring screening of national trade policies.

Finally, the Organization cooperates with the main actors and policy-makers of the global economy, first and foremost with the IMF and the International Bank for Reconstruction and Development (IBRD), which was the only organization of the WB Group existing at the time of the conclusion of the former GATT 1947. Cooperation with these two agencies mainly focuses on technical assistance to developing countries.

While Article III:5 explicitly mentions only the latter organizations (IMF and IBRD), nothing precludes the WTO from entering into relations with other international organizations and non-governmental organizations (NGOs). This capacity can be inferred from other provisions of the WTO Agreement, such as Article V:1-2, which allows appropriate arrangements for effective cooperation with other intergovernmental organizations having responsibilities related to those of the WTO. On this basis, cooperation arrangements have been established with the World Intellectual Property Organization (WIPO) and the United Nations Conference on Trade and Development (UNCTAD). Apart from the existence of formal arrangements, the WTO may consult with relevant stakeholders or actors. For example, the WTO collaborates with the World Health Organization (WHO) on issues related to trade and health and, during the COVID-19 pandemic, the two organizations strengthened their cooperation and mutual assistance.

Beyond the functions listed in Article III, the WTO also performs some *extra ordinem* functions, including building trade capacity in the interest of developing or least-developed countries (LDCs), representing over three-quarters of WTO Members. In this sense, the Organization's action is two-fold. On the one hand, it monitors the implementation of special treatments accorded to developing countries by virtually all WTO agreements. On the other hand, the WTO provides technical assistance and training to developing economies and government officials from all over the world, especially from African countries.

4.4. Membership, Accession, and Withdrawal

The WTO has a universal membership and vocation. As of 30 August 2024, the WTO counts 166 Members, including the US and all the BRICs, namely Brazil, Russia, India, and China; China and Russia joined the Organization in

2001 and 2012, respectively. The EU has been an original member in its own right since 1 January 1995. Individual EU countries are also members separately from the EU, which, however, speaks for them through the European Commission at almost all WTO meetings. As a matter of fact, this means that WTO Members cover around 98% of world trade.

States other than original Members may accede pursuant to the accession clause provided in Article XII of the WTO Agreement. According to this provision, the Ministerial Conference shall approve and decide upon applications for accession by a two-thirds majority of the WTO Members.

Besides, WTO membership remains open not only to States but also to separate customs territories possessing full autonomy in the conduct of its external commercial relations. Hong Kong, Macau and Chinese Taipei have joined the WTO in this capacity.[1]

In this context, it is worth noting that the composition of WTO Members is very diverse. Developing and LDCs represent two-thirds and one-fifth of the membership, respectively. As will be pointed out below (Section 4.11), they benefit from special and differential treatment (S&DT) under many of the WTO agreements. For States to qualify as developing countries, there is no settled definition, so this status depends on self-designation and may generate controversies at the admission stage. Contrariwise, in relation to LDCs, the WTO relies upon the qualifications made by the United Nations.

Members retain the right to withdraw from the Organization. Article XV:1 of the WTO Agreement explicitly provides that Members may withdraw from the same Agreement at their convenience. Based on the single undertaking principle (Section 4.5.2), however, such withdrawal would immediately affect the withdrawing Member's participation in multilateral trade agreements. In other terms, a Member is precluded from picking and choosing which agreements to remain part of. Withdrawal only takes effect six months after the party's intention to withdraw has been duly notified to the WTO Director-General.

4.5. Sources

The Marrakesh Agreement and its six Annexes are the primary sources shaping the WTO normative framework. The latter includes sources of institutional law governing the Organization's functioning as well as substantive rules regulating different branches of international trade.

---

[1] See *supra,* Chapter 2, Section 2.2.

The institutional part is mainly designed by the WTO Agreement, which is a very short text of just sixteen provisions. It represents a sort of "constitution" of the Organization as it sets up its general objectives, functioning, internal structure, the competencies of the different bodies in which the Organization is articulated, and the capacity to enter into relations with other subjects of international law.

The institutional architecture of the Organization is further completed by Annex 2 and 3 of the WTO Agreement. The former instrument contains the Understanding on Rules and Procedures Governing the Settlement of Disputes (Dispute Settlement Understanding or DSU). The DSU is the source of the procedural rules governing the dispute settlement system, which has made the WTO one of the most effective mechanisms of interstate dispute resolution for at least two decades and will be further discussed below (Section 4.9). Annex 3, on the other hand, contains the TPRM Agreement, a set of procedural rules applicable to the TPRM, which reviews Members' national trade policies.

Turning to the substantive part of WTO law, it primarily consists of three major multilateral agreements contained in Annexes 1A, 1B and 1C, which are dedicated to trade in goods, trade in services and trade-related aspects of intellectual property rights, respectively. Here, the reference goes to the 1994 General Agreement on Tariffs and Trade (GATT 1994), which is the most important treaty on trade in goods, the General Agreement on Trade in Services (GATS), and the Agreement on Trade-Related Aspects of Intellectual Property Rights (TRIPS Agreement).

Even though, as will be argued below (Section 4.5.1), the GATT 1994 is an instrument legally distinct from the GATT 1947, the experience gathered and the practices settled under the former regime may still provide useful guidance in the case of a lacuna in the WTO system. According to Article XVI:1 of the WTO Agreement, the WTO shall be guided by the decisions, procedures and customary practices followed by the Contracting Parties to the GATT 1947 and the bodies established in the framework of GATT 1947.

4.5.1. The GATT 1994 and Other Multilateral Trade Agreements

The GATT 1994 has a pretty peculiar structure as a text and does not constitute an entirely new treaty. On the contrary, it has incorporated the substantive rules set out in the GATT 1947 by reference. Paragraph 1 of Annex 1A of the WTO Agreement states indeed that *"[the GATT 1994] shall consist of (a) the provisions in the General Agreement on Tariffs and Trade, dated 30 October 1947 […]*". Therefore, even if the GATT 1947 was formally terminated in 1996, its substantial rules have survived and have been substantially incorporated into the GATT 1994.

In addition to the rules of its predecessor, paragraph 1 of Annex 1A also includes in the GATT 1994 (b) decisions taken by the contracting parties between 1948 and 1994, (c) the Understandings they have agreed upon during the Uruguay Round, and (d) the Marrakesh Protocol to the GATT 1994.

As will be explained below (Section 4.10), the GATT 1994 contains some fundamental provisions constituting the cornerstones not only of the agreement itself but also of other multilateral and plurilateral trade agreements and of WTO law more generally. They include the most favored nation treatment (MFN) under Article I and the national treatment (NT) under Article III, which both represent the two principal mechanisms of the multilateralization of trade relations among WTO Members.

The prohibition of quantitative restrictions provided in Article XI should also be mentioned before moving on to the flexibilities that the GATT 1994 provides to reconcile trade liberalization with non-economic concerns. Here, the reference goes to the general exceptions listed in Article XX, the national security exception under Article XXI, which has become more frequently invoked in recent times in light of the so-called "securitization" of international relations, and the regional economic integration clause within the meanings of Article XXIV. Substantive obligations and exceptions will be further examined below (Section 4.10 and 4.11).

Besides the GATT 1994, Annex 1A includes twelve other multilateral agreements relating to the trade in goods in more specific branches of international trade. Among them, it is worth mentioning the Agreement on Agriculture (AoA), the Agreement on the Application of Sanitary and Phytosanitary Measures (SPS Agreement), the Agreement on Textiles and Clothing (ATC), the Agreement on Technical Barriers to Trade (TBT Agreement), the Agreement on Trade-Related Investment Measures (TRIMS Agreement), the Agreement on the Implementation of Article VI of the General Agreement on Tariffs and Trade 1994 (Anti-Dumping Agreement), the Agreement on Subsidies and Countervailing Measures (SCM Agreement).

Compared to the provisions of the GATT 1994, the multilateral trade agreements provide for more detailed rules applicable to trade in goods in a specific branch of international trade. As a consequence, the latter could conflict with the general rules contained in the former treaty. In the event a conflict occurs between the GATT 1994 and one of the other multilateral trade agreements listed in Annex 1A, the Interpretative Note to Annex 1A states that the multilateral trade agreement shall prevail to the extent of the conflict as *lex specialis ratione materiae*.

4.5.2. The Single Undertaking Principle

According to Article II:2 of the WTO Agreement, multilateral trade agreements, alongside the WTO Agreement itself, are equally binding upon all Members.

As pointed out by the Appellate Body, a standing body of seven judges that hears appeals from decisions of first instance issued in disputes brought by WTO Members (see Section 4.9.3 below), "*the WTO Agreement is a single treaty instrument which was accepted by the WTO Members as a 'single undertaking'*".[2] Another statement from the same Appellate Body later echoed this finding. In the case *Argentina – Footwear* (1999), it found that the GATT 1994 and another multilateral agreement relevant to the case at hand constituted "*an inseparable package of rights and disciplines which have to be considered in conjunction*".[3] This means that virtually every agreement is part of a whole and indivisible package of rights and obligations so that State parties to the negotiations cannot agree upon them separately. On the one hand, the single undertaking principle reflects the *substantive notion* of "treaty" adopted by Article 2(a) of the 1969 Vienna Convention on the Law of Treaties (VCLT). According to this provision, in the relevant part, "*'treaty' means an international agreement concluded […] in written form and governed by international law, embodied in more related instruments*". On the other hand, unlike other treaties, the instruments composing the Marrakesh Agreement can only be accepted or refused in an all-or-nothing fashion. Here, it is worth noting that the principle of treaty flexibility, which allows States to accept only certain instruments of the treaty or to limit the application of the treaty as regards some parts of it, gives way to the more rigid principle of treaty integrity insofar as the contracting parties wanted to establish a virtually uniform regime for their international trade relations, biding upon all of them.

However, the single undertaking principle does not exclude that conflicts may arise between the individual treaties composing it, as they are the outcomes of negotiations conducted in parallel but in different Committees during the Uruguay Round. For this purpose, Article XVI:3 of the WTO

---

[2] *Brazil – Measures Affecting Desiccated Coconut*, Report of the Appellate Body, 21 February 1997, WT/DS22/AB/R, para. 177.

[3] *Argentina – Safeguard Measures on Imports of Footwear*, Report of the Appellate Body, 14 December 1999, WT/DS121/AB/R, para. 81.

Agreement contains a subordination clause that provides that in the event of a conflict between a provision of the WTO Agreement and a provision of any of the multilateral trade agreements, the former treaty shall prevail to the extent of the conflict.

4.5.3. Plurilateral Trade Agreements

Annex 4 lists two plurilateral trade agreements which fall outside the scope of the single undertaking principle and, therefore, may have different membership. As a result, they are binding only upon those individual contracting parties who have accepted them separately, as stated in Article II:3 of the WTO Agreement; they are the Agreement on Trade in Civil Aircraft and the Agreement on Government Procurement. The International Dairy Agreement and the International Bovine Meat Agreement were originally included in Annex 4 of the WTO Agreement but were later terminated in 1997 and consequently deleted from Annex 4 by two decisions of the General Council (WT/L/251, WT/L/252).

4.5.4. Regional Trade Agreements

In the last decade, multilateralism entered into crisis due to economic and social disruptions and the advent of nationalist movements. As a consequence, economic cooperation has developed more at the regional level than the global one. Today, besides multilateral and plurilateral agreements, the WTO also administers around 300 regional agreements. Based on the levels of commitment by the contracting parties, it is possible to distinguish different types of instruments such as Preferential Trade Areas, Free Trade Areas, Custom Unions, Common Markets, Economic Union and Full integration. This issue will be further discussed below (Section 4.11).

4.6. Interpretation of WTO Law and General International Law

In the past, it was sometimes argued that the WTO is a self-contained regime, as if it were a closed box. As the Appellate Body has acknowledged, however, WTO law "*is not to be read in clinical isolation from public international law*".[4]

On the contrary, Article 3(2) of the DSU confirms that WTO law

[4] *United States – Standards for Reformulated and Conventional Gasoline*, Report of the Appellate Body, 29 April 1996, WT/DS2/AB/R, p. 17.

should be understood as a branch of the international legal system, to which it remains anchored. Pursuant to this provision, interpretation must be carried out in accordance with customary rules of interpretation of public international law, namely Articles 31-33 of the VCLT.

The following lines provide a few examples of this approach, where general rules on treaty interpretation, other customary norms or general principles of law were resorted to by panels and the Appellate Body in interpreting WTO agreements. A first instance can be traced in the twenty-seven Ministerial Decisions and Declarations, which, alongside the WTO Agreement, formed together the Final Act adopted in Marrakesh on 15 April 1994 and formally concluding the Uruguay Round of negotiations. In interpreting the WTO Agreement and its Annexes, these instruments must be taken into consideration as relevant (external) context to the extent that they represent agreements relating to the treaty which were made between all the parties in connection with the conclusion of the treaty, within the meaning of Article 31(2)(a) of the VCLT.

In similar terms, decisions adopted at Ministerial Conferences following the conclusion of the Marrakesh Agreement should also be taken into account as subsequent agreements between the parties regarding the interpretation of the WTO Agreement or the application of its provisions, pursuant to Article 31(3)(a) of the VCLT. In *US – Clove Cigarettes* (2012), the Appellate Body was called to clarify the interpretation of the term "reasonable interval" under Article 2(12) of the TBT Agreement. Paragraph 5.2 of the Doha Ministerial Decision on Implementation-Related Issues and Concerns specified that those terms generally mean a period of at least six months. In this context, the Appellate Body noted that "*a decision adopted by Members, other than [an authoritative] decision adopted pursuant to Article IX:2 of the WTO Agreement, may constitute a 'subsequent agreement' on the interpretation of a provision of a covered agreement under Article 31(3)(a) of the Vienna Convention*".[5]

A further example can be found in *US – Tuna II (Mexico)* (2012), where the Appellate Body faced the same question. To find a solution, however, this time it relied upon the decision taken by the TBT Committee on Principles for the Development of International Standards, Guides and Recommendations with Relation to Articles 2, 5, and Annex 3 to the [TBT] Agreement. In relation to this instrument, the judges pointed out that

> "*the TBT Committee Decision can be considered as a 'subsequent agree-*

[5] *United States – Measures Affecting the Production and Sale of Clove Cigarettes*, Report of the Appellate Body, 4 April 2012, WT/DS406/AB/R, para. 260.

ment' within the meaning of Article 31(3)(a) of the Vienna Convention. The extent to which this Decision will inform the interpretation and application of a term or provision of the TBT Agreement in a specific case, however, will depend on the degree to which it 'bears specifically' on the interpretation and application of the respective term or provision".[6]

As a further authority, it is worth mentioning *Australia – Tobacco Plain Packaging (Indonesia)* (2018), where the dispute concerned the application of the TRIPS Agreement. To justify the contention that each and every provision of this treaty needs to be interpreted in light of its object and purpose, as expressed in particular in its objectives and principles, the Panel recalled that paragraph 5 of the Doha Declaration explicitly invited the interpreter to follow this line of reasoning. Discussing in turn the authority of this instrument, panel experts concluded that "*[t]his paragraph of the Doha Declaration may, in our view, be considered to constitute a 'subsequent agreement' of WTO Members within the meaning of Article 31(3)(a) of the Vienna Convention*".[7]

Moving on to systemic integration pursuant to Article 31(3)(c) of the VCLT, some guidance can be traced in the *Brazil – Aircraft (Article 22.6 - Brazil)* (2002) arbitration. On 10 May 2000, as Brazil did not comply with the recommendations of the Dispute Settlement Body (DSB), Canada requested authorization from the DSB to take "appropriate countermeasures" (see Section 4.9.5), pursuant to Article 4(10) of the SCM Agreement and Article 22(2) of the DSU, in an amount of CanD 700 million per year. Brazil objected to such an amount and requested the matter be referred to arbitration pursuant to Article 22(6) of the DSU and Article 4(11) of the SCM Agreement. In determining what should be meant as "appropriate countermeasures", the arbitral tribunal concluded that "*a countermeasure is 'appropriate',* inter alia, *if it effectively induces compliance*", noting that Article 47 of the (then Draft) Articles on State Responsibility provided that "*countermeasures are meant to 'induce [the State which has committed an internationally wrongful act] to comply with its obligations'*".[8] In response

[6] *United States – Measures Concerning the Importation, Marketing and Sale of Tuna and Tuna Products*, Report of the Appellate Body, 16 May 2012, WT/DS381/AB/R, para. 372.

[7] *Australia – Certain Measures Concerning Trademarks, Geographical Indications and Other Plain Packaging Requirements Applicable to Tobacco Products and Packaging*, Report of the Panel, 28 June 2018, WT/DS435/R, WT/DS441/R, WT/ DS458/R, WT/DS467/R, paras. 7.2409-7.2410.

[8] *Brazil – Export Financing Programme for Aircraft – Recourse to Arbitration by Brazil under Article 22.6 of the DSU and Article 4.11 of the SCM Agreement*, Decision by the

to Canada's argument that since the Articles were not a binding source of international law, they could not be relevant for treaty systemic integration under Article 31(3)(c) of the VCLT, the arbitrators replied that they should have been taken into account to the extent they reflected rules of general international law.

In *Brazil – Desiccated Coconuts* (1997), the Appellate Body found that Article 32(3) of the SCM Agreement did not conflict with the general principle of non-retroactivity of treaties, as codified in Article 28 of the VCLT, since the same Article 32(3) states that "*the provisions of this Agreement shall apply to investigations, and reviews of existing measures, initiated pursuant to applications which have been made on or after the date of entry into force for a Member of the WTO Agreement*".

In *US – Gasoline* (1996), the Appellate Body observed that

> *"[o]ne of the corollaries of the 'general rule of interpretation' in the Vienna Convention is that interpretation must give meaning and effect to all the terms of the treaty. An interpreter is not free to adopt a reading that would result in reducing whole clauses or paragraphs of a treaty to redundancy or inutility".* [9]

A few years later, the same Appellate Body further highlighted that *"[a] fundamental tenet of treaty interpretation flowing from the general rule of interpretation set out in Article 31 is the principle of effectiveness* (ut res magis valeat quam pereat*)".* [10] On other occasions, the Appellate Body clarified that the interpretative principle *in dubio mitius* is a supplementary means of interpretation within the meaning of Article 32 of the VCLT. [11]

Arbitrator, WT/DS46/ARB, 28 August 2000, paras. 3.42-3.44, in particular footnotes 46 and 48.

[9] *United States – Standards for Reformulated and Conventional Gasoline* (note 4), p. 23. In the same sense, see *India – Measures Concerning the Importation of Certain Agricultural Products*, Report of the Appellate Body, WT/DS430/AB/R, 4 June 2015, para. 5.24; *Korea – Definitive Safeguard Measure on Imports of Certain Dairy Products*, Report of the Appellate Body, 14 December 1999, WT/DS98/AB/R, paras. 80-81.

[10] *Japan – Taxes on Alcoholic Beverages*, Report of the Appellate Body, 4 October 1996, WT/DS8/AB/R, WT/DS10/AB/R, WT/DS11/AB/R, p. 12.

[11] *European Communities – EC Measures Concerning Meat and Meat Products (Hormones)*, Report of the Appellate Body, 16 January 1998, WT/DS26/AB/R, WT/DS48/AB/R, p. 67, footnote 154; *China – Measures Affecting Trading Rights and Distribution Services for Certain Publications and Audiovisual Entertainment Products*, Report of the Appellate Body, 21 December 2009, WT/DS363/AB/R, para. 411.

4.6.1. The Application of General International Law Norms in the WTO System

The case law just mentioned concerned general rules on treaty interpretation, other customary norms or general principles of law resorted to by panels and the Appellate Body in interpreting WTO agreements. A different and much more disputed question may arise regarding the direct application of norms of general international law in the WTO system, in the case where this normative framework shows a lacuna. This issue is not settled by any rule of WTO agreements. Nonetheless, the case law of the dispute settlement system provides some guidance on the matter.

In *Korea – Procurement* (2000), the Panel has taken a clear stance on this issue, noting that:

> *"the relationship of the WTO agreements to customary international law is broader than [that underling the application of rules on interpretation]. Customary international law applies generally to the economic relations between the WTO Members. Such international law applies to the extent that the WTO treaty agreements do not 'contract out' from it. To put it another way, to the extent there is no conflict or inconsistency, or an expression in a covered WTO agreement that implies differently, we are of the view that the customary rules of international law apply to the WTO treaties and to the process of treaty formation under the WTO".*

A significant number of other cases seem to corroborate, explicitly or implicitly, the conclusion that norms of general international law may apply to the extent that the matter is not (or at least not entirely) governed by WTO agreements.

In *EC – Bananas* (1997), the Appellate Body was confronted with an objection concerning the legitimacy of the representation appointed by Saint Lucia in the pending proceedings. In upholding the legitimacy of the delegation, the judges stated that they could not find anything in either

> *"the Marrakesh Agreement Establishing the World Trade Organization (the 'WTO Agreement'), the DSU or the Working Procedures, nor in customary international law or the prevailing practice of international tribunals, which prevents a WTO Member from determining the composition of its delegation in Appellate Body proceedings".* [12]

[12] *European Communities – Regime for the Importation, Sale and Distribution of Bananas*, Report of the Appellate Body, 9 September 1997, WT/DS27/AB/R, para. 10.

In *US – Wool Shirts and Blouses* (1997), the Appellate Body pointed out that "it is a generally accepted canon of evidence in *civil law, common law and, in fact,* most jurisdictions, that the burden of proof rests upon the party, *whether complaining or defending, who asserts the affirmative of a particular claim or defence*".[13]

In *India – Patents (US)* (1998), India sought to challenge the first instance report, alleging that the Panel had erred in its treatment of India's domestic law, because domestic law is a fact that must be established before an international tribunal by the party relying on it, and that the Panel should have sought guidance from India on matters relating to the interpretation of Indian law. In dismissing India's insidious argument, the Appellate Body recalled the famous judgment rendered by the Permanent Court of International Justice in the *Upper Silesia* case. It pointed out that, according to a settled rule of international law, domestic law is a mere fact, not a legal source international courts and tribunals could be called to interpret as such, but for the purpose of assessing whether India's conduct was in breach of its obligations under the TRIPS Agreement.[14]

In *Canada – Dairy* (1999), the Panel was called to assess whether the Canadian Dairy Commission could constitute a government agency providing direct subsidies within the meaning of Article 9(1)(a) of the AoA. In answering in the affirmative to what was an issue of attribution, the Panel emphasized that customary international law, as codified in Article 7(2) of the Articles on State Responsibility, provided that

> *"[t]he conduct of an organ of an entity which is not part of the formal structure of the State or of a territorial governmental entity, but which is empowered by the internal law of that State to exercise elements of the governmental authority, shall also be considered as an act of the State under international law, provided that organ was acting in that capacity in the case in question".*[15]

In other cases, panels and the Appellate Body resorted to general principles of law. In *US – Shrimp* (1998), for example, the Appellate Body had the occasion to clarify that the *chapeau* of Article XX of the GATT 1994

---

[13] *United States – Measures Affecting Imports of Woven Wool Shirts and Blouses from India*, Report of the Appellate Body, 25 April 1997, WT/DS33/AB/R, p. 14.

[14] *India – Patent Protection for Pharmaceutical and Agricultural Chemical Products*, Report of the Appellate Body, 19 December 1997, WT/DS50/AB/R, paras. 64-66.

[15] *Canada – Measures Affecting the Importation of Milk and the Exportation of Dairy Products*, Report of the Panel, 13 October 1999, WT/DS103/R, WT/DS113/R, para. 7.77, in particular footnote 427.

> *"is, in fact, but one expression of the principle of good faith. This principle, at once a general principle of law and a general principle of international law, controls the exercise of rights by States. One application of this general principle, the application widely known as the doctrine of* abus de droit, *prohibits the abusive exercise of a State's rights and enjoins that whenever the assertion of a right 'impinges on the field covered by [a] treaty obligation, it must be exercised* bona fide, *that is to say, reasonably'".* [16]

In the same case, interpreting the notion of "arbitrary discrimination" as a preliminary issue precluding the application of the general exceptions under Article XX of the GATT 1994, the Appellate Body recalled the due process principle, noting that "*it is only reasonable that rigorous compliance with the fundamental requirements of due process should be required in the application and administration of a measure which purports to be an exception to the treaty obligations of the Member imposing the measure*". [17]

4.7. The Legal Value of Judicial Precedents

The WTO ensures that its Members comply with its agreements and rules through the WTO Dispute Settlement System (Section 4.9), a structured mechanism that parties must resort to when they cannot resolve trade disputes among them through mutual agreement. In principle, the WTO system does not adhere to the doctrine of the *stare decisis*. Formally, the rulings delivered by the WTO dispute settlement panels or the Appellate Body only bind the parties to an individual proceeding. In practice, however, WTO judicial authorities and WTO Members could hardly disregard the previous case law, especially if adopted by the Appellate Body. The WTO dispute settlement system does not provide for advisory jurisdiction. Therefore, the main sources of clarifications and interpretations of WTO law are the decisions taken by panels and the Appellate Body in the exercise of contentious jurisdiction, which are usually followed in later disputes on the same matter. In other words, the WTO system adheres to the so-called "taking into account approach", which is crucial to ensure that the dispute settlement system serves its function of providing security and predictability to the multilateral trading system (Article 3(2) of the DSU).

While Article 3(2) of the DSU emphasizes the boundaries of judicial

[16] *United States – Import Prohibition of Certain Shrimp and Shrimp Products*, Report of the Appellate Body, 12 October 1998, WT/DS58/AB/R, para. 158.

[17] *Ibid.*, para. 182.

decisions' interpretative authority where it points out that rulings of the DSB cannot "*add to or diminish the rights and obligations provided in the covered agreements*", the Appellate Body has firmly stated that both adopted panels' and Appellate Body reports create legitimate expectations among WTO Members, and should therefore be taken into account where they are relevant to any dispute.[18] As a matter of fact, panels are expected to follow the Appellate Body's conclusions in earlier disputes, especially where the matter at issue is the same.[19] It is worth mentioning that the disagreement with this approach was cited by the US as one of the reasons for its current blockage of the appointment and reappointment of the Appellate Body members (Section 4.9.6).

Finally, although unadopted panel reports have no formal legal status in the GATT or WTO system and, therefore, cannot create legitimate expectations (Section 4.9.1), the rationale presented in such reports can still offer valuable guidance to a panel or the Appellate Body in future cases dealing with the same legal issues.[20]

4.8. Institutional Structure

The WTO, as an international organization, presents a rather complex institutional architecture. Just like any other intergovernmental organization, it includes the so-called classical triad, namely a set of three organs consisting of a plenary body with decision-making powers (the Ministerial Conference), an executive council responsible for enforcement (General Council) and a Secretariat. However, WTO's internal organization is not limited to this basic structure and includes several other bodies.

Indeed, Article IV of the WTO Agreement sets up the Ministerial Conference, the General Council, the DSB and the Trade Policy Review Body (TPRB), as well as three specialized councils and other committees. The WTO Secretariat is established under Article VI.

The Ministerial Conference constitutes the plenary body with decision-making powers, consisting of representatives of all the Members who act in the name of their State or international organization. It convenes on a regular basis, at least once every two years. The Ministerial Conference has gen-

[18] *Japan – Taxes on Alcoholic Beverages* (note 10), p. 14.

[19] *United States – Sunset Reviews of Anti-Dumping Measures on Oil Country Tubular Goods from Argentina*, Report of the Appellate Body, 29 November 2004, WT/DS268/AB/R, para. 188.

[20] *Japan – Taxes on Alcoholic Beverages*, Report of the Panel, 11 July 1996, WT/DS8/R, WT/DS10/R, WT/DS11/R, para. 6.10.

eral competencies as it carries out the functions of the WTO, defines the general policy of the Organization and, under certain circumstances, takes decisions on all matters under any of the multilateral trade agreements. Other functions of the Ministerial Conference include the capacity to adopt authoritative interpretations of WTO agreements (Article IX:2 of the WTO Agreement) and to amend such agreements (Article X of the WTO Agreement). Additionally, it decides on the accession of new Members (Article XII of the WTO Agreement), appoints the Director-General, which is the chief of the Secretariat (Article VI:2 of the WTO Agreement), and may also set up subsidiary bodies such as additional committees not provided in any of the WTO agreements, providing them with such powers as it may deem appropriate for the performance of its own functions. Based on this prerogative, the Ministerial Conference established the Committee on Trade and Environment (CTE) to pursue the WTO's general objectives of preserving the environment and reconciling environmental concerns with economic development. The CTE constitutes a permanent forum where WTO Members may convene and discuss both the impact of trade policies on the environment and that of environment policies on trade.

The Ministerial Conference itself, under different names but with the same composition, serves in the capacity of General Council, DSB and TPRB.

Under Article IV:2 of the WTO Agreement, the General Council is therefore equally composed of representatives of all the Members. As the executive body of the Organization, it performs the functions, both regulatory and executive, of the Ministerial Conference in the intervals between the latter's meetings. To this end, it convenes as appropriate. Beyond this, within the terms of Article VII:3 of the WTO Agreement, the General Council considers the annual budget of the Organization as presented by the Director-General and reviewed by the Committee on Budget, Finance and Administration and approves it by a two-thirds majority comprising more than half of WTO Members. Lastly, it is competent for relations with other entities playing a role in international trade. Pursuant to Article V of the WTO Agreement, it makes appropriate arrangements for cooperation with other intergovernmental organizations and non-governmental organizations.

The same plenary body, in the same composition, also serves as the DSB. According to Article IV:3 of the WTO Agreement, the General Council indeed discharges the responsibilities the DSU attributes to the DSB. For this purpose, it appoints a chairman and adopts its rules of procedure. The competence and functioning of the DSB within the dispute settlement system will be addressed below in more detail (Section 4.9.1).

As for its third and last capacity, according to Article IV:4 of the WTO Agreement, the General Council convenes as appropriate to perform the duties of the TPRB as provided by the TPRM Agreement. As already mentioned above (Section 4.8), this body is entrusted with improving all Members' adherence to rules, disciplines and commitments put in place under the multilateral trade agreements.

Article IV:5 of the WTO Agreement also established three additional bodies: the Council for Trade in Goods, the Council for Trade in Services, and the Council for Trade-Related Aspects of Intellectual Property Rights (Council for TRIPS). Each of them has been entrusted with the task of overseeing the functioning and effectiveness of a specific trade regime. While the second and the third of these bodies monitor Members' compliance with the GATS and the TRIPS Agreement, respectively, the first one exercises its functions in relation to the GATT 1994 and all the other multilateral agreements on trade in goods listed in Annex 1A. The three Councils discharge the duties assigned to them by their respective agreements or the General Council, under whose guidance they operate. They consist of the representatives of all WTO Members and may convene as necessary.

Finally, the Committee on Trade and Environment, the Committee on Balance-of-Payments Restrictions (BOP Committee) and the Committee on Budget, Finance and Administration close the series of bodies provided in Article IV of the WTO Agreement and established by the Ministerial Conference. Membership in these Committees is open to representatives of all Members.

As for the Committee on Trade and Development (CTD), it is entrusted to periodically review the S&DT that multilateral trade agreements accord in favor of LDC Members, and to report to the General Council for proper consideration.

Under the GATT 1994 and other WTO agreements, import restrictions are meant as a temporary relief and not the optimal form of restoring equilibrium to the balance-of-payments position. To this end, in the presence of such kind of national policies, the BOP Committee must consult with WTO Members, according to the consultation procedures laid down in Article XV:2 of the GATT 1994, every time the Members maintain import restrictions for balance-of-payments reasons, with a view to removing such measures as soon as possible. The IMF may be invited to intervene in the consultation process.

As in other international organizations, the Secretariat represents the administrative body. The WTO Secretariat, set up by Article VI of the WTO Agreement, is composed of the Organization's staff, acting under the authority of the Director-General. As already mentioned above (Section

4.8), the Director-General is an individual civil servant directly appointed by the Ministerial Conference, which also defines its powers, duties, conditions of service and term of office.

The Secretariat staff personnel, in turn, is recruited and appointed by the Director-General through the office for human resources based on considerations of efficiency, competence, integrity and geographical representation, in accordance with regulations adopted by the Ministerial Conference.

The Secretariat is generally understood as a neutral and independent body representing the organization's only interests. Article VI:4 of the WTO Agreement reflects this general assumption as it provides that the responsibilities of the Director-General and the Secretariat shall be exclusively international in character. A twofold consequence stems from the recognition of the international character of these bodies. First, they are precluded from seeking or accepting instructions from any government or any other authority external to the WTO and, more broadly, must refrain from any action that might impinge on their position as international officials. Second, and symmetrically, WTO Members are called upon to respect the international character of both the Secretariat and the Director-General and, therefore, must abstain from seeking to influence them in the discharge of their duties.

4.9. The WTO Dispute Settlement System

As mentioned above (Section 4.7), the WTO has established its own dispute settlement system, which the parties must resort to in case of a disagreement arising from the interpretation and application of the WTO-covered agreements, when they are unable to reach a mutually agreed solution. The following sections will delve into the rationale of the system as well as its institutions, procedural aspects and current challenges.

The current dispute settlement system was created as part of the WTO Agreement during the Uruguay Round, and its procedure and rules are defined in the DSU, which can be found in Annex 2 of the WTO Agreement. Under Article 3(7) of the DSU, although a mutually agreed solution remains the preferable option, in cases where it is not achievable, the parties can resort to the adjudicative organs of the dispute settlement system.

The WTO settlement system, which has tried to overcome the weaknesses of its predecessor, has been reformed to be able to perform a twofold objective: resolving the disputes concerning the rights and obligations resulting from the provisions of the WTO Agreement (Article 1(1) of the

DSU) and providing security and predictability to the multilateral trading system (Article 3(2) of the DSU). The dispute settlement system is also competent to clarify the existing provisions of the General Agreement and the other covered agreements. It is worth recalling here that, under Article 3(2) of the DSU, this function must be carried out in accordance with customary rules on interpretation, namely Articles 31-33 of the VCLT, and that the General Agreement should be read in the more general framework of public international law (Section 4.6).

The following sections will be dedicated to the three main institutions created for these purposes: the DSB, the *ad hoc* dispute settlement panels and the standing Appellate Body. While the first is a political institution, the other two are quasi-judicial authorities.

The analysis will show how, despite being prolifically operational for more than two decades, the WTO dispute settlement system is nowadays facing a crisis, with the US becoming very critical and paralyzing the current system (Section 4.9.6).

4.9.1. The Dispute Settlement Body

The DSB is a political institution emanating from the WTO's General Council. Composed of representatives of all WTO Members, its function is to oversee the entire dispute settlement process under the DSU and specifically "*to establish panels, adopt panel and Appellate Body reports, maintain surveillance of implementation of rulings and recommendations, and authorize suspension of concessions and other obligations under the covered agreements*" (Article 2(1) of the DSU).

The DSB is thus involved at every stage of the WTO dispute resolution process, from the establishment of a panel to the implementation and enforcement of panel and Appellate Body reports, which have no binding value without the intervention of this political organ. In other words, panels, as will be pointed out below (Section 4.9.2), are not equivalent to established tribunals: first, they are quasi-judicial bodies established on an *ad hoc* basis upon the request of the complaining party; second, their reports only become binding upon the parties to the dispute at a later stage, once the DSB adopts them. In the GATT 1947 system, both the establishment of a panel and the adoption of its reports depended upon the approval of *all* contracting parties based on the so-called "consensus" rule. As a result, any GATT Member could vote against and prevent both the establishment of a panel (as a respondent party) or the adoption of its decisions (as a losing party), making the GATT 1947 dispute settlement system clearly ineffective. The WTO system addressed this major limitation with the implementation of the "reverse consensus" rule, which has made both the establishment of a panel and the adoption of its reports practically automatic, as will now be explained.

Generally speaking, the DSB takes decisions by consensus (or "positive" consensus; Article 2(4) of the DSU), namely a decision-making process without a vote and based on the absence of formal objections by the members of a given body. However, there are a few exceptions where it decides by a "reverse" or "negative" consensus, meaning that the decision is approved unless there is a consensus against it. This is the case when the DSB establishes panels, adopts panel and Appellate Body reports, and authorizes countermeasures (Articles 6(1), 16(4), 17(14) and 22(6) of the DSU). In practice, this means that these types of decisions are adopted unless all DSB Members vote against them. However, this outcome is practically impossible since there is always a DSB Member who places the decision request on the agenda, making it highly unlikely that they would then proceed to vote against it. Therefore, these key decisions are usually taken automatically. This voting procedure was considered one of the main perks of the new WTO dispute settlement system aimed at overcoming the shortcomings of the one provided by the GATT 1947, where, as mentioned above (Section 4.9.1), the key decisions required the consensus of *all* 1947 GATT Members, allowing a single negative vote (even from the respondent or losing party) to block the whole system.

The DSB meets as often as necessary to carry out its functions under the rules established by the DSU, acting under its own rules of procedure and under the leadership of an *ad hoc* appointed chairperson.

In the new institutional framework assumed by the dispute settlement system, the DSB is only formally assigned to the contentious functions but rather has a limited role compared to the other two institutions part of the system, with the predominance of the jurisdictional element over the diplomatic one.

4.9.2. Panels

The disputes occurring between WTO Members are adjudicated at the first-instance level by quasi-judicial bodies instituted *ad hoc*: temporary panels which are dissolved once they have accomplished their task. Established by the DSB, the panels are composed of three (five if the parties so agree) governmental and/or non-governmental experts whose nominations are proposed by the WTO Secretariat and approved by the parties to the dispute.

Panel members should be selected with a view to ensuring their independence, a sufficiently diverse background and a broad spectrum of expertise. Therefore, nationals of Members whose governments are either parties or third parties to the dispute[21] cannot serve on a panel concerned with that dispute unless the other parties agree otherwise. Panelists act in their individual capacities, and not as representatives of their home States, providing assurance of impartiality, independence and competence (Article 8 of the DSU).

The function of panels is to assist the DSB in discharging its responsibilities under the DSU and the covered agreements. Accordingly, panelists should make an objective assessment of the factual and legal aspects of the case and consult regularly with the parties to the dispute to give them adequate opportunity to develop a mutually satisfactory solution (Article 11 of the DSU). Finally, they submit a report to the DSB, which will adopt it by reverse consensus, as explained above (Section 4.9.1). Only after its adoption by the DSB does the report become a binding decision for the parties to the proceedings.

4.9.3. The Appellate Body

The Appellate Body is a standing quasi-judicial body established by the DSB to hear appeals from panel cases, providing final rulings on legal interpretations of WTO agreements (Section 4.7).

The body is composed of seven Members that the DSB appoints by positive consensus for a four-year term, with the possibility of reappointing each person once. The Appellate Body should comprise people of recognized authority with demonstrated expertise in law, international trade and the subject matter of the covered agreements generally. The Appellate Body members should be independent and unaffiliated with any government. Furthermore, the DSB takes into account factors such as different geographical areas, levels of development, and legal systems when appointing them, as they should be broadly representative of membership in the WTO. To ensure their impartiality, they may not participate in the consideration of any appeal that would create a direct or indirect conflict of interest.

The Appellate Body hears the appeals in divisions of three of its Mem-

[21] In the WTO dispute settlement system, the expression "third party" refers to those Members who are not parties to a dispute but might nonetheless hold an interest towards its outcome, usually because the dispute's resolution could impact their economies or trade interests. The DSU provides several ways for third parties to participate in the proceedings at different stages, i.e. in consultations (Article 4 of the DSU), before the panels (Article 10 of the DSU) and before the Appellate Body (Article 17 of the DSU).

bers, serving in rotation. The decision is taken by the division to which the appeal is assigned after an exchange of views on the issues raised with the Appellate Body members who are not in the division.

The Appellate Body reviews specific legal issues, such as the interpretation of WTO agreements and how these were applied by the panel in its decision. It can uphold, modify, or reverse the legal findings of the panel, but it cannot re-examine facts or evidence presented during the initial dispute. Once the Appellate Body issues its report, it is adopted by the DSB by reverse consensus, as explained above (Section 4.9.1). Also in this case, the report becomes binding on the parties to the proceedings only after its adoption by the DSB.

4.9.4. Jurisdiction: Nature and Scope

The nature of the WTO jurisdiction can be described as compulsory, exclusive and contentious.

The *compulsory* nature of WTO jurisdiction is explained in Article 6 of the DSU, which states as follows:

> *"If the complaining party so requests, a panel shall be established at the latest at the DSB meeting following that at which the request first appears as an item on the DSB's agenda, unless at that meeting the DSB decides by consensus not to establish a panel".*

In other words, membership in the WTO is sufficient to establish the jurisdiction of the WTO dispute settlement system. If a dispute arises under the WTO agreement, all Members are bound to subject it to the dispute settlement system. The panel is established at the request of the complaining party, and there is no need for further acceptance or consensus from the other parties.[22]

---

[22] Nowadays, all WTO Members have also signed (at least one) regional trade agreements (RTAs) that establish their own regional dispute settlement bodies (Sections 4.5.4 and 4.11.3). Hence, if RTAs do not include clauses to prevent the possibility of overlapping jurisdiction, Members to both the WTO and the RTA might be able to choose between the two *fora*. The WTO system does not answer the question of which dispute settlement system should prevail in this case, neither did the Appellate Body ever completely clarify the matter in its case law. See *Mexico – Tax Measures on Soft Drinks and Other Beverages*, Report of the Appellate Body, 6 March 2006, WT/DS308/AB/R, paras. 47-55 and M.A. Forere, *The Relationship of WTO Law and Regional Trade Agreements in Dispute Settlement: From Fragmentation to Coherence*, Wolters Kluwer, 2015.

Within the WTO system, jurisdiction is also *exclusive*, which means that a complaining Member is obliged to bring any dispute arising under the covered agreements to the WTO dispute settlement system. For this purpose, Article 21(1) of the DSU provides as follows:

> *"When Members seek the redress of a violation of obligations or other nullification or impairment of benefits under the covered agreements or an impediment to the attainment of any objective of the covered agreements, they shall have recourse to, and abide by, the rules and procedures of this Understanding".*

The rationale behind this exclusivity is to protect the WTO system from unilateral conduct. For this reason, Members are prohibited from unilaterally determining that a violation has occurred except through recourse to dispute settlement and are bound to make any such determination consistent with the findings contained in the panel or Appellate Body report adopted by the DSB or an arbitration award rendered under the DSU (Article 23(2)(a) of the DSB).

Finally, the jurisdiction in the WTO system can only be *contentious*, which means that it does not contemplate the possibility for its adjudicative bodies to render advisory opinions, i.e. legally non-binding decisions issued for the sole purpose of clarifying legal questions related to the interpretation and application of legal sources: in this case, the WTO agreements. Hence, it is only within the context of contentious jurisdiction that interpretation can be clarified (Sections 4.6 and 4.7).

Moving on to examine the scope of WTO jurisdiction, under Article 3(3) of the DSU, the contentious system covers disputes arising when "*a member considers that any benefits accruing to it directly or indirectly under the* covered agreements *are being impaired by* measures taken by another member".

The "covered agreements" include all the multilateral WTO agreements listed in Appendix 1 of the DSU, so not only the agreements which materially regulate the various aspects of international trade but also the main institutional agreements, such as the Agreement Establishing the World Trade Organization and the DSU itself, considered independently or in combination with other covered agreements. The TPRM provided for in Annex 3, on the other hand, is excluded, because it only imposes obligations on Members *vis-à-vis* the Organization and not in their mutual relations. Therefore, it is not considered likely to produce disputes between Members.

Regarding the measures that can be subject to WTO dispute settlement proceedings, the Appellate Body has clarified that the expression "*measures taken by another Member*" refers to any act or omission attributable to a WTO Member.[23] This general statement was further specified to include also some "atypical" measures such as: (i) actions of private parties attributable to a Member State; (ii) measures that are no longer in force because they have expired or have been withdrawn during the proceedings; (iii) legislative acts as such, independently from their concrete application; (iv) unwritten norms or practices of Member States; (v) ongoing conduct of Member States; (vi) measures by regional or local authorities.

4.9.5. Implementation and Enforcement

The submission of the panel report and, if any, of the Appellate Body report to the DSB marks the end of the adjudicative phase. Where a panel or the Appellate Body concludes that a measure is inconsistent with a covered agreement, it recommends to the Member concerned to bring the measure into conformity with that agreement. In addition to its recommendations, the panel or Appellate Body may suggest ways in which the Member concerned could implement the recommendations (Article 19(1) of the DSU). Contrary to recommendations, these suggestions are not binding.

The adoption of these rulings and/or recommendations by the DSB marks the start of the enforcement stage, regulated by Articles 21-22 of the DSU. These provisions describe three different ways of achieving the implementation of DSB recommendations: the spontaneous withdrawal of the WTO-inconsistent measure, compensation and the adoption of countermeasures. The choice between the three is not completely free and must follow the order established by Article 3(7) of the DSU. According to this provision, the first objective of the settlement system is to secure the withdrawal of the WTO inconsistent measures. Therefore, the measure of compensation should be resorted to only if the immediate withdrawal of the measure is impracticable and as a temporary measure. Furthermore, the possibility of adopting countermeasures, namely the suspension of the application of concessions or other obligations, should be considered only as a last resort.

As for the *spontaneous withdrawal of the inconsistent measures*, within 30 days after the date of adoption of the panel or Appellate Body report, the DSB holds a meeting where the Member concerned is required to pro-

---

[23] *United States – Sunset Review of Anti-Dumping Duties on Corrosion-Resistant Carbon Steel Flat Products from Japan*, Report of the Appellate Body, 15 December 2003, WT/DS244/AB/R, para. 81.

vide information regarding its plans for implementing such rulings. According to established case law, compliance or implementation of rulings of the DSB consists in the withdrawal or modification of the WTO-inconsistent measure or part of it.[24] If immediate compliance is impracticable, the Member State will be given a reasonable period of time to do so (Article 21(3) of the DSU). The latter can be established in three different ways: (i) at a Member's proposal approved by the DSB; (ii) by agreement between the parties; or (iii) if none of these options is viable, through resort to arbitration under Article 21(3)(c) of the DSU. In any case, unless the parties to the dispute agree otherwise, the period from the establishment of a panel until the date of determination of the reasonable period of time must not exceed 15 months (Article 21(4) of the DSU).

During this period of time, the infringing Member must modify or withdraw the WTO-inconsistent behaviors. However, it is frequent for the parties to disagree on whether the losing member has implemented the recommendations and rulings. In this occurrence, under Article 21(5) of the DSU, either of the parties can request the dispute to be decided through recourse to the same settlement procedures discussed above, including, where possible, resorting to the original panel. The panel shall circulate its report within 90 days after the date of referral of the matter to it. This arbitral procedure, like the one established to determine the reasonable period of time in Article 21(3)(c) of the DSU, is designed to prevent delays in the proceedings caused by stalling tactics from the losing State. As for the scope of the panel jurisdiction, the Appellate Body has clarified that it is not limited to examining whether the implementing measure fully complies with the recommendations and rulings adopted by the DSB but also covers the assessment of the new measure in its totality, including its consistency with a covered agreement.[25]

If the losing Member fails to bring its measure into conformity with its WTO obligations within a reasonable period of time, the complaining

---

[24] *United States – Continued Dumping and Subsidy Offset Act of 2000, Arbitration under Article 21.3(c) of the Understanding on Rules and Procedures Governing the Settlement of Dispute*, Award of the Arbitrator, 13 June 2003, para. 49 and *Argentina – Measures Affecting the Export of Bovine Hides and the Import of Finished Leather, Arbitration under Article 21.3(c) of the Understanding on Rules and Procedures Governing the Settlement of Disputes*, Award of the Arbitrator, 31 August 2001, para. 40.

[25] *Canada – Measures Affecting the Export of Civilian Aircraft – Recourse by Brazil to Article 21(5) of the DSU*, Report of the Appellate Body, 21 July 2000, WT/DS70/AB/RW, paras. 40-41 and *United States – Import Prohibition of Certain Shrimp and Shrimp Products – Recourse to Article 21(5) of the DSU by Malaysia*, Report of the Appellate Body, 22 October 2001, WT/DS58/AB/RW, paras. 85-87.

Member is entitled to resort to temporary measures, namely compensation and retaliation.

Under Article 22(1) of the DSU, the payment of *compensation* is voluntary and mutually agreed. At the request of any party having invoked the dispute settlement procedures, the implementing Member must enter into negotiations with a view to developing mutually acceptable compensation. When the complaining Member so requests, the infringing one is obliged to take part in negotiations, but it is not bound to reach an agreement, which (if reached) should be concluded within 20 days after the expiration of the reasonable period of time defined by Article 21(3) of the DSU. Compensation must be WTO-consistent, which means that it must respect, among others, the MFN obligation under Article I of the GATT 1994. This requirement has been considered one of the reasons why this temporary measure can be a less attractive choice.[26] Compliance with Article I of the GATT 1994 means WTO Members other than the complainant could also benefit from the compensation, depending on its form. As for the latter, compensation does not consist in monetary payment but in the offer of a benefit (e.g., a tariff reduction) equivalent to the benefit which the respondent has nullified or impaired through its non-compliance.

In practice, it is frequent for the parties not to be able to reach a consensus over the compensation within the 20-day timeframe provided by Article 22(2) of the DSU. This is where *retaliation* comes into play, as the Member affected by the infringement is given the possibility to ask the DSB for authorization to claim the suspension of treaty obligations towards the defaulting Member. Being a last resort (Article 3(7) of the DSU), recourse to such countermeasures should be temporary and they should be symmetrical. For this purpose, under Article 22(4) of the DSU, the level of the suspension of concessions or other obligations authorized by the DSB shall be equivalent to the level of the nullification or impairment. The DSB must decide upon the rule of reverse consensus whether to grant the authorization to suspend obligations within 30 days of the expiry of the reasonable period of time. If the parties disagree on the complainant's proposed form of retaliation, the matter shall be referred to arbitration (Article 22(6) of the DSU). Such arbitration shall be carried out by the original panel, if Members are available, or by an arbitrator appointed by the Director-General, and shall be completed within 60 days after the date of expiry of the reasonable period of time. As for its form, we already mentioned that retaliation might imply the suspension of concessions or obligations. The

[26] World Trade Organization, *A Handbook on the WTO Dispute Settlement System*[2], CUP, 2017, p. 140.

former occurrence is for sure the most frequent and can consist, for instance, in the suspension of tariff reduction commitments which WTO Members have made in multilateral trade negotiations. It should be noted that resorting to authorized countermeasures is not the most frequent case, and the respondent Member usually complies with the recommendations and rulings of the DSB. In any case, designed as temporary remedies, these measures should be removed immediately upon subsequent compliance with the DSB's recommendations and decisions (Article 22(8) of the DSU).

The whole implementation and enforcement process is supervised by the DSB (Article 21(6) of the DSU). During the reasonable time period and for as long as there is no implementation, the DSB keeps under surveillance the implementation of adopted recommendations or rulings. Any Member can, at any time following their adoption, raise an issue about the implementation. Unless the DSB decides otherwise, the issue of implementation of the recommendations or rulings shall be placed on the agenda of the DSB meeting after six months following the date of establishment of the reasonable period of time and shall remain on the DSB's agenda until the issue is resolved. At least 10 days prior to each such DSB meeting, the Member concerned shall provide the DSB with a status report in writing of its progress in the implementation of the recommendations or rulings.

4.9.6. A Paralyzed System: Current Challenges and Future Perspectives

Over the years, the WTO has been quite successful with its Members increasingly inclined to solve their disputes through its dispute settlement system. However, this process has not developed without criticism. The whole system has faced challenges in recent years, mainly because, since 2017, the US has finally acted out its criticism by preventing the appointment and reappointment of the Appellate Body members. Although, as mentioned above (Section 4.9.1), many of the key decisions in the WTO system are now adopted by "reverse" consensus – and are taken, therefore, automatically –, the appointment of the Appellate Body members still follows the "positive" consensus rule, allowing any WTO Member to block the process (Section 4.9.3). Before 2017, under the Obama Administration, the US had already manifested its concerns towards the system, specifically accusing the Appellate Body of "judicial activism" and advocating for a more flexible and case-by-case approach, avoiding general interpretations and "guiding" precedents. The US had also voiced its frustration over a series of Appellate Body decisions deeply affecting its economic and political interests, namely the ones regarding subsidies and State-owned enterprises. Decisions whose effectiveness the US did not have any chance to block since their adoption was subject to the "reverse" consensus rule. Notably, as explained, the new WTO system was more efficient than its predecessor in this regard. Hence, in 2017, the Trump Administration used one of the few loopholes left in the WTO system and took a more assertive stance, blocking the appointment of the Appellate Body members. As a result, the Appellate Body has been unable to function effectively since December 2019, when the number of judges fell below the minimum of three required to hear an appeal.

State parties to the WTO have tried several solutions to address the current paralysis of the Appellate Body. First, instead of defining the conduct of the US as abusive and contrary to good faith (Article 3(10) of the DSU), they advanced some proposals to improve the system. On 15 October 2019, the WTO Facilitator issued a Report to the WTO General Council proposing a Draft GC Decision on Functioning of the Appellate Body.[27] The recommendations included transitional rules for outgoing Members, enforcing a 90-day deadline for appeals, and clarifying that municipal law should be treated as fact, not subject to appeal. The Appellate Body was advised to avoid addressing issues not raised by the parties or beyond the dispute at hand (this attitude might be interpreted as the provision of an advisory opinion, a function which falls outside the scope of the competencies Article 17(12) of the DSU attributes to the dispute settlement system). Previous rulings were not to create binding precedents, and panels were urged to avoid overreach. Additionally, annual dialogues between WTO Members and the Appellate Body were suggested to discuss broader issues.[28]

Since the US did not accept these proposals, WTO Members have resorted to alternative dispute resolution mechanisms. Article 25 of the DSU provides for the possibility of recurring to arbitration instead of the regular dispute settlement system. On this basis, in March 2020, sixteen WTO Members set up a Multi-Party Interim Appeal Arbitration Arrangement (MPIA), which was then joined by other Members for a total of 27 States adhering in 2024, including China, Japan, and the EU.[29] However, several

---

[27] WTO, *Agenda Item 4: Informal Process on Matters Related to the Functioning of the Appellate Body – Report by the Facilitator, H.E. Dr. David Walker (New Zealand)*, Doc. JOB/GC/222, 15 October 2019.

[28] See more broadly on this point G. Sacerdoti, "Adjudication of International Trade Disputes: From Success to Crisis. What's Next?", in *The Law & Practice of International Courts and Tribunals*, 2023, 22(2), pp. 419-449, 439-440 and P. Van den Bossche, D. Prévost, *Essentials of WTO Law*², CUP, 2021, pp. 51-53.

[29] As of now (2024), the MPIA participants list includes the following States: Australia, Colombia, Iceland, Nicaragua, Switzerland, Benin, Costa Rica, Japan, Norway,

key WTO Members did not sign on the MPIA. Besides the US, States such as India, South Korea, Russia, and Turkey were hesitant to join because of the voluntary nature of the MPIA, whose effectiveness and decision enforcement are limited compared to the Appellate Body's binding decisions.

The MPIA works as an alternative appeal system, operating under the WTO appellate review rules, to which disputing parties can appeal panel decisions by virtue of specific bilateral agreements between them.

The MPIA is a temporary alternative for disputes among those WTO Members that are party to it, designed to remain in place only for as long as the Appellate Body is not functioning. The efficacy and longevity of this system remain uncertain, but much of its success will depend on the authority of its decisions and on the alternative solutions that the US and other Members will find. For instance, some have questioned the enforceability of the awards rendered under the MPIA as they may lack the same legal status as the WTO panel or Appellate Body reports.[30] In the same vein, others have highlighted how the hibernation of the Appellate Body might lead to WTO Members settling their disputes by negotiation or other means, with already some evidence of panel proceedings being suspended by joint requests of the parties in view of reaching a settlement.[31]

4.10. Substantial Obligations: The Multilateralization of International Trade

International trade law substantive rules revolve around two fundamental obligations, which together represent two formidable instruments of liberalization to the extent that they multilateralize commercial treatments WTO Members may have granted to third parties (also non-Members) or their own national economic operators by extending those treatments to all WTO Members.

These two key institutions are the MFN obligation and the NT obligation, respectively.[32] Within the WTO system, they have been enshrined

---

Ukraine, Brazil, Ecuador, Macao, China, Pakistan, Uruguay, Canada, European Union, Mexico, Peru, China, Guatemala, Montenegro, Philippines, Chile, Hong Kong, New Zealand and Singapore.

[30] C. Carmody, "Procedural aspects of WTO dispute settlement", in J. Gomula, S. Wittich (eds.), *Research Handbook on International Procedural Law*, Edward Elgar Publishing, 2024, p. 153.

[31] G. Sacerdoti (note 28), pp. 419-449.

[32] The MFN and NT obligations also apply in international investment law. See Chapter 3, Sections 3.3.3 and 3.3.4, respectively.

most notably in the GATT 1994 as well as under other multilateral trade agreements such as the GATS,[33] the TBT Agreement,[34] and the TRIPS Agreement.[35] For the limited scope of this volume, we will only address the two normative mechanisms as provided in Articles I and III of the GATT 1994, respectively.

In line with the general purpose of eliminating "discriminatory treatment in international trade relations", as stated in the Preamble of the GATT 1994, the MFN and the NT obligations are essentially aimed at establishing a uniform legal framework for international trade among WTO Members by prohibiting illegitimate discriminations among them. The two norms provide treaty-based expressions of the general principle of non-discrimination.

4.10.1. The Most-Favored-Nation Treatment

As it has been acknowledged in the jurisprudence of the WTO dispute settlement system, the MFN treatment is an obligation of a "*pervasive character*", a "*cornerstone of the GATT and is one of the pillars of the WTO trading system*".[36] An archetype of the MFN obligation is provided in Article I:1 of the GATT 1994. Under the latter provision,

> *"[w]ith respect to customs duties and charges of any kind imposed on or in connection with importation or exportation or imposed on the international transfer of payments for imports or exports, and with respect to the method of levying such duties and charges, and with respect to all rules and formalities in connection with importation and exportation, and with respect to all matters referred to in paragraphs 2 and 4 of Article III, any advantage, favor, privilege or immunity granted by any contracting party*

[33] Under the GATS, the MFN obligation and the NT obligation can be found in Article II:1 and Article XVII:1, respectively.

[34] Under the TBT Agreement, Article 2(1) and Article 5(1)(1) enshrine both obligations in relation to technical regulations and conformity assessment procedures, respectively.

[35] Under the TRIPS Agreement, the two obligations can be traced in Article III (NT) and Article IV (MFN).

[36] *Canada – Certain Measures Affecting the Automotive Industry*, Report of the Appellate Body, 31 May 2000, WT/DS139/AB/R, WT/DS142/AB/R, paras. 69 and 82; *European Communities – Measures Prohibiting the Importation and Marketing of Seal Products*, Report of the Appellate Body, 22 May 2014, WT/DS400/AB/R, WT/DS401/AB/R, para. 5.86; *European Communities – Conditions for the Granting of Tariff Preferences to Developing Countries*, Report of the Appellate Body, 7 April 2004, WT/DS246/AB/R, para. 101.

to any product originating in or destined for any other country shall be accorded immediately and unconditionally to the like product originating in or destined for the territories of all other contracting parties".

According to the MFN obligation, if a Member grants any advantage to any product originating in the territory of any other country (which does not necessarily need to be a WTO Member), it must extend immediately and unconditionally the same treatment to like products originating from or destined to all other Members. This means that the MFN obligation entails a general prohibition of discrimination, including both *de jure* and *de facto* discrimination. In this respect, in *Canada – Autos* (2000), the Appellate Body pointed out that

> *"the words of Article I:1 do not restrict its scope only to cases in which the failure to accord an 'advantage' to like products of all other Members appears on the face of the measure, or can be demonstrated on the basis of the words of the measure. Neither the words* de jure *nor* de facto *appear in Article I:1. [The latter provision] does not cover only 'in law', or* de jure, *discrimination[, it] also covers 'in fact', or* de facto, *discrimination".*[37]

To assess whether an individual national measure may constitute a violation of the MFN obligation, a four-tier test has been established in the case law of the Appellate Body.[38] In particular, four conditions must be satisfied: (i) the measure at issue must fall within the scope of application of Article I:1; (ii) the imported or exported products at issue must be "like products"; (iii) the measure at issue must confer an "advantage, favor, privilege, or immunity" on a product originating in the territory of any country; (iv) the advantage so accorded must not have been extended "immediately and unconditionally" to like products originating in the territory of all WTO Members.

Starting with the first requirement, a measure falling within the scope of Article I:1 of the GATT 1994 may either impose duties and charges of any kind, affect the method of levying such duties and charges or provide rules and formalities in connection with importation and exportation. It is worth noting that "*'in connection with importation' as used in Article I, not only encompasses measures which directly relate to the process of importation but could also include those measures [...] which relate to other aspects of the*

---

[37] *Canada – Certain Measures Affecting the Automotive Industry* (note 36), para. 78.

[38] *European Communities – Measures Prohibiting the Importation and Marketing of Seal Products* (note 36), para. 5.86.

importation of a product or have an impact on actual importation".[39] The same rationale applies to exportations.

In relation to the notion of "charge" within the meanings of Article I:1 of the GATT 1994, judicial practice has generally understood it as referring to "*'pecuniary burden, cost', 'expense', or '[a] price required or demanded for service rendered or goods supplied'*".[40] In addition, it is settled in the case law that relevant measures may include not only positive actions but also apparently omissive conducts such as selective exemption from the imposition of a customs fee. In *US – Customs User Fee* (1997), the Panel noted that "*[e]xemptions from the fee fell within the category of 'advantage, favor, privilege or immunity' which Article I:1 required to be extended unconditionally to all other contracting parties. Such preferential exemptions, therefore, constituted a breach of the obligation of non-discrimination of Article I:1*".[41] Furthermore, the MFN obligation covers not only tariff barriers but also non-tariff ones; for example, in *EC – Bananas III*, the relevant measure was a less burdening licensing procedure.

The MFN obligation under Article I:1 shows a very wide scope of application. Its all-encompassing nature, however, can only be understood by reference to the matters covered in Article III:2 and 4. This brings within the scope of the MFN obligation "internal taxes or other internal charges of any kind" applied to like products as well as "all laws, regulations and requirements affecting their internal sale, offering for sale, purchase, transportation, distribution or use".

Turning to the second requirement, the imported or exported products at issue must be "like products" within the meaning of Article I:1. However, likeness finds no definition in the GATT 1994, and this assessment must be conducted on a case-by-case basis. A combined reading of the Agreement's provisions and the case law of the dispute settlement system may assist the interpreter in applying this notion in a particular case. In this respect, it is first worth noting that, as the rationale of Article I:1 is to protect the equality of competitive opportunities, assessing the likeness of two products involves a determination that competitive relationships exist between them.[42]

---

[39] *United States – Certain Measures Affecting Imports of Poultry from China*, Report of the Panel, 29 September 2010, WT/DS392/R, para. 7.410.

[40] *China – Measures Related to the Exportation of Various Raw Materials*, Report of the Panel, 5 July 2011, WT/DS394/R, WT/DS395/R, WT/DS398/R, para. 7.820.

[41] *United States – Customs User Fee*, Report of the Panel, 25 November 1997, L/6264, B.I.S.D. 35S/245, para. 122.

[42] *European Communities – Measures Affecting Asbestos and Asbestos Containing Products*, Report of the Appellate Body, 12 March 2001, WT/DS135/AB/R, paras. 91

Thus, like products are "*products that share a number of identical or similar characteristics or qualities*".[43] In determining whether two products are "like products", in *Spain – Unroasted Coffee* (1981), the Panel established a three-tier test. In particular, it considered: (i) their physical characteristics, such as their properties, natures, and qualities; (ii) their end-use in the given market; and (iii) tariff classification and corresponding applicable tariff regime of other Members.

Spain – Unroasted Coffee provides an instructive example in this context. The case arose from the fact that Spain did not apply customs duties to the coffee varieties Colombian mild and other mild, while imposing a 7 per cent customs duty on three other types of unroasted coffee. Brazil mainly exported unwashed Arabica and robusta coffee, to which the tariff applied, and therefore decided to start proceedings against Spain, alleging a violation of the MFN obligation under Article I:1.

The Panel established in the case had to assess whether the different types of coffee – affected and exempted from the measure – were like products. In this regard, it noted that Spain justified the differential treatment on the basis of the organoleptic properties of the coffee varieties, as resulting from geographical factors, cultivation and processing of the coffee beans, and genetic factors.

However, on the basis of three elements, it excluded that such differences were sufficient reason to allow for a different tariff treatment. First, it noted that "*it was not unusual in the case of agricultural products that the taste and aroma of the end-product would differ because of one or several of the above-mentioned factors*".[44] Second, it underlined that "*unroasted coffee was mainly, if not exclusively, sold in the form of blends, combining various types of coffee, and that coffee in its end-use, was universally regarded as a well-defined and single product intended for drinking*".[45] It further highlighted that "*no other contracting party applied its tariff régime in respect of unroasted, non-decaffeinated coffee in such a way that different types of coffee were subject to different tariff rates*".[46] For these reasons, the Panel concluded that unroasted, non-decaffeinated cof-

and 99; *Philippines – Taxes on Distilled Spirits*, Report of the Appellate Body, 21 December 2011, WT/DS396/AB/R, WT/DS403/AB/R, para. 170.

[43] *European Communities – Measures Affecting Asbestos and Asbestos Containing Products* (note 42), para. 91.

[44] *Spain – Tariff Treatment of Unroasted Coffee*, Report of the Panel, 27 April 1981, L/5135, para. 4.6.

[45] *Ibid.*, para. 3.12.

[46] *Ibid.*, para. 4.8.

fee beans should be considered as like products within the meaning of Article I:1.

This test was later expanded within the context of the likeness test for the purpose of the NT obligation under Article III:2 and 4, so as to include the consumers' tastes and habits as an additional requirement. Still, the latest version may apply to the MFN obligation under Article I:1, as "*both these provisions are concerned with 'prohibiting discriminatory measures' and ensuring 'equality of competitive opportunities' between products that are in a competitive relationship*".[47] Yet, none of the conditions mentioned is *per se* conclusive, as the assessment of likeness is a relative one and "*will always involve an unavoidable element of individual, discretionary judgment*".[48] Furthermore, subsequent practice conducted to a simplified hypothetical like product analysis where the products' origin constitutes the only difference between them. Under such circumstances, likeness can be presumed.[49]

Moving to the third step of the test, the measure at issue must confer an "advantage, favor, privilege, or immunity" on a product originating in the territory of any country. In this respect, it must be highlighted that "*[t]he words of Article I:1 refer not to some advantages [...] but to 'any advantage'; not to some products, but to 'any product'; and not to like products from some other Members, but to like products originating in or destined for 'all other' Members*".[50]

Lastly, the advantage so accorded must not have been extended "immediately and unconditionally" to like products originating in the territory of all WTO Members, as the MFN obligation would require. The former term insists on the temporal dimension of the advantage accorded, which must be extended to all WTO Members since its introduction. The *unconditionally* requirement, on the other hand, precludes WTO Members from making any trade advantages available based on any criteria that are not related to the imported product itself.

---

[47] *European Communities – Measures Prohibiting the Importation and Marketing of Seal Products* (note 36), para. 5.82.

[48] *Japan – Taxes on Alcoholic Beverages* (note 10), pp. 20-21.

[49] *Indonesia – Certain Measures Affecting the Automobile Industry*, Report of the Panel, 2 July 1998, WT/DS54/R, WT/DS55/R, WT/DS59/R, WT/DS64/R, para. 14.113; *Canada – Certain Measures Affecting the Automotive Industry*, Report of the Panel, 11 February 2000, WT/DS139/R, WT/DS142/R, para. 10.74; *India – Measures Affecting the Automotive Sector*, Report of the Panel, 21 December 2001, WT/DS146/R, WT/DS175/R, paras. 7.174-7.176.

[50] *Canada – Certain Measures Affecting the Automotive Industry* (note 36), para. 79; *European Communities – Regime for the Importation, Sale and Distribution of Bananas* (note 12), para. 206.

However, as the Appellate Body explained,

"as Article I:1 is concerned, fundamentally, with protecting expectations of equal competitive opportunities for like imported products from all Members, it does not follow that Article I:1 prohibits a Member from attaching any conditions to the granting of an 'advantage' within the meaning of Article I:1. Instead, it prohibits those conditions that have a detrimental impact on the competitive opportunities for like imported products from any Member. Conversely, Article I:1 permits regulatory distinctions to be drawn between like imported products, provided that such distinctions do not result in a detrimental impact on the competitive opportunities for like imported products from any Member". [51]

4.10.2. The National Treatment

The NT obligation is the second substantive obligation that pursues the general aim of prohibiting and preventing discriminatory treatment in international trade. As already mentioned, this principle is enshrined in various WTO agreements. In this Section, the analysis will focus on the NT obligation provided for in Article III of the GATT 1994. It is first worth noting that unlike the MFN obligation, which intends to prohibit WTO Members from applying a differentiated treatment to products of another Member in relation to the treatment accorded to like products of any third party taken as a term of reference, the NT obligation is aimed at prohibiting differentiated treatments between domestic products and products imported from other WTO Members, once they have entered the domestic market, cleared through customs duties. In other words, the rationale of the obligation is to ensure (or not to alter) the fairness of competitive conditions [52] or opportunities, [53] and to protect the expectations existing in this regard [54] by prohibiting protectionist policies that affect imported products to the benefit of domestic ones. [55]

---

[51] *European Communities – Measures Prohibiting the Importation and Marketing of Seal Products* (note 36), para. 5.88.

[52] *European Communities – EC Measures Concerning Meat and Meat Products (Hormones)* (note 11), para. 98.

[53] *European Communities – Measures Prohibiting the Importation and Marketing of Seal Products* (note 36), para. 582.

[54] *Japan – Taxes on Alcoholic Beverages* (note 10), p. 16.

[55] *Korea – Taxes on Alcoholic Beverages*, Report of the Appellate Body, 18 January 1999, WT/DS75/AB/R, WT/DS84/AB/R, p. 120.

As the Appellate Body emphatically pointed out in *Japan – Alcoholic Beverages* (1996),

> *"The broad and fundamental purpose of Article III is to avoid protectionism in the application of internal tax and regulatory measures. More specifically, the purpose [...] 'is to ensure that internal measures not be applied to imported or domestic products so as to afford protection to domestic production'. Toward this end, Article III obliges Members of the WTO to provide equality of competitive conditions for imported products in relation to domestic products. [...] Moreover, [...] Article III protects expectations not of any particular trade volume but rather of the equal competitive relationship between imported and domestic products. Members of the WTO are free to pursue their own domestic goals through internal taxation or regulation so long as they do not do so in a way that violates Article III".*[56]

In more detail, Article III:1 of the GATT 1994 enshrines a corollary of the WTO law general principle of non-discrimination, which here prevents the introduction of national measures affecting products imported from another WTO Member so as to protect domestic production. In its terms, it provides that

> *"The contracting parties recognize that internal taxes and other internal charges, and laws, regulations and requirements affecting the internal sale, offering for sale, purchase, transportation, distribution or use of products, and internal quantitative regulations requiring the mixture, processing or use of products in specified amounts or proportions, should not be applied to imported or domestic products so as to afford protection to domestic production".*

The first paragraph of Article III states the general objective of the provision, its rationale, and one of the general objectives of the GATT 1994 as a whole. In addition, it constitutes the normative context in which the subsequent paragraphs setting forth more specific and operational substantive obligations regarding internal taxation and regulation are to be read. It follows that paragraph 1 must always guide the interpretation and application of the subsequent paragraphs under Article III in order for them to produce meaningful effects.[57]

As to the scope of Article III, it extends beyond tariff concessions. According to the Appellate Body,

---

[56] *Japan – Taxes on Alcoholic Beverages* (note 10), p. 16.

[57] *Ibid.*, p. 17 ff.

> *"The broad purpose of Article III of avoiding protectionism must be remembered when considering the relationship between Article III and other provisions of the WTO Agreement. Although the protection of negotiated tariff concessions is certainly one purpose of Article III, [...t]he sheltering scope of Article III is not limited to products that are the subject of tariff concessions under Article II. The Article III national treatment obligation is a general prohibition on the use of internal taxes and other internal regulatory measures so as to afford protection to domestic production. This obligation clearly extends also to products not bound under Article II".*[58]

Although Article III deals primarily with "internal measures", whether of tariff or otherwise nature, it may nevertheless also cover border measures. In this respect, the Interpretive Note *Ad* Article III, contained in Annex I of the GATT 1994, clarifies that

> *"Any internal tax or other internal charge, or any law, regulation or requirement of the kind referred to in paragraph 1 which applies to an imported product and to the like domestic product and is collected or enforced in the case of the imported product at the time or point of importation, is nevertheless to be regarded as an internal tax or other internal charge, or a law, regulation or requirement of the kind referred to in paragraph 1, and is accordingly subject to the provisions of Article III".*

On the other hand, the same Interpretative Note *Ad* Article III implicitly excludes that the provision applies to processes and production methods, as long as it only speaks of "products". In the words of the Panel in *US – Tuna II (Mexico)* (2011), "*Article III:4 calls for a comparison of the treatment of imported tuna* as a product *with that of domestic tuna as a product. Regulations governing the taking of dolphins incidental to the taking of tuna could not possibly affect tuna* as a product".[59]

Turning to the following paragraphs of Article III, it should be emphasized that they clarify the twofold scope of the NT obligation. On the one hand, Article III:2 provides that the NT obligation applies to internal taxation. It shows here a further internal subdivision. The provision's first sentence states the NT obligation regarding internal taxation on "like products", while the second sentence extends the NT obligation to measures on "directly competitive or substitutable products". On the other hand, Arti-

---

[58] *Ibid.*, pp. 16-17.

[59] *United States – Measures Concerning the Importation, Marketing and Sale of Tuna and Tuna Products*, Report of the Panel, 15 September 2011, WT/DS381/R, para. 5.15.

cle III:4 requires the contracting parties to ensure the NT standard with regard to internal regulation.

4.10.2.1. ...for Internal Taxation on Like Products

Starting with the NT for internal taxation on like products, the first sentence of Article III:2 provides that "*The products of the territory of any contracting party imported into the territory of any other contracting party shall not be subject, directly or indirectly, to internal taxes or other internal charges of any kind in excess of those applied, directly or indirectly, to like domestic products*".

To assess whether an internal tax is compatible with the NT obligation under the first sentence of Article III:2, a three-tier test applies. First, a preliminary requirement needs to be met in the sense that the internal measure must constitute an "internal tax or other internal charge of any kind". Once this first question (i) is answered in the affirmative, it must be determined (ii) whether imported and domestic products are "like products" and (iii) whether imported products are taxed in excess of domestic products.

Regarding the first element, it must be stated that this is an assessment to be made on a case-by-case basis, taking into account the substantive characteristics of the measure at issue. In this respect, the time at which the internal tariff burden is actually imposed,[60] the *nomen iuris* and the characterization of the measure under domestic law, and the intention of the legislature do not constitute decisive criteria.[61] Typically, VATs fall within the scope of Article III:2 of the GATT 1994, whereas customs duties and other tariff charges levied at the border are not covered by the provision.

As regards the second element, to determine whether domestic products and products imported from the territory of one of the GATT 1994 contracting parties are like products for the purposes of Article III:2, a case-by-case assessment must be made. To this end, the case law of the WTO dispute settlement system has developed a four-tier test, which requires consideration of the following four elements: (i) the products' properties, nature and quality, (ii) their end-uses in a given market, (iii) consumers' tastes and habits, and (iv) the tariff classification of the products based on the Harmonized System.[62]

---

[60] *China – Measures Affecting Imports of Automobile Parts*, Report of the Appellate Body, 15 December 2008, WT/DS339/AB/R, WT/DS340/AB/R, WT/DS342/AB/R, para. 162.

[61] *Ibid.*, para. 178.

[62] *Mexico – Tax Measures on Soft Drinks and Other Beverages*, Report of the Panel, 7

It is here worth recalling that the Harmonized System (Harmonized Commodity Description and Coding System, or HS) is a multipurpose international product nomenclature established by the World Customs Organization (WCO). As of today, more than 200 countries or territories apply it. Even though the GATT 1994 does not oblige WTO Members to follow the Harmonized System, most of them are also contracting parties to the International Convention on the Harmonized Commodity Description and Coding System (HS Convention). This circumstance makes the HS relevant to the interpretation of WTO agreements. As noted by the Appellate Body in *EC – Chicken Cuts* (2005),

> *"The Harmonized System is not, formally, part of the WTO Agreement, as it has not been incorporated [...] into that Agreement. Nevertheless, the concept of 'context', under Article 31 [of the VCLT], is not limited to the treaty text – namely, the WTO Agreement – but may also extend to 'any agreement relating to the treaty which was made between all the parties in connection with the conclusion of the treaty', within the meaning of Article 31(2)(a) of the Vienna Convention [...].*
>
> *[P]rior to, during, as well as after the Uruguay Round negotiations, there was broad consensus among the GATT Contracting Parties to use the Harmonized System as the basis for their WTO Schedules [...]. In our view, this consensus constitutes an 'agreement' between WTO Members 'relating to' the WTO Agreement that was 'made in connection with the conclusion of' that Agreement, within the meaning of Article 31(2)(a) of the Vienna Convention. As such, this agreement is 'context' under Article 31(2)(a) for the purpose of interpreting the WTO agreements [...]. In this light, we consider that the Harmonized System is relevant for purposes of interpreting tariff commitments".* [63]

Turning to the last step of the three-tier test, it requires an assessment of whether imported products are taxed in excess of like domestic products. In this respect, it must be said that there is no *de minimis* threshold so that even a slight disproportion could constitute a violation of Article III:2 of the GATT 1994. [64] Moreover, this provision is intended to prohibit dis-

---

October 2005, WT/DS308/R, para. 8.29. In less explicit and schematic terms, the test was already applied in these same terms in *Japan – Taxes on Alcoholic Beverages* (note 10), pp. 19-22, in line with the Report of the Working Party on Border Tax Adjustments, BISD 18S/97, para. 18.

[63] *European Communities – Customs Classification of Frozen Boneless Chicken Cuts*, Report of the Appellate Body, 12 September 2005, WT/DS269/AB/R, WT/DS286/AB/R, paras. 195 and 199.

[64] *Japan – Taxes on Alcoholic Beverages* (note 10), pp. 27-28.

criminatory treatments as such, regardless of whether they have actual trade effects on the volume of imported products. As the Appellate Body observed in *Japan – Alcoholic Beverages* (1996),

> *"it is irrelevant that 'the trade effects' of the tax differential between imported and domestic products, as reflected in the volumes of imports, are insignificant or even non-existent; Article III protects expectations not of any particular trade volume but rather of the equal competitive relationship between imported and domestic products".* [65]

4.10.2.2. ...for Internal Taxation on Directly Competitive or Substitutable Products

The second sentence of Article III:2 of the GATT 1994 provides that "*no contracting party shall otherwise apply internal taxes or other internal charges to imported or domestic products in a manner contrary to the principles set forth in paragraph 1*". This provision extends the contracting parties' NT obligation for internal taxation to directly competitive or substitutable products. In this respect, paragraph 2 of the Interpretative Note *Ad* Article III, contained to the GATT 1994, specifies that "*A tax conforming to the requirements of the first sentence of paragraph 2 would be considered to be inconsistent with the provisions of the second sentence only in cases where competition was involved between, on the one hand, the taxed product and, on the other hand, a directly competitive or substitutable product which was not similarly taxed*".

Compared to the first sentence of Article III:2, the second sentence shows a wider scope of application. Thus, if an internal taxation measure is found incompatible with the first sentence, there is no need for an examination under the second sentence.

To assess whether an individual measure of internal taxation is compatible with the NT obligation under Article III:2, second sentence, of the GATT 1994 to the extent that it alters the conditions of competitiveness between domestic products and directly competitive or substitutable imported products to the advantage of the former, a four-tier test has been established in the case law of the WTO dispute settlement system. First of all, it is necessary that the measure at issue constitutes an "internal tax or other internal charge". In this respect, the considerations already made above apply (Section 4.10.2.1). If this question can be answered in the affirmative, the further elements of the test must be examined. In *Mexico – Soft Drinks* (2005), the Panel pointed out that

---

[65] *Ibid.*, p. 16.

> *"There are three elements to be considered [...]: first, whether the imported products and the domestic products are 'directly competitive or substitutable products' which are in competition with each other; second, whether the directly competitive or substitutable imported and domestic products are 'not similarly taxed'; and third, whether the dissimilar taxation of the directly competitive or substitutable imported and domestic products is 'applied ... so as to afford protection to domestic production'"*.[66]

Starting from the first of these requirements, two compared products may be considered directly competitive or substitutable "*when they are interchangeable or if they offer [...] alternative ways of satisfying a particular need or taste*".[67] In this assessment, the decisive element "*is whether they have common end-uses,* inter alia, *as shown by the elasticity of substitution*".[68] Conversely, an important but not decisive factor can be found in cross-price elasticity, i.e. the effect of changes in the price of one good on the quantity demanded of another good.

As to the second requirement concerning "dissimilar taxation", whereas the first sentence of Article III:2 does not allow even the slightest difference, the second sentence intends to prohibit only tariff differential treatments exceeding a minimum threshold that can alter the competitive relationships between the two products.

As a third and last condition, it is necessary to ascertain that the measure at issue was designed "so as to afford protection to domestic production". To this end, consideration should be paid to certain characteristics of the measure, such as the design, architecture, structure and overall application it has in practice.

4.10.2.3. ...for Internal Regulation

The NT obligation under Article III of the GATT 1994 covers not only internal taxation but also internal regulation. As a matter of fact, Article III:4 requires that

> *"[t]he products of the territory of any contracting party imported into the territory of any other contracting party shall be accorded treatment no less favorable than that accorded to like products of national origin in respect of all laws, regulations and requirements affecting their internal sale, offering for sale, purchase, transportation, distribution or use"*.

---

[66] *Mexico – Tax Measures on Soft Drinks and Other Beverages* (note 62), para. 8.66.

[67] *Korea – Taxes on Alcoholic Beverages* (note 55), para. 115.

[68] *Japan – Taxes on Alcoholic Beverages* (note 10), p. 25.

Again, as the Appellate Body stated in *Korea – Various Measures on Beef* (2001), a three-tier test applies.[69] Three requirements should be satisfied: (i) that the measure at issue is a "law, regulation, or requirement affecting their internal sale, offering for sale, purchase, transportation, distribution, or use"; (ii) that the imported and domestic products at issue are "like products"; and (iii) that the imported products are accorded "less favorable" treatment than that accorded to like domestic products.

Starting with the first requirement, it is necessary that the internal measure *affects* – has an impact on – any of the commercial activities related to imported products, from sale to transport, distribution or use. In other words, it must be able to alter the existing competitive conditions on the market between the products in relation to one of these activities. In this respect, it does not matter whether the domestic measure lays down substantive or procedural rules and requirements. Minimum price requirements, advertising restrictions, highway transport costs for imported products, and limitations of distribution channels, among other things, fall within the scope of Article III:4 of the GATT 1994.

Likeness is the second requirement. It is formally required for the purposes of Article III:4 and Article III:2, first sentence, in addition to the MFN obligation under Article I. However, although both Article III:2, first sentence, and Article III:4 refer to "like products" and belong to the same provision, the concept must be understood differently in the two cases.

For the purposes of Article III:2, first sentence, the notion must be interpreted narrowly since competitive relationships between products not covered by that provision may nevertheless fall within the scope of Article III:2, second sentence, by reason of direct competitiveness or elasticity of substitution. On the contrary, under Article III:4, likeness covers the entire scope of the provision. In this regard, in *Japan – Alcoholic Beverages II* (1996), the Appellate Body noted that

> *"In construing Article III:4, the same interpretive considerations do not arise, because the 'general principle' articulated in Article III:1 is expressed in Article III:4, not through two distinct obligations, as in the two sentences in Article III:2, but instead through a single obligation that applies solely to 'like products'. Therefore, the harmony that we have attributed to the two sentences of Article III:2 need not and, indeed, cannot be replicated in interpreting Article III:4. Thus, we conclude that, given*

---

[69] *Korea – Measures Affecting Imports of Fresh, Chilled and Frozen Beef*, Report of the Appellate Body, 11 December 2000, WT/DS161/AB/R, WT/DS169/AB/R, para. 133.

the textual difference between Articles III:2 and III:4, the 'accordion' of 'likeness' stretches in a different way in Article III:4". [70]

At the same time, however, it has been clarified that "*the product scope of Article III:4, although broader than the first sentence of Article III:2, is certainly not broader than the combined product scope of the two sentences of Article III:2 of the GATT 1994*".[71]

In interpreting the concept of likeness for the purposes of Article III:4 of the GATT 1994, one must take into account, as relevant content, the general principle stated in Article III:1, which intends to prohibit differential treatments between imported and like domestic products directed to afford protection to domestic production. Although this general principle is not explicitly invoked in Article III:4, it nonetheless informs the latter provision. It follows that the terms "like products" in Article III:4 must be interpreted so as to give effective meaning to this principle. Consequently, Article III:4 can only apply to products that are in competitive relationships in a given marketplace. Precisely on this basis, the Appellate Body reached the conclusion that the "*determination of 'likeness' under Article III:4 is, fundamentally, a determination about the nature and extent of a competitive relationship between and among products*".[72] The reference to the nature and extent of the competitive relationships implies both qualitative and quantitative considerations.

Turning to the last step of the test, the less favorable treatment of imported products in relation to like domestic products must be identified. This requirement is necessary because not every differential treatment of imported products entails an alteration of competitive conditions in the market, just as not every equal treatment is able to exclude it *a priori.*

According to the settled case law of the WTO dispute settlement system, internal regulation results in less favorable treatment whenever it alters the existing competitive conditions within the market to the detriment of imported products compared to like domestic products.

---

[70] *European Communities – Measures Affecting Asbestos and Asbestos-Containing Products* (note 42), paras. 95-96.

[71] *European Communities – EC Measures Concerning Meat and Meat Products (Hormones)* (note 11), para. 99.

[72] *Ibid.*

4.11. Derogations and Flexibilities

As a general rule, Article XVI, paras. 4 and 5 of the Establishing Agreement provide that accession to the WTO requires full adaptation of State laws, regulations and administrative procedures to the obligations enshrined in the WTO and other annexed agreements, except for express exceptions. Therefore, within the WTO system, States can escape their treaty obligations only in exceptional cases. This provision was introduced with the aim of mitigating the flexibility that had previously characterized the GATT, ensuring, at the same time, the possibility for States to derogate from their WTO obligations (mainly the MFN principle) when overriding public interest comes into play. The following paragraphs deal with these exceptions with the aim of clarifying the conditions and modalities for their application and defining the supervisory powers exercised by the WTO system in this context.

4.11.1. General Exceptions

Article XX of the GATT 1994, entitled "General Exceptions", provides that

> *"[s]ubject to the requirement that such measures are not applied in a manner which would constitute a means of arbitrary or unjustifiable discrimination between countries where the same conditions prevail, or a disguised restriction on international trade, nothing in this Agreement shall be construed to prevent the adoption or enforcement by any contracting party of measures"*

which might protect several societal values or overriding public interests such as public morals (lett. a), human, animal or plant life or health (lett. b), importations or exportations of gold or silver (lett. c), national treasures of artistic, historical or archaeological value (lett. f) and natural resources (lett. g). Furthermore, Article XX also refers to measures aimed at securing compliance with laws or regulations which are not inconsistent with the provisions of the GATT 1994, including those relating to customs enforcement, the enforcement of monopolies, the protection of patents, trademarks and copyrights, and the prevention of deceptive practices (lett.d); measures relating to products of prison labor (lett. e); measures undertaken in pursuance of obligations under any intergovernmental commodity agreement (lett. h); measures involving restrictions on exports of domestic materials necessary to ensure essential quantities of such materials to a domestic processing industry during periods when the domestic price of such materials is held below the world price as part of a governmental stabilization plan (lett. i); measures essential to the acquisition or distribution of products in general or local short supply (lett. j).

The scope of this provision is limited. Since the expression "in this agreement" only refers to the GATT, a Member cannot invoke Article XX of the GATT 1994 to justify the adoption of a measure inconsistent with any other WTO agreement, unless the latter has incorporated, even implicitly, the provision at hand.

The paragraphs of Article XX set forth *limited* and *conditional* exceptions from the obligations of the substantive provisions of the GATT. Any measure, to qualify for exception, must also satisfy the requirements of the *chapeau*, i.e. the introductory clause of Article XX.[73] Therefore, the possibility to invoke these general exceptions is subject to two conditions: (i) the GATT inconsistent measure must be included in the exhaustive list provided for in paragraphs (a) to (j); (ii) the respect of the *chapeau* of Article XX of the GATT 1994.[74]

In practice, the first step (i) consists of the identification and examination of the specific exception threatened with abuse. Then, the interpreter must assess if the exception at hand also satisfies the requirements of the *chapeau* (ii), namely if the measure does not constitute arbitrary or unjustifiable discrimination between countries where the same conditions prevail or a disguised restriction on international trade.

The Appellate Body has clarified how this assessment must be conducted. Notably, according to established case law, "*the line of equilibrium between rights and obligations set by the Members in the* chapeau *of Article XX is not fixed and unchanging, rather the line moves as the kind and the shape of the measures at stake vary and as the facts making up specific cases differ*".[75] Since the *chapeau* is an expression of the principle of good faith (Section 4.6.1), the interpreter must strike a balance between the Member's right to invoke an exception for legitimate societal goals and the rights of other Members under various substantive provisions (e.g., Article XI of the GATT 1994).[76] The aim is to preserve the balance of rights and obligations

---

[73] *United States – Import Prohibition of Certain Shrimp and Shrimp Product* (note 16), para. 157 and *United States – Section 337 of the Tariff Act of 1930*, Report of the GATT Panel, 7 November 1989, L/6439, para. 5.9.

[74] The exhaustive nature of the list enshrined in Article XX was clarified in *ibid.*, para. 5.9.

[75] *United States – Import Prohibition of Certain Shrimp and Shrimp Product* (note 16), para. 159.

[76] *Ibid.* paras. 158-159. The Appellate Body referring to the *chapeau* expressing a principle of good faith is yet another proof of the WTO settlement dispute system using

constructed by the Members themselves in the Agreement and enshrined in Article XX of the GATT 1994, and the *chapeau* serves the purpose of preventing any abuse of exceptions.

For instance, in *EC – Seal Products* (2014), the Appellate Body was called to review a panel report concerning the adoption by the EU of a regulation generally prohibiting the importation and placing on the market of seal products, with certain exceptions, including for seal products derived from hunts conducted by Inuit or indigenous communities (IC exception) and hunts conducted for marine resource management purposes (MRM exception). The EU had justified the measure under Article XX(a), arguing that it was necessary to protect animal welfare, particularly in relation to the hunting of seals for their fur. Both the Panel and the Appellate Body asserted that despite the measure could fit the exception provided by Article XX(a), it could not however be considered compatible with the *chapeau* of the same provision. The Appellate Body found

> *"several features of the EU Seal Regime [indicating] that the regime is applied in a manner that constitutes a means of arbitrary or unjustifiable discrimination between countries where the same conditions prevail, in particular with respect to the IC exception".* [77]

The same mechanism provided by Article XX of the GATT 1994, although with some differences concerning the conditions required, is established in the GATS for trade in services. Hence, WTO Members can justify otherwise GATS inconsistent measures by invoking the general exceptions provided by Article XIV of the GATS. [78]

4.11.2. Security Exceptions

Under Article XXI of the GATT 1994, Members are allowed to take otherwise GATT-inconsistent measures for national or international security and peace reasons in three cases.

---

general international law, in this case a general principle of law, to ground and support its decisions. On this issue see more broadly P. Van den Bossche and W. Zdouc, *The Law and Policy of the World Trade Organization: Text, Cases, and Materials*[5], CUP, 2021, pp. 62-72.

[77] *European Communities – Measures Prohibiting the Importation and Marketing of Seal Products* (note 36), para. 5.338.

[78] A thorough and updated analysis of this provision and its judicial interpretation can be found in DS Report, *WTO ANALYTICAL INDEX GATS – Article XIV*, available at www.wto.org.

According to Article XXI(a), Members can avoid furnishing any information the disclosure of which they consider to be contrary to their essential security interests.

Furthermore, under Article XXI(b), if they consider it necessary for the protection of their essential security interests, Members can take measures: (i) relating to fissionable materials or the materials from which they are derived; (ii) relating to the traffic in arms, ammunition and implements of war and to such traffic in other goods and materials as is carried on directly or indirectly for the purpose of supplying a military establishment; (iii) taken in time of war or other emergency in international relations.

Finally, Article XXI(c) allows Members to take GATT-inconsistent measures in order to pursue their obligations under the United Nations Charter for the maintenance of international peace and security. The reference is to the measures ordered by the Security Council under Chapter VII of the UN Charter.[79]

Over the years, the expression "which it considers" in the *chapeau* of Article XXI(b) has prompted a debate as to whether this provision represents a "self-judging" clause or not, i.e. a provision through which States retain their right to derogate from an international obligation based on a unilateral appreciation of the relevant grounds.[80] In several instances, Members invoking Article XXI(b) have argued that every WTO Member retains the authority to determine for itself those matters that it considers necessary for the protection of its essential security interests, as "reflected" in the text of the provision.[81] The matter has been recently set in the case

[79] In the past, some authors have argued that the rule enshrined in Article XXI(c) would merely identify just one example of the several provisions contained in the broader category of *ius cogens* obligations aimed at protecting the essential interests of the international community as a whole. According to this view, an interpretation of Article XXI compatible with general international law would allow States to derogate from their GATT and WTO obligations whenever there is a violation of such imperative norms. In this sense, see P. Picone, A. Ligustro, *Diritto dell'Organizzazione mondiale del commercio*, Cedam, 2002, pp. 347-348. On the notion of peremptory norms of general international law (*ius cogens*), see *supra,* Chapter 2, Section 2.8.2.

[80] Article XXI(b) in the relevant part provides as follows: "*Nothing in this Agreement shall be construed [...] (b) to prevent any contracting party from taking any action* which it considers *necessary for the protection of its essential security interests [...]*".

[81] It must be noted that, before 2019, the invocation of Article XXI had been rare and, in no case had a panel affirmed its jurisdiction over the motives behind it. On the contrary, in a case regarding the imposition by the US of a trade embargo on Nicaragua, the Panel denied its jurisdiction, stating that "*it was not authorized to examine the justification*" for the invocation of Article XXI by the sanctioning State. At the same time, the Panel raised some general issues concerning the correct application of the security exception and recommended the Contracting Parties to take them into consideration.

Russia – Traffic in Transit (2019), where the Panel rejected the view that Article XXI(b) is totally "self-judging" or "non-justiciable".[82] On the one hand, Members have some latitude to determine what their essential security interests are, and the necessity of action to protect those interests.[83] However, on the other hand, in order to avoid abuses, under Article XXI(b), panels have the power to review whether the requirements of the enumerated subparagraphs were met.[84]

In general, Article XXI has been rarely invoked, and the recent surge in disputes concerning its interpretation and application was mainly linked to the constant economic confrontation between the US and China, on the one hand, and the conflict between Russia and Ukraine, on the other.[85] In this context, Article XXI has come under close judicial scrutiny and some of its terms – as partially already mentioned before – have been better clarified. For instance, the expression "emergency in international relations" under Article XXI(b)(iii) has been interpreted to refer generally to "*a situation of armed conflict, or of latent armed conflict, or of heightened tension or crisis, or of general instability engulfing or surrounding a State*".[86] Therefore, the provision does not operate in case of mere tensions and differences in international relations, unless the situation they give rise to is of a truly grave character that it implicates, in practice, a breakdown or near-breakdown in those relations.[87]

Article XXI of the GATT 1994 finds its equivalent for trade in services in Article XIV *bis* of the GATS, that establishes the conditions upon which Members are allowed to take otherwise GATS inconsistent measures for national and international security and peace reasons.

As a result, this report was never adopted. *United States – Trade Measures Affecting Nicaragua*, Report of the GATT Panel, 13 October 1986, L/6053, paras. 5.3 and 5.17. For an overview on the past and possible future invocations of Article XXI see F. Kawashima, "Trade Sanctions against Russia and their WTO Consistency: Focusing on Justification under National Security Exceptions", in *International Community Law Review*, 2024, 26(1-2), pp. 121-150.

[82] *Russia – Measures Concerning Traffic in Transit*, Report of the Panel, 5 April 2019, WT/DS512/R, para. 7.102.

[83] *Ibid.*, para. 7.98.

[84] *Ibid.*, para. 7.100.

[85] See M. Herdegen, *Principles of International Economic Law*[3], OUP, 2024, pp. 259-265.

[86] *Russia – Measures Concerning Traffic in Transit* (note 82), para. 7.76.

[87] *United States – Origin Marking Requirement*, Report of the Panel, 21 December 2022, WT/DS597/R, para. 7.289.

4.11.3. Regional Integration

The "regional integration exceptions" or exceptions for "regional trade agreements" (RTAs) allow Members to sign RTAs, despite it being clearly in contrast with the MFN principle.[88] In fact, RTAs are agreements that grant their parties a more favorable treatment in trade matters than they do in relation to other (non-parties) WTO Members. At the same time, regional trade liberalization can lead to substantial economic growth within the region, which may subsequently stimulate increased trade with the rest of the world.

Therefore, WTO Members are allowed to form RTAs under specific conditions designed with the aim of ensuring that these agreements facilitate trade between the constituent territories and do not raise barriers to the trade of other Members with such territories.[89]

As for trade in goods, Article XXIV of the GATT 1994 provides that, under specific conditions, Members are allowed to adopt three kinds of RTAs, namely customs unions, free-trade areas or interim agreements necessary for the formation of one of the two.

Customs unions are the substitution of a single customs territory for two or more customs territories so that almost all the internal trade restrictions are eliminated, and a common external trade regime is adopted towards the rest of the world (Article XXIV:8(a) of the GATT 1994). Currently, 16 customs unions have been notified to the World Trade Organization.[90] As mentioned, they generally implement a common external tariff applying to all goods, but exceptions are possible. For instance, while the EU's customs union encompasses all goods, Turkey's customs union with the EU does not include primary agricultural products, coal, or steel.

Free trade areas (FTAs) consist of a group of countries that have mutually agreed to limit or eliminate tariffs and non-tariff barriers among them (Article XXIV:8(b) of the GATT 1994). An example of such an RTA is the United States-Mexico-Canada Agreement (USMCA), which replaced the North American Free Trade Agreement (NAFTA) in 2020. Under this agreement, the United States, Mexico, and Canada committed to eliminat-

---

[88] The term regional refers to the fact that these agreements were initially concluded by States coming from the same region (e.g., MERCOSUR). However, nowadays these treaties also involve countries coming from different regions and are also referred to as "preferential trade agreements". We consider the two expressions to be interchangeable but will refer to them as regional trade agreements.

[89] Article XXIV:4 of the GATT 1994. See also the Preamble to the Understanding on the Interpretation of Article V of the GATT 1994.

[90] The updated list is available at https://rtais.wto.org/UI/PublicMaintainRTAHome.aspx.

ing tariffs and reducing trade barriers on goods and services exchanged between them.

In order to satisfy these definitions, Article XXIV:8 of the GATT 1994 establishes a standard for both the internal and external trade between the Members.

To respect the *internal trade requirement*, the constituent Members of a customs union or an FTA must eliminate duties and other restrictive regulations of commerce with respect to *substantially all the trade* between them. There is no consensus among the WTO Members regarding the interpretation of the word "substantially". However, in *Turkey – Textiles* (1999), the Appellate Body has clarified "*that 'substantially all the trade' is not the same as all the trade, and also that 'substantially all the trade' is something considerably more than merely some of the trade*".[91]

According to the *external trade requirement*, the duties and all the other regulations of commerce applicable after the formation of the customs union or FTA should not be higher or more restrictive than the general incidence of the duties and other regulations of commerce applicable prior to their formation. For customs unions, Article XXIV:8(a) additionally requires the constituent Members of a customs union to apply *substantially the same duti*es and other regulations of commerce to external trade with third countries. Thus, the constituent Members of a customs union must apply a common external trade regime, relating to both duties and other regulations of commerce. Once again, in *Turkey – Textiles* (1999), the Appellate Body noted that the expression "substantially the same" offers a certain degree of flexibility to the constituent Members of a customs union in the creation of a common commercial policy, and it does not require each constituent member of the union to apply the same duties and other regulations of commerce as other constituent Members with respect to trade with third countries.[92]

Finally, Article XXIV of the GATT 1994 refers to *interim agreements* that must lead to the establishment of a customs union or a free-trade area – established upon the requirements mentioned above – within a reasonable period of time, which should not exceed 10 years (Understanding on the Interpretation of Article V of the GATT 1994).

For RTAs on trade in services, Article V of the GATS establishes a similar mechanism that enables Members, upon strict requirements, to adopt economic integration agreements notwithstanding the MFN principle.

---

[91] *Turkey – Textiles*, Report of the Appellate Body, 22 October 1999, WT/DS34/AB/R, para. 48.

[92] *Ibid.*, para. 50.

4.11.4. Enabling Clause

The Decision of the GATT Contracting Parties of 28 November 1979 on "Differential and More Favorable Treatment, Reciprocity, and Fuller Participation of Developing Countries" (1979 Decision) introduced derogations to the MFN principle in favor of developing countries Members. Commonly referred to as the "Enabling Clause", this exception allows, under specific conditions, contracting parties to adopt measures that accord differential and more favorable treatment to developing countries, without according such treatment to other contracting parties.

Article 2(a) of the 1979 Decision allows developed contracting parties to adopt Generalized System of Preferences (GSP) programs that accord preferential *tariff treatment* to products originating in developing countries. For instance, the European Union's GSP provides reduced or zero tariffs for goods imported from eligible developing countries, with the aim of promoting their economic growth and integration into the global economy. The preferences beneficial to the developing countries must be "*generalized, non-reciprocal and non-discriminatory*".[93] Thus, despite the provision not explicitly authorizing or prohibiting the granting of different tariff preferences to different GSP beneficiaries, it is clear from the ordinary meanings of "non-discriminatory" that preference-granting countries must make available identical tariff preferences to all similarly situated beneficiaries.[94] This is always true but in the case of Article 2(d) of the 1979 Decision, that allows for a *"[s]pecial treatment on the least developed among the developing countries in the context of any general or specific measures in favor of developing countries"*.

Article 2(b) of the 1979 Decision allows for a differential and more favorable treatment of developing countries with respect to the provisions of the General Agreement concerning non-tariff measures governed by the provisions of instruments multilaterally negotiated under the auspices of the GATT.

Finally, Article 2(c) of the 1979 Decision allows for FTAs (regional or global arrangements) entered into amongst LDC Members for the mutual reduction or elimination of tariffs and for the mutual reduction or elimination of non-tariff measures on products imported from one another. The Appellate Body has clarified that an FTA adopted under paragraph 3(c) may be "non-discriminatory" even if "identical" tariff treat-

---

[93] See footnote 3 to Article 2(a) of the 1979 Decision.

[94] *European Communities – Conditions for the Granting of Tariff Preferences to Developing Countries* (note 36), para. 154.

ment is not accorded to "all" beneficiaries. Moreover, paragraph 3(c) suggests that tariff preferences under FTAs may be "non-discriminatory" when the relevant tariff preferences are addressed to a particular development, financial or trade need and are made available to all beneficiaries that share that need.[95] Both the assessment regarding the existence of such a need and the determination as to whether developing-country Members are similarly situated must be examined according to an objective standard.

Unlike the other exceptions to the MFN principle, the Enabling Clause does not have an equivalent for trade in services in the GATS. However, this gap has been temporarily filled in at the 8th Ministerial Conference held in Geneva in 2011, when WTO Members adopted a waiver to allow preferential treatment for services and service suppliers from least-developed countries. The use of such a waiver to Article 11 GATS must be notified to the Council for Trade in Services and is conditional upon its approval. In 2015, the duration of this waiver has been extended until the end of 2030.[96]

References

Adinolfi, G. (2001). *L'Organizzazione mondiale del commercio: profili istituzionali e normativi*, Cedam.

Adinolfi, G., Baetens, F., Caiado, J., Lupone, A., Micara, A.G. (eds.) (2017). *International Economic Law: Contemporary Issues*, Springer.

Carmody, C. (2024). "Procedural aspects of WTO dispute settlement", in J. Gomula, S. Wittich (eds.), *Research Handbook on International Procedural Law*, Edward Elgar Publishing.

Chaisse, J., Rodríguez-Chiffelle C. (2023). *The Elgar Companion to the World Trade Organization*, Edward Elgar Publishing.

Choukroune, L., Nedumpara, J.J. (2021). *International Economic Law: Text, Cases and Materials*, Cambridge University Press.

Collins, D. (2019). *Foundations of International Economic Law*, Edward Elgar Publishing.

[95] *Ibid.*, para. 165. It should be noted that according to the Appellate Body "*paragraph 3(c) does not authorize any kind of response to any claimed need of developing countries, [rather] the types of needs to which a response is envisaged are limited to 'development, financial and trade needs'*". *Ibid.*, para. 163.

[96] *Implementation of Preferential Treatment in Favour of Services and Service Suppliers of Least-Developed Countries and Increasing LDC Participation in Services Trade*, WT/L/982, adopted 19 December 2015.

Daunton, M., Narlikar, A., Stern, R.M. (eds.) (2012). *The Oxford Handbook on The World Trade Organization*, Oxford University Press.

de Andrade, M.C. (2023). *International Custom and General Principles of Law in WTO Dispute Settlement*, Editoriale Scientifica.

Elsig, M., Hoekman, B.M., Pauwelyn, J. (2017). *Assessing the World Trade Organization: Fit for Purpose?*, Cambridge University Press.

Fabbricotti, A. (2009). *Gli accordi di integrazione economica regionale e il diritto dell'Organizzazione mondiale del commercio*, Aracne.

Folsom, R.H. (2018). *Principles of International Trade Law : Including the World Trade Organization, Technology Transfers, and Import/Export/Customs Law*, 2nd ed., West Academic Publishing.

Forere, M.A. (2015). *The Relationship of WTO Law and Regional Trade Agreements in Dispute Settlement: from Fragmentation to Coherence*, Wolters Kluwer.

Herdegen, M. (2024). *Principles of International Economic Law*, 3rd ed., Oxford University Press.

Kawashima, F. (2024). "Trade Sanctions against Russia and their WTO Consistency: Focusing on Justification under National Security Exceptions", in *International Community Law Review*, 26(1-2), pp. 121-150.

Lowenfeld, A.F. (2008). *International Economic Law*, 2nd ed., Oxford University Press.

Matsushita, M., Schoenbaum, T.J., Mavroidis, P.C., Hahn, M.J. (2015). *The World Trade Organization: Law, Practice, and Policy*, 3rd ed., Oxford University Press.

Mauro, M.R. (2019). *Diritto internazionale dell'economia. Teoria e prassi delle relazioni economiche internazionali*, Edizioni Scientifiche Italiane.

Narlikar, A. (2005). *The World Trade Organization: A Very Short Introduction*, Oxford University Press.

Picone, P., Ligustro, A. (2002). *Diritto dell'Organizzazione mondiale del commercio*, Cedam.

Sacerdoti, G. (2023). "Adjudication of International Trade Disputes: From Success to Crisis. What's Next?", in *The Law & Practice of International Courts and Tribunals*, 22(2), pp. 419-449.

Sacerdoti, G., Castren, K., "Article I GATT, Annexes A, B, C, D, E, F, G GATT, Enabling Clause, Preferential Tariff Treatment for Least-Developed Countries Waiver", in R. Wolfrum, P.-T. Stoll, H.P. Hestermeyer (eds.) (2011). *Max Planck Commentaries on World Trade Law: WTO-Trade in Goods*, Vol. 5, Martinus Nijhoff Publishers, pp. 53-77.

Van den Bossche, P., Zdouc, W. (2021). *The Law and Policy of the World Trade Organization: Text, Cases, and Materials*, 5th ed., Cambridge University Press.

Van den Bossche P., Prévost, D. (2021). *Essentials of WTO Law*, 2nd ed., Cambridge University Press.

Venturini, G. (ed.) (2015). *L'Organizzazione Mondiale del Commercio*, 3rd ed., Giuffrè.

World Trade Organization (2017). *A Handbook on the WTO Dispute Settlement System*, 2nd ed., Cambridge University Press.

Chapter 5
INTERNATIONAL FINANCIAL LAW

Domenico Pauciulo

ABSTRACT: *This chapter addresses the legal framework surrounding international financial relations, analyzing the role of intergovernmental fora of discussion in establishing guidelines on economic cooperation, and the role played by the International Monetary Fund and the institutions of the World Bank Group, identifying functions, activities and principles governing their operations. Additionally, this chapter provides an overview of the functioning of the accountability mechanisms created by these institutions, in order to better align with norms pertaining to other sectors of international law, especially with the rules promoting and protecting fundamental human rights.*

KEYWORDS: *G20 – International Monetary Fund – World Bank – Inspection Panel – accountability of international organizations – lending – International Financial Corporation.*

SUMMARY: 5.1. Introduction. – 5.2. The G20 and the Intergovernmental Dimension of International Financial Law. – 5.3. The International Monetary Fund. – 5.3.1. Internal Structure. – 5.3.2. The Functions of the IMF: Surveillance and Capacity Development. – 5.3.3. Lending Activities. – 5.4. The World Bank Group. – 5.4.1. The International Bank for Reconstruction and Development. – 5.4.2. Internal Structure. – 5.4.3. The International Development Association. – 5.4.4. Functions of the World Bank: Analytics and Policy Advice. – 5.4.5. Financing Activities. – 5.4.6. The International Finance Corporation and Its Support to the Private Sector. – 5.4.7. The Multilateral Investment Guarantee Agency. – 5.5. The Relationship between the Bretton Woods Institutions and International Law. – 5.5.1. The IMF and Human Rights. – 5.5.2. The World Bank "Environmental and Social Framework". – 5.6. Accountability of International Financial Institutions. – 5.6.1. The IMF Independent Evaluation Office. – 5.6.2. The World Bank Accountability Mechanism. – 5.6.2.1. The Inspection Panel. – 5.6.2.2. Procedural Steps before the Inspection Panel. – 5.6.2.3. The Dispute Resolution Service. – 5.6.3. The IFC/MIGA Compliance Advisory Ombudsman. – 5.7. Final Remarks. – References.

5.1. Introduction

International economic law has an important role in supporting economic development, promoting peaceful and prosperous relations among nations, and enhancing global well-being. Such functions are developed through various mechanisms of cooperation, that include financing of development projects; economic contributions aimed at facing temporary situations of deficit or economic stagnation; and a generic promotion of the "regulation" of globalized financial markets. Therefore, international economic law encourages States' financial stability, preventing economic crises and the systemic risk of contagion from one country or region to others. Additionally, international economic law regulates economic aid for development. [1] For the purpose of this chapter, this author will refer to this body of law as "international financial law", since it is connected to the global financial architecture. These rules have been put in place to regulate a wide range of initiatives applicable to States, private companies, banks, financial institutions, capital markets, sovereign debt, and many other activities relevant to global finance. The design of such an international legal framework to govern economic operations has emerged in two main forms: inter-governmental and treaty-based.

In particular, the main bodies of law regulating financial activities surfaced pursuant to the Articles of Agreement that established the International Monetary Fund (IMF) and the International Bank for Reconstruction and Development (IBRD, which was later to become the World Bank). Negotiated mainly between the United States and the United Kingdom, the rules and principles embodied in these institutions were said to be informed by the universally valid and beneficial tenets of free trade theory. [2] The IMF and the IBRD were established at the United Nations Monetary and Financial Conference, held in Bretton Woods, New Hampshire,

---

[1] See L. Choukroune, J.J., Nedumpara, *International Economic Law. Text, Cases, Materials*, CUP; 2021, pp. 683-724. The current agenda for development in synthetized in the Sustainable Development Goals (SDGs) adopted by the United Nations in 2015 with the resolution *Transforming Our World – The 2030 Agenda for Sustainable Development* (A/RES/70/1). Activities, policies and projects functional to the realization of the SDGs necessitates a constant financial flow: the UN, its specialized agencies, international organizations, States and private actors contribute to the mobilization of these resources, in compliance with the principles set forth by the *Addis Ababa Action Agenda*, adopted during the Third International Conference on Financing for Development (13-16 July 2015).

[2] However, as newly independent countries soon claimed, these rules favored the economic interests of developed countries by promoting liberalization of their competitive sectors while permitting discrimination in those in which developing countries were supposed to have comparative advantage (as agriculture). The demands of least-developed countries were mainly put forward in the UN General Assembly with the adoption of resolutions proclaiming a "New International Economic Order" based on i) the right of the territorial State to exercise permanent sovereignty over natural resources and economic activities without external interference; ii) the principle of common heritage of mankind on resources located outside the jurisdiction of any State; iii) the duty to cooperate; iv) the principles of equity and interdependence.

USA, in July 1944.[3] These institutions were envisaged as two of the three "economic pillars" of a new international order that would follow the conclusion of the Second World War[4]. In broad terms, the IMF was to be dedicated to international monetary stability, and the IBRD - being concerned with both "reconstruction' and 'development" as the name suggests - with the reconstruction of Europe after the War's end. However, the IBRD's resources were never sufficient to finance the reconstruction of Europe and were quickly overshadowed by funding provided through the US "Marshall Plan". By the 1950s, the IBRD's attention had turned towards development and today the World Bank is the major source of both development finance and knowledge about development, and it has become the most important development institution in the world. In contrast to the Bank, the IMF does not define itself by reference to development. At Bretton Woods, it was given two basic roles. The first involved overseeing and governing a global system of stable exchange rates. The second major role envisaged the provision of short-term finance to States facing balance-of-payments difficulties.[5] This financing role remains central to the IMF's work today and now extends beyond the role imagined at Bretton Woods.

This chapter, therefore, will first analyze intergovernmental summits of States aimed at discussing cooperation in financial matters (Section 5.2.), and will then proceed to scrutinize the functioning and activities of the IMF (Section 5.3.) and of the IBRD, which later evolved in the World Bank Group, a set of independent institutions with common objectives and operational profiles (Section 5.4.). The following sections deal with the relationship of international financial law – through the activities of its main institutional players – with the wider spectrum of international law. Indeed, while trade law and investment law are nowadays permeated by principles,

---

[3] The IMF and IBRD are constituted by separate Articles of Agreement. These Articles were adopted at Bretton Woods in 1944, but only came into effect in December 1945, following their ratification by the necessary number of States. The first meeting of the board of governors of the IMF and IBRD took place in 1946. The IBRD started operations in 1946, and the IMF in 1947.

[4] See Chapter 4, Section 4.2.

[5] According to the *IMF Balance of Payments Manual*, the balance of payments is a statistical statement that systematically summarizes, for a specific time-period, the economic transactions of an economy with the rest of the world. Transactions, for the most part between residents and non-residents, consist of those involving goods, services, and income; those involving financial claims on, and liabilities to, the rest of the world; and those (such as gifts) classified as transfers, which involve offsetting entries to balance – in an accounting sense – one-sided transactions. The balance of payments, therefore, reveals the country's financial and economic strength, and it informs its government's fiscal and monetary policy.

rules and values protected by other areas of international law, [6] international financial law is often conceived as a specialized body of law that presents almost no interactions with other rules of international law. This conception is favored, of course, by the high technicalities of financial operations and by philosophical motives: neoliberalism doctrines, indeed, believe that economic activity does belong to the sphere of the private, the unpolitical, as to exclude public intervention also at the international level, avoiding "contamination" with principles established in other fields of cooperation. In international financial law, this problem has interested primarily the impacts on human rights of the activities of international financial institutions (Section 5.5.). Such an issue has been solved mostly through the establishment of internal accountability mechanisms in charge of evaluating the respect of internal standards and policies on social and environmental concerns by these institutions (Section 5.6.). The activities of these mechanisms have privileged, at least in the field of human rights and environmental protection, a higher consideration of rules of international law in the context of international financial law (Section 5.7.).

5.2. The G20 and the Intergovernmental Dimension of International Financial Law

First, international economic cooperation has been pursued at the intergovernmental level through specific fora of States which are entrusted to discuss (and face) complex economic issues. The main example is constituted by the Group of 20 (G20), an informal group of 19 countries and the European Union, created as a mechanism connected to the Bretton Woods institutions for informal dialogue "on key economic and financial policy issues among systematically significant economies and to promote cooperation to achieve stable and sustainable world growth that benefits all". [7]

The G20 was created as a deliberative rather than decisional body: it is therefore an instrument of informal consultation, lacking a structure with permanent bodies and a founding agreement, which therefore cannot be considered a true international organization. Moreover, the G20 has no permanent secretariat: instead, the Chair country provides administrative and organizational support. In addition, formal requirements for membership are absent. The primary need, at the time of its establishment, was

[6] See Chapter 1, Section 1.2.

[7] *Statement of G7 Finance Ministers and Central Bank Governors*, Washington DC, 25 September 1999, para. 19. See P.I. Hajnal, *The G20. Evolution, Interrelationship, Documentation*², Routledge, 2019.

identified in the involvement of emerging economies in the reform of the international financial architecture, ensuring an appropriate geographical balance.[8] Today, G20 Member countries account for two-thirds of the world's population, about 80 percent of the world's GDP and 75 percent of the world's trade.

The informality embodied in the G20's operational modalities characterizes the decisions that are adopted at the end of its annual summits. Generally, the G20 adopts recommendations for the Members of the Group. The content of these documents is essentially negotiated by representatives of the leaders (so-called *sherpas*) during preparatory meetings: the main documents are the "Leaders' Declaration", which contains guidelines to governments aimed at harmonizing national and supranational policies, and the "Communiqués of the Finance Minister and Central Bank Governors", which normally summarize common positions on the economic situation. Very often these acts are accompanied or preceded by the adoption of variously named policy documents ("Action Plans", "Principles", "Policy Priorities", "Frameworks" or even "Conclusions") that serve to detail much more general provisions contained in statements and declarations. Clearly, under international law, such instruments do not create obligations of a conventional nature, falling squarely within the category of soft law.[9] International organizations (particularly the IMF and the World Bank), by virtue of their close relationship with the G20, contribute to the implementation of the objectives and actions decided during the summits through the adoption of their own acts. Indeed, the inclusion of the President of the World Bank, the Managing Director of the IMF (as well as the Chairpersons of the International Monetary and Financial Committee and of the Development Committee) will ensure that the G20 process is well

---

[8] The G20 was convened for the first time in 1999 as a meeting between Ministers of Finance and Central Bank Governors to address the severe crisis in Asian markets. This forum originated from the summits that began from the 1970s, which, in their various "composition", were used primarily to discuss international cooperation, peace and security, but also macroeconomic policy, international trade and relations with developing countries, as the G7 or G8. Member countries of the G20 include Argentina, Australia, Brazil, Canada, China, France, Germany, India, Indonesia, Italy, Japan, Mexico, Russia, Saudi Arabia, South Africa, South Korea, Turkey, the United Kingdom, the United States and the European Union. The Managing Director of the IMF and the President of the World Bank, as well as the Chairpersons of the International Monetary and Financial Committee and Development Committee of the IMF and World Bank, will participate fully in the discussions. These countries are joined by Spain, a "permanent guest", and by the representatives of other States and of international and regional organizations (often represented by their Chair), invited by the country holding the Presidency to participate as observers.

[9] See Chapter 3, Section 3.7.

integrated with the activities of these institutions: indeed, the potential for the development of common positions on complex issues among G20 Members clearly stimulates and expedite the decision-making process in other fora.

Together with the G20, other summits and periodic conferences discuss and influence the legal framework regarding international economic cooperation. Certain States, from diverse regional areas, have established in 2009 the "BRICS Annual Summit" with a focus on improving the global economic situation and reforming the international financial architecture. This group was conceived as a geopolitical and geoeconomic counterweight to the Western-dominated financial institutions, and it promotes ways for developing countries to become more involved in international affairs and to supersede the perceived US dollar (USD) "dominance" as international reserve assets.[10] Members of the BRICS are Brazil, Russian Federation, India, China and South Africa: starting from 2024, other countries were invited to join the group, such as Ethiopia, Egypt, Iran, Saudi Arabia and the United Arab Emirates. Together, BRICS States represent almost 40 percent of the world population and over 20 percent of the global economy. Another intergovernmental mechanism for economic cooperation is the Asian Pacific Economic Forum, which represents a regional forum established in 1999 with 21 Member States joined in a cooperative process concerned primarily with trade and economic issues.[11]

Some of these intergovernmental mechanisms have specific competences: for example, the Financial Stability Board (FSB) promotes global financial stability by coordinating the development of regulatory, supervisory and other financial sector policies, together with monitoring and advisory functions.[12] The FSB was founded during the 2009 G20 Head of States and Governments meeting in Pittsburgh as a non-treaty-based organization, but more as a coordinating body, driving the agenda of its Members to strengthen financial stability. Its decisions are not legally binding. In-

---

[10] D. Monyae, B. Ndzendze, *The BRICS Order. Assertive or Complementing the West?*, Springer, 2021.

[11] I. Yamazawa, *Asia Pacific Economic Cooperation (APEC). Challenges and Tasks for the Twenty First Century*, Routledge, 2001.

[12] According to Article 5 of the FSB Organizational Charter, eligible members are: authorities from jurisdictions responsible for maintaining financial stability, such as ministries of finance, central banks, and supervisory and regulatory authorities; international financial institutions; and international standards settings, regulatory, supervisory and central banks bodies. Currently, 14 international organizations and entities (including the IMF and the World Bank) and 24 States are Members of the FSB (with a number of representatives based on their economic positions in the global market).

stead, the FSB operates by moral suasion and peer pressure, setting internationally agreed policies and minimum standards that its Members commit to implement at the national level. [13]

Special competence is also recognized to the "Paris Club", which was established in 1956 as an informal group of creditors whose role is to find coordinated and sustainable solutions to the payment difficulties experienced by debtor countries: it therefore deals with sovereign debt. [14] The Paris Club consists of 22 Permanent Members, representing the main creditor States, around 20 Associate Members and observers, including international organizations such as the IMF, the World Bank, regional development banks, and the EU. The Club operates in a highly informal approach based on six agreed principles, [15] taking decisions on a case-by-case basis and by consensus. It lacks, therefore, the institutional structure typical of international organizations.

The Club deals with debt restructuring, i.e. the conclusion of an agreement by which the original terms of a loan (rates, maturities, currency, guarantee period) are modified to ease the debtor's burden, in order to avoid the debtor State's default. The request for restructuring is presented by the debtor country and discussed with the main creditor States in a negotiation. When a State asks the Club to restructure its external debt, a "cut-off date" is set, by virtue of which the debt accrued up to that time will be restructured; debt that the State may accrue thereafter will not, in principle, be subject to restructuring. [16] The negotiation is aimed at draw-

---

[13] See Article 23 of the FSB Organizational Charter, that states "This Charter is not intended to create any legal rights or obligations".

[14] F. Gianviti, *The International Monetary Fund and the external debt*, in *Recueil des Cours*, vol. 215, Brill, 1989, p. 233, endorses a definition of debt commonly accepted by the main institutional lenders as "the amount, at any given time, of disbursed and outstanding liabilities of residents of a country to non-residents to repay principal, with or without interest, or to pay interest, with or without principal". Sovereign debts are therefore loans contracted by State organs, including its central bank, agencies, or territorial ramifications, and by State-controlled entities.

[15] Even if the Paris Club has no legal basis or structure, its work is based on a number of rules and principles agreed by creditor countries, which facilitates decision-making and the conclusion of agreements. The Six Principles informing its activities are: solidarity (all Members of the Paris Club agree to act as a group in their dealings); consensus; information sharing; case-by-case (the Club tailors its action to each debtor country's individual situation); conditionality (the Paris Club only negotiates debt restructurings with debtor countries that have a current program of reforms supported by an appropriate arrangement with the IMF); comparability of treatment (thus, a debtor country should not accept from its non-Paris Club debtors terms of treatment of its debt less favorable to the debtor than those agreed with the Paris Club).

[16] Eligible credits, i.e. those for which the Club is responsible, are only medium- and

ing up a restructuring program, which must be signed by all the States concerned. This document, however, does not qualify as an international agreement, as it is merely an understanding reached by consensus within the Paris Club. Subsequently, creditor States can conclude bilateral agreements with the debtor country, which must conform to the understanding signed within the Club. To conclude such agreements, compliance with the principle of conditionality must be ensured, therefore the debtor State must demonstrate that it is the beneficiary of assistance by the IMF. [17]

The development of international financial law is especially favored by a treaty-based architecture and the existence of so-called "International Financial Institutions" (IFIs). Other than the IMF and the World Bank, an example is constituted by the Organization for the Economic Cooperation and Development (OECD), founded in Paris in 1960 with the mission of promoting, at a global level, policies that improve the economic and social well-being of citizens, through the integration of markets and the realization of the highest levels of economic growth and sustainable employment, fostering investment and competitiveness while maintaining financial stability. The OECD is one of the world's largest and most trusted sources of statistics, data and policy analysis, that may help to inform debates in international fora, parliaments, the media, civil society, and research work. Its structure revolves around a Council, the highest decision-making body, composed of one representative from each of the 38 Member States as well as from the EU. More than 300 Substantive Committees, established pursuant to Article 9 of its Convention, engage with data and propose solutions, policy actions, adopting also standards and guidelines.

---

long-term public debts (with a maturity of one more than one year). Debts owed by private entities and guaranteed by the public sector are considered to be part of the public debts. However, the Paris Club also excludes from restructuring the loans to countries that do not have significant exposure, as well as debt that has already been restructured and whose instalments fall due during the period covered by a new negotiation.

[17] A. Viterbo, *Sovereign Debt Restructuring. The Role and Limits of Public International Law,* Giappichelli, 2020. It must be highlighted that, through the Heavily Indebted Poor Countries (HIPC) Initiative, the IMF and the World Bank ensure debt relief to countries facing an unsustainable debt burden. In 2005, to accelerate progress toward the United Nations' Sustainable Development Goals, the HIPC Initiative was supplemented by the Multilateral Debt Relief Initiative. This allows countries completing the HIPC Initiative process to receive 100 percent relief on eligible debts by the IMF, the World Bank, and certain regional institutions.

5.3. The International Monetary Fund

According to Article I of its Articles of Agreement, the purposes of the IMF are

> *"(i) To promote international monetary cooperation through a permanent institution which provides the machinery for consultation and collaboration on international monetary problems. (ii) To facilitate the expansion and balanced growth of international trade, and to contribute thereby to the promotion and maintenance of high levels of employment and real income and to the development of the productive resources of all Members as primary objectives of economic policy. (iii) To promote exchange stability, to maintain orderly exchange arrangements among Members, and to avoid competitive exchange depreciation. (iv) To assist in the establishment of a multilateral system of payments in respect of current transactions between Members and in the elimination of foreign exchange restrictions which hamper the growth of world trade. (v) To give confidence to Members by making the general resources of the Fund temporarily available to them under adequate safeguards, thus providing them with opportunity to correct maladjustments in their balance of payments without resorting to measures destructive of national or international prosperity. (vi) In accordance with the above, to shorten the duration and lessen the degree of disequilibrium in the international balances of payments of Members".* [18]

Therefore, the objective of the IMF is to assist its Member States in developing economic policies that promote financial stability and monetary cooperation, which are essential to foster growth, economic welfare, productivity and job creation. Consequently, each Member undertakes to cooperate with the Fund and other Members to maintain orderly exchange arrangements and to promote a stable system of exchange rates, and to conduct its economic and financial policies with the objective of promoting economic growth.

At present, the IMF has 191 Members: each Member is allocated a quota expressed in Special Drawing Rights (SDRs), an interest-bearing international reserve asset created by the IMF in 1969 to complement other reserve assets of Member countries. An SDR is based on a basket of international currencies (the US dollar, the Japanese yen, the euro, the pound ster-

---

[18] Articles of Agreement of the International Monetary Fund, adopted at the United Nations Monetary and Financial Conference (Bretton Woods) on July 22, 1944. See H. Aufricht, *The International Monetary Fund - Legal Basis, Structure, Functions*, Stevens & Sons, 1964, and E. Denters, A. Viterbo, *International Monetary Fund*, Springer, 2013.

ling and the Chinese renminbi).[19] SDRs are allocated according to the quota each country pays to the IMF,[20] which normally reflects the Member's relative position in the world economy. Quotas determine the number of shares owned by a Member State, but also the maximum amount of financial resources a Member is required to provide to the IMF, as well as the maximum amount of resources a Member can receive in loans from the IMF under normal access. Quotas are also an important determinant of voting power in the IMF's decision-making process.[21]

5.3.1. Internal Structure

According to Article XII(1) of its Articles of Agreement, the Fund shall have a Board of Governors, an Executive Board, a Managing Director and a staff, and a Council.[22] Unlike other international organizations, where

---

[19] Special Drawing Rights (SDRs) are neither a currency nor a claim on the IMF, but rather a right to acquire freely usable currencies of IMF Members. The value of an individual SDR is determined daily by the IMF on the basis of fixed amounts of the currencies in the SDR basket and the daily market exchange rates between the currencies in the SDR basket. SDRs can be held and used by Member countries, the IMF and certain designated official entities, known as "prescribed holders", but cannot be held, for example, by private entities or individuals. There are currently 20 prescribed holders: 4 central banks (the European Central Bank, the Bank of Central African States, the Central Bank of West African States and the Eastern Caribbean Central Bank); 3 intergovernmental monetary institutions (the Bank for International Settlements, the Latin American Reserve Fund and the Arab Monetary Fund); and 13 development institutions (African Development Bank, African Development Fund, Asian Development Bank, Caribbean Development Bank, Development Bank of Latin America - known as Corporación Andina de Fomento- , European Bank for Reconstruction and Development, European Investment Bank, Inter-American Development Bank, International Bank for Reconstruction and Development and International Development Association, Islamic Development Bank, Nordic Investment Bank and International Fund for Agricultural Development).

[20] The IMF conducts "General Reviews" of quotas at least every 5 years, reviewing the size of an overall quota increase and the distribution of the increase among Members. The most recent General Review (the 16th) was completed on 15 December 2023 and approved a 50 percent increase in IMF Members' quotas (SDR 238.6 billions, or USD 320 billions).

[21] The United States detains the highest number of shares, which represent the 17.42 percent of the total votes, followed by Japan (6,47 percent), China (6,4 percent), Germany (5,59 percent), France (4,23 percent), United Kingdom (4.23 percent), Italy (3,16 percent), Russian Federation (2,71 percent), Canada (2,31 percent), Brazil (2,23 percent), Saudi Arabia (2,10 percent), Spain (2 percent).

[22] To date, the Council has not been activated. The Board of Governors, according to the Articles of Agreement, shall decide to establish the Council by a majority of 85

each country has one vote, the IMF's voting power and decision-making reflect the relative economic positions of its Members: each Member has 250 basic votes. The remaining votes are based on quota shares and are denominated in the IMF's Special Drawing Rights (SDRs): one vote per 100,000 SDRs of quota. The voting system applies to all decisions to be taken by the Fund's organs, with adjustments when the vote concerns a temporary waiver of economic conditions for access to credit or decisions on ineligibility to use the IMF's general resources.

The Board of Governors is the highest decision-making body of the IMF. It consists of one Governor and one Alternate Governor for each Member country, who serve without remuneration from the Fund. The Governor is appointed directly by the Member country: usually he/she is the Minister of Finance or the Governor of the Central Bank. In accordance with Article XII(2) of the IMF Articles of Agreement, the Board of Governors may delegate to the Executive Board the power to exercise any of the powers of the Board of Governors, except the right to approve quota increases, SDR allocations, the admission of new Members, the compulsory withdrawal of Members, and amendments to the Articles of Agreement and to the By-Laws of the Fund (which contain provisions supplementary to the Articles of Agreement). The Board of Governors also elects or appoints Executive Directors and is the final arbiter on questions of interpretation of the IMF's Articles of Agreement. Each Governor shall be entitled to cast the number of votes allotted to him by the Members who appointed him during any meeting of the Board of Governors.[23]

The IMF Board of Governors is advised by two ministerial committees, the International Monetary and Financial Committee (IMFC) and the Development Committee. The IMFC has 24 Members drawn from the pool of 191 governors: the Committee advises and reports to the IMF Board of Governors on the oversight and management of the international monetary and financial system, including responses to emerging events that could disrupt the system. It also considers proposals by the Executive Board to

---

percent of the total voting power, and to apply provisions contained into Appendix D of the Articles of Agreement that regulate powers, composition and functioning of the Council. See A. Abrams, *The IMF Council of Governors*, in R. Lamdany, L. Martinez-Diaz (eds.), *Studies of IMF Governance. A Compendium*, International Monetary Fund, 2009, pp. 43-57.

[23] Under Article XII(2)(c) and d of the IMF Articles of Agreement, meetings of the Board of Governors shall be convened as provided by the Board of Governors or called by the Executive Committee, or at the request of 15 Members or of Members holding one quarter of the total number of votes. The quorum shall consist of a majority of the Governors representing at least two-thirds of the total voting power.

amend the Articles of Agreement and advises on any other matters that may be referred to it by the Board of Governors. Although the IMFC has no formal decision-making powers, in practice it has become a key instrument for providing strategic direction to the Fund's work and policies. The Development Committee, which has 25 Members (usually Ministers of Finance or of Development), was established in October 1974 to advise the Boards of Governors of the IMF and of the World Bank on critical development issues and on the financial resources needed to promote economic development.

The Executive Board conducts the day-to-day business of the Fund and exercises the powers delegated to it by the Board of Governors and those conferred on it by the Articles of Agreement. It is composed of 24 Executive Directors and the Managing Director, who serves as its Chair.[24] Each Executive Director appoints an Alternate with full powers to act in his/her absence; in addition, an Executive Director elected from a constituency composed of a number of Member States determined by the Board of Governors may appoint two Alternates.

The Executive Board operates in continuous session at the Fund's main office in Washington, DC, and meets as often as the business of the IMF requires.[25] The Executive Board discusses all aspects of the Fund's work and normally takes decisions by consensus, but sometimes formal votes are taken. In such a case, each Executive Director is entitled to cast the number of votes of the constituency he or she represents.

The Executive Board shall elect a Managing Director who shall not be a Governor or Executive Director. He or she shall be appointed by the Executive Committee for a renewable term of 5 years. The Managing Director is the head of the Fund's operational staff and, under the direction of the Board, conducts the ordinary business of the IMF, including the organization, appointment and dismissal of the Fund's staff. In addition, the Managing Director is the Chairman of the Executive Board, but has no vote, except a casting vote in the event of an equality of votes; he may also attend meetings of the Board of Governors but with no vote.

---

[24] Previously, the 5 Member countries with the largest quotas each had the right to appoint one Executive Director, while 19 were elected by the remaining Member countries through a system of electoral constituencies (composed of a group of Member States). With the entry into force of the Board Reform Amendment on 26 January 2016, the all-elected Executive Board has been in place since the subsequent election took effect on 1 November 2016.

[25] Article XII(3)(h) of the Articles of Agreement requires a quorum for any meeting of the Executive Board consisting in a majority of the Executive Committee Members holding at least half of the total voting rights.

5.3.2. The Functions of the IMF: Surveillance and Capacity Development

The IMF has several core responsibilities in relation to the global economy. In general terms, these activities highlight stability risks to Member countries and advise governments on possible policy adjustments: this function is also known as "surveillance". In particular, the IMF monitors the international monetary system and global economic developments ("multilateral surveillance") while also conducting regular health checks on the economic and financial policies of its Members ("bilateral surveillance").

Bilateral surveillance and policy advice is governed by Article IV of the IMF Articles of Agreement and normally involves annual visits to Members.[26] Based on these meetings, the IMF staff prepares country assessments for wide-ranging policy recommendations for reform, known as "Article IV Consultations". These reports are then shared with Member governments for consultation. At the conclusion of the Article IV consultation, the staff report is presented to the IMF Executive Board. The Board then discusses the report, and its views are summarized and presented in the final Article IV report alongside the staff report.

In addition to bilateral surveillance, the IMF mandates Members to undergo financial stability assessments, known as the "Financial Sector Assessment Programme" (FSAP). When the FSAP program began in 1999, the assessments were voluntary: over time, the IMF made them mandatory for certain Members (now 47) that it considered to have systematically important financial sectors. The FSAP provides a comprehensive, in-depth analysis of the resilience of a country's financial sector: it includes "stress tests" of financial institutions, an assessment of the quality of supervision and regulation of the sector, and an evaluation of the crisis management framework.

At the multilateral level, the IMF monitors regional and global economic trends and analyses the impact of Members' policies on neighboring countries and the global economy. It issues regular reports and analysis on these trends. The findings of all multilateral reports are brought together in the "Global Policy Agenda", which proposes responses to perceived challenges for the IMF and its Member countries. Between these reports, the "World Economic Outlook" provides analysis and projections of the world

---

[26] During these visits, IMF staff meets with government's and Central Bank's officials, as well as with parliamentarians and representatives of business, labor, and civil society, addressing risks to domestic and global stability, and policies and reforms to address these risks.

economy over the short and medium term, while the "Global Financial Stability Report" provides an assessment of the global financial system and markets. In addition to these studies, the IMF publishes "Regional Economic Reports", which examine economic developments within regions and the policies of monetary unions.[27]

A second core function of the IMF is known as "capacity development": this involves technical assistance and training, which is available to all Members upon request and is tailored to a country's specific needs. In general, IMF assistance aims to help countries modernize their monetary and exchange rate policies, develop their legal systems, or strengthen governance. In practice, IMF staff provides expert advice to country officials, both in-country and remotely from headquarters. Such visits focus on specific issues and are initiated at the request of the Member country; staff may therefore be in-country for a short period or detached in a national office for a longer period, depending on the request of the country authorities. In addition, a network of IMF Regional Capacity Development Centers provides assistance to countries under the guidance of the IMF: these Regional Centers are jointly funded by the IMF, external development partners and Member countries. The IMF also provides in-person and online training to government officials on selected macroeconomic and financial topics, or to the general public through open online courses.

5.3.3. Lending Activities

The IMF's core activity is to provide financial support to countries in crisis or to prevent crises by easing their economic and financial situation while they implement policies that can restore economic stability and growth. Such crises can be caused by domestic or external factors, or a combination of both: the former include inappropriate fiscal and monetary policies, which can lead to budget deficits and high public debt; an exchange rate fixed at an inappropriate level; a fragile financial system; and political instability. External factors, on the other hand, include shocks ranging from natural disasters to large fluctuations in commodity prices. The COVID-19 pandemic was an example of an external shock that affected countries

[27] These reports are based on annual and separate consultations with the regional institutions responsible for common policies in 4 monetary unions (the Euro Area, the Eastern Caribbean Currency Union, the Central African Economic and Monetary Union, and the West African Economic and Monetary Union).

around the world and to which the IMF responded with unprecedented financial support.[28]

Resources for IMF lending come from three sources: Members' quotas are the main source. In addition, the IMF can draw on resources from the "New Arrangement to Borrow" (NAB), under which 40 countries have agreed to lend additional resources to the IMF, or from "Bilateral Borrowing Agreements" (BBAs) with Member States.

Technically, IMF loans are disbursed or drawn by the borrower's purchase of foreign currency assets from the IMF with its own currency or with SDRs: repayment of the loan is therefore achieved by the borrower's repurchase of its own currency from the IMF with foreign currency.[29] However, under Article V(3)(b)(ii) of the IMF Articles of Agreement, the Member must represent problems in its reserve position or in the balance of payments.

IMF lending is usually conditional on a request from a Member country, followed by a discussion between the government and IMF staff on the country's economic and financial situation: this process is continued, as IMF lending can be redefined to meet countries' changing needs. Typically, the Member's government and the IMF agree on a program of corrective policy measures before the Fund lends to the country: these adjustments are conditions of IMF loans and are known as "policy conditionality".[30] Once the terms are agreed upon, the arrangement is presented to the IMF's Executive Board in a "Letter of Intent" and detailed in a "Memorandum of Understanding".[31] In some cases, there is a "Memorandum of Economic Policies" (MEP), which details the reforms and measures to be implemented. Sometimes, there is also a "Technical Memorandum of Understanding"

---

[28] The COVID-19 outbreak and the associated global economic turmoil created a critical need to support the Fund's Members, including exceptional support for the poorest countries especially impacted by the pandemic. In direct response to the COVID-19 crisis the IMF Executive Board has adopted some immediate enhancements to its emergency facilities (Rapid Credit Facility, Rapid Financing Instrument, Catastrophe Containment and Relief Trust), also adjusting existing lending agreements in order to accommodate urgent needs arising from the pandemic.

[29] Article XXX(c) of the Articles of Agreement.

[30] Conditionality generally involves the implementation of neo-liberal reforms (collectively known as "Washington consensus") deemed necessary by the IMF to enable the recipient State to balance its balance of payments and stimulate growth in its economy. Conditionality requirements range from a general commitment to cooperate with the IMF in setting various policies to the formulation of a specific plans for monetary, fiscal and trade policies ("stabilization programme" and "structural adjustment programme").

[31] See Chapter 2, Section 2.7

(TMU), which sets out the economic variables. Afterward, the IMF staff makes a recommendation to the Executive Board to endorse the country's policy objectives and offers financing. After the Executive Board approves the loan, the IMF monitors how Members implement the policy actions.

The IMF offers different types of loans (called instruments or programs) to governments, depending on their specific circumstances and income classification. The first lending instrument available to all Member States is the reserve tranche: Members can withdraw part of their quota contribution at any time, without authorization from the Fund and without having to comply with any specific conditions or being subject to any repayment obligations. Any Member State may also make additional purchases over and above its reserve quota (so-called "credit tranches"), but these are not automatic and are subject to eligibility conditions, which become stricter the larger the amount involved. All IMF Member States are eligible to borrow from the "General Resources Account" (GRA) at market-based interest rates, while only low-income countries are eligible to borrow at concessional rates (currently at 0 percent interest rates) through the "Poverty Reduction and Growth Trust" (PRGT). As anticipated, how much a country can borrow depends on their IMF quota share, which is determined by a formula that considers the size of their economic output and other factors.

The IMF's main lending instruments are "Stand-By Arrangements" (SBA), which are intended for emerging and advanced market economies to address short-term or potential balance of payments problems. The SBA is open to any Member State and covers a period of no more than 36 months (typically 12 to 24 months), and repayments are due within 3 to 5 years. This facility requires access to IMF resources in tranches ("phasing"): consequently, disbursements are conditional on the observance of certain criteria and on the implementation of structural measures that are critical to the achievement of the objectives of the program. Any Member country experiencing a temporary balance of payments imbalance has access to an amount currently equal to 200 percent of its quota on an annual basis and 600 percent of its quota on a cumulative basis. The IMF Executive Board conducts periodic program reviews to assess whether the program is on track or needs to be adjusted in light of new developments.

Other instruments available to Member States include: the "Standby Credit Facility" (SCF), designed to address short-term or potential balance of payments problems of low-income countries under the PRGT, with a grace period of 4 years and a final maturity of 8 years; the "Extended Fund Facility" (EFF), usually approved for 3 years, intended for emerging and advanced market economies where the impediments to growth are considered structural; the "Extended Credit Facility" (ECF), provided to low-income countries under the PRGT for an initial period of 3 years; the "Rapid Financing Instrument" (RFI), which can be used for a range of urgent needs, such as natural disasters, conflicts and commodity price shocks, and should be repaid within 3 and a quarter to 5 years; the "Rapid Credit Facility" (RCF), which is available to low-income countries under the PRGT;[32] the "Flexible Credit Line" (FCL), which is intended for countries that have a strong policy framework and a track record of economic performance, therefore does not involve conditionality and functions as a renewable credit line of 1 to 2 two years; the "Short-Term Liquidity Line" (SLL), for Members with very strong policy frameworks that face potential, moderate, short-term liquidity needs due to external shocks; the "Precautionary and Liquidity Line" (PLL), which is intended to cover the liquidity needs of countries whose economic framework is considered sound by the IMF, but which have remaining problems that prevent them from drawing on the FCL; the "Resilience and Sustainability Facility" (RSF), which provides long-term financing and it is linked to specific reform progress; the "Catastrophe Containment and Relief Trust" (CCRT), which allows the IMF to provide grants (rather than loans) to the poorest countries in the form of debt relief in the event of catastrophic natural or public health disasters; the "Policy Coordination Instrument" (PCI), that allows low-income Members to secure IMF advice without financial assistance, thereby leveraging financing from other sources thanks to the "reputational" effect of receiving IMF assistance. In addition, Member countries that are not yet in a position to implement IMF programs can access the "Staff Monitored Programme" (SMP), an informal arrangement between an IMF Member country and the IMF staff to monitor the Member country's economic program.

5.4. The World Bank Group

The International Bank for Reconstruction and Development (IBRD or Bank) is the second product of the efforts to rebuild the international economy after the War. As originally conceived, the IBRD was established to catalyze private capital to support post-war reconstruction in Europe and the development of economically disadvantaged nations; however, its mandate has evolved over the past 60 years to become the principal "poli-

[32] Unlike the other facilities, the RCF and RFI are provided in a single disbursement, meaning that no conditionality needs to be met during the program prior to disbursement.

cymaker" for developing countries, while its function of financing industry, infrastructure and agriculture has been significantly reduced by the Bank's promotion of macroeconomic and institutional reforms. [33] The IBRD is the best-known of a larger set of international institutions called the "World Bank Group" (WBG), which first includes the International Development Association (IDA), conceived as specialized institutions complementary to IBRD, which provides financing to the poorest country of the world. The term "World Bank" (WB), therefore, refers to IBRD and IDA jointly. The Group also comprises the International Finance Corporation (IFC), the International Centre for Settlement of Investment Disputes (ICSID), and the Multilateral Investment Guarantee Agency (MIGA). As such, the WBG does not have its own legal personality, but merely implies that there are significant links between the Member organizations at the administrative, institutional and operational levels. [34]

On the operational level, the WBG has set two ambitious goals in its Strategy, adopted during the 2013 Spring Meeting: end extreme poverty, by reducing the percentage of people living on less than 1,25 USD a day to 3 percent by 2030; promote shared prosperity, fostering income growth of the bottom 40 percent of the population in every country. These goals, and the partnership to achieve them, are aligned with the previous international effort to reach the Millennium Development Goals and also with the current development agenda synthesized in the Sustainable Development Goals adopted in 2015.

5.4.1. The International Bank for Reconstruction and Development

Under Article I of its Articles of Agreement, the IBRD purposes are:

> *"(i) To assist in the reconstruction and development of territories of Members by facilitating the investment of capital for productive purposes, including the restoration of economies destroyed or disrupted by war, the reconversion of productive facilities to peacetime needs and the encouragement of the development of productive facilities and resources in less*

---

[33] World Bank, *A Guide to the World Bank*[3], World Bank Group, 2011.

[34] For example, membership in the WBG institutions is conditional upon IBRD's membership. In addition, the President of the IBRD is ex-officio President of the IDA and chairs the executive bodies of all four WBG Member organizations. In addition, the Executive Directors and Alternate Executive Directors of the IBRD are ex officio Executive Directors and Alternate Executive Directors of the IDA (Article VI(4) of the IDA Articles of Agreement) and the IFC (Article IV(4) of the IFC Articles of Agreement), subject to the conditions set out in their respective Statutes.

developed countries. (ii) To promote private foreign investment by means of guarantees or participations in loans and other investments made by private investors; and when private capital is not available on reasonable terms, to supplement private investment by providing, on suitable conditions, finance for productive purposes out of its own capital, funds raised by it and its other resources. (iii) To promote the long-range balanced growth of international trade and the maintenance of equilibrium in balances of payments by encouraging international investment for the development of the productive resources of Members, thereby assisting in raising productivity, the standard of living and conditions of labor in their territories. (iv) To arrange the loans made or guaranteed by it in relation to international loans through other channels so that the more useful and urgent projects, large and small alike, will be dealt with first. (v) To conduct its operations with due regard to the effect of international investment on business conditions in the territories of Members and, in the immediate postwar years, to assist in bringing about a smooth transition from a wartime to a peacetime economy".[35]

The Bank, consequently, has two main functions: to facilitate and encourage investment, particularly private investment, for reconstruction and development;[36] and to support, by providing loans or guarantees, operations that facilitate the productive use of a Member's resources when private capital is not available on reasonable terms.

The IBRD operates as a cooperative made up of 189 Member States. In order to be participate in the IBRD, a State must be a Member of the IMF (Article II(1) of the IBRD Articles of Agreement). The quota allocated by the IMF is used to determine the number of shares held in the context of the IBRD. Each Member, therefore, by paying its quota, subscribes a number of shares of the Bank. Two percent of the quota is to be paid immediately in USD or gold; 18 percent is to be paid, at the Bank's request, in national currency if the Bank needs it for its operations; and the remaining 80 percent is to be paid by all Members, again at the Bank's request (so-called

---

[35] Articles of Agreement of the International Bank for Reconstruction and Development, adopted at the United Nations Monetary and Financial Conference (Bretton Woods) on July 22, 1944.

[36] IBRD pursues the first objective through the Group's two private sector-related agencies, the IFC and the MIGA: the IFC, indeed, supports private enterprises through the provision of financing for productive investments, while the MIGA encourages foreign investment in developing countries through the provision of guarantees and insurance policies against political or non-commercial risks. This objective is also indirectly pursued by the ICSID, which, having jurisdiction over the settlement of disputes between a State and a foreign private party, is an important instrument for investment promotion and protection, see Chapter 3, Section 3.6.1.

"calls for subscribed capital"), when the organization needs it to meet its obligations in relation to loans granted or in which it participates or for guarantees, following Article II(5)(ii) of the Articles of Agreement.

As for the IMF, in the IBRD system shares determine each Member's voting rights: State receive votes consisting of share votes (one vote for each share of the Bank's capital stock held by the Member) plus basic votes (calculated so that the sum of all basic votes is equal to 5.55 percent of the sum of basic votes and share votes for all Members).[37] However, unlike in the IMF, where quotas are the basis for access to resources, the IBRD Articles of Agreement provide for no limitations related to loans from shares held. Loans are made when Members have difficulty obtaining financial resources in other ways on reasonable terms.

5.4.2. Internal Structure

According to Article V(1) of the IBRD Articles of Agreement, the Bank shall have a Board of Governors, Executive Directors, a President and such other officers and staff to perform such duties as the Bank may determine. The structure of the Bank, therefore, resembles that of the IMF.

All the powers of the Bank shall be vested in the Board of Governors, consisting of one Governor and one Alternate appointed by each Member in such manner as it may determine, which shall serve for five years and may be reappointed.[38] States normally appoint their Ministers of Finance or Governors of the Central Bank.[39] The IBRD Articles of Agreement establish that the Board of Governors may delegate to the Executive Directors authority to exercise any powers of the Board, except the power to: (i) admit new States and determine the conditions of their admission; (ii) in-

[37] At the time of the Bank's institution, the authorized capital stock was set at 10,000 millions USD in effect on 1 July 1944: the capital was then divided in 100,000 shares having a par value of 100,000 USD each, available for subscription only by Members. In October 2024, the capital of the 269,938 millions of 1944 USD.

[38] Under Article V(2)(d) of the IBRD Articles of Agreement, the Board is convened at least once a year at the request of the Executive Directors, of 5 Members, or of a number of Members representing one-fourth of the votes cast or whenever it deems appropriate. The quorum for valid meetings of the Board of Governors is fixed at the majority of Governors, representing at least 2/3 of the total votes.

[39] If the country is a Member of the Bank and also a Member of the IFC or IDA, then the appointed Governor and his or her Alternate serve ex-officio as the Governor and Alternate also on the IFC and IDA Boards of Governors. They also serve as representatives of their country on the Administrative Council of ICSID unless otherwise decided.

crease or decrease the capital stock; (iii) suspend a Member; (iv) decide appeals from interpretations of this Agreement given by the Executive Directors; (v) make arrangements to cooperate with other international organizations (other than informal arrangements of a temporary and administrative character); (vi) decide to suspend permanently the operations of the Bank and to distribute its assets; (vii) determine the distribution of the net income of the Bank.[40]

The Board of Executive Directors is responsible for the daily business of the IBRD. This body, entailing 25 Executive Directors, is made up of representatives of the Bank's Member countries that appoint them or elect them. Indeed, under the current system, each of the 6 Members having the largest number of shares (United States, France, China, United Kingdom, Japan and Germany) appoints an Executive Director, while the remaining Members elect the other Executive Directors through a system of electoral constituencies. Executive Directors shall be appointed or elected every two years.[41]

The Board of Executive Directors is in charge of conducting the Bank's general operations and, to this end, it exercises the powers delegated to them by the Board of Governors. In particular, the Executive Directors decide on the Bank's lending activities, ruling on the conditions attached to loans and guarantees. Indeed, this Board shall function in continuous session at the principal office of the Bank and shall meet as often as the business of the Bank may require.[42] During meetings, each appointed Director shall be entitled to cast the number of votes allotted to the Member appointing him, while each elected Director shall be entitled to cast the number of votes which counted toward his election.

The Executive Directors shall select a President who shall not be a Governor or an Executive Director or an Alternate for either. The President acts as Chairman of the Executive Directors without voting rights, except the power to cast a deciding vote in case of an equal division. He/she may participate in meetings of the Board of Governors but shall not vote at such meetings. The President shall be the chief of the operating staff of the Bank and shall conduct, under the direction of the Executive Directors, the ordinary business of the Bank. Subject to the general control of the Execu-

[40] Article V(2) of the IBRD Articles of Agreement.

[41] Under Article V(4)(c) of the IBRD Articles of Agreement, each Director shall appoint an Alternate with full power to act for him when he is not present. In the other cases, Alternates may participate in meetings but shall not vote.

[42] Under, Article V(4)(f) of the IBRD Articles of Agreement, the quorum for meetings of the Executive Directors is a majority of Executive Directors having at least half of the total votes.

tive Directors, he shall be responsible for the organization, appointment and dismissal of the officers and staff.

In addition, Article V(6) of the IBRD Articles of Agreement establishes an Advisory Council, composed of experts, chosen by the Board of Governors, from the banking, commerce, industry, labor, and agriculture sectors; it must be as representative as possible of the various States and gives opinions on the Bank's general policy.

5.4.3. The International Development Association

The International Development Association (IDA) is the section of the World Bank that helps low-income countries, supplementing IBRD's activities. Established in 1960, the IDA, which has 175 Members and a tripartite structure like the IBRD, with which it shares the Board of Governors and the President, while the Council of Executive Directors is autonomous (Article VI of the IDA Articles of Agreement). As said, IDA membership is conditional upon participation in the IBRD (Article II(1) of the IDA Articles of Agreement).

According to Article I of its Articles of Agreement, IDA promotes economic development "by providing finance to meet their important developmental requirements on terms which are more flexible and bear less heavily on the balance of payments than those of conventional loans". The Association, therefore, provides financing to further development in the less-developed areas of the world included within its membership, for purposes which in the opinion of the IDA are of high developmental priority in the light of the needs of the area concerned: financing, except in special circumstances, is therefore provided for specific projects.

Eligibility for IDA support depends first and foremost on a country's relative poverty, defined as gross national income (GNI) per capita below an established threshold and updated annually (1,335 USD, in the fiscal year 2025), risk of debt distress, and population size. Moreover, IDA countries shall lack creditworthiness to borrow on market terms: the Association indeed does not provide financing if in its opinion such funding is available from private sources on terms which are reasonable for the recipient or could be provided by a loan of the type made by the Bank (Article V(1)(c) of the IDA Articles of Agreement). [43]

---

[43] The status of IDA-only country can be, therefore, temporary, but certain low-income countries may remain eligible for IDA loans even if they exceed the GNI per capita for IDA-eligibility for more than 2 consecutive years, but they are not yet credit-

5.4.4. Functions of the World Bank: Analytics and Policy Advice

The World Bank (IBRD and IDA) provides "Advisory Service and Analytics" (ASA) to inform the national and global development agendas, in line with its strategy of ending extreme poverty and promoting shared prosperity. These non-lending activities support the design of better development policies and strategies through the adoption of reports, studies, policy notes, and training programs. Some of these services are provided in response to a request from – and paid for by – clients (governments, subnational entities, State-owned enterprises or other organizations).

These activities are the basis of medium and long-term strategies for the benefit of Member countries, and they allow the WB to avoid financial intervention to meet occasional needs. Indeed, the World Bank's approach is tailor-made to the profile of the country that requires assistance. The WB's engagement is framed by the "Country Partnership Framework" (CPF), which identifies key objectives and development results through which the WBG intends to support a Member country, outlining a selective and flexible program. This document is normally prepared every 4 to 6 years on the basis of a "Systematic Country Diagnostic" (SCD), an assessment in close dialogue with national authorities, citizens and other stakeholders of the constraints a country has to address.[44] At the end of the CPF period, the World Bank Group completes a self-assessment and issues a "Completion and Learning Review" (CLR) that assesses the program's performance. All these steps are developed in close consultation with governments, through several ministries and agencies at various levels. This method refines the approach already undertaken by the WB with the adoption of the "Country Assistance Strategy" (CAS),[45] and the "Poverty Reduction Strategy Paper" (PRSP).[46]

---

worthy to borrow from IBRD (so-called "gap countries") or if their creditworthiness for IBRD loans is established (so-called "blend countries").

[44] The WB engages with the country in a continuous process of results monitoring. Every two years during the implementation of a CPF, or at midterm, the WB produces a "Performance Learning Review" (PLR), which focuses on key country developments since the issuance of the CPF, and on program progress and performance, with a view to draw lessons learned from implementation, introducing midcourse adjustments, updating the results framework, and extending the CPF period as necessary, see World Bank Group, *Directive on Country Engagement*, OPCS 5.01-DIR.01, 1 July 2014.

[45] A CAS, now replaced by the CPF model, involved a "diagnosis" of a country's development challenges, particularly the incidence, trends and causes of poverty and set out the indicative level and type of assistance the WBG had to provide to a country, usually for a 4 years period. The documents were introduced in 1990 for countries borrowing from the IDA and were extended to all borrowers in 1994.

[46] Launched in late 1999 by the World Bank and the IMF, the PRSP was prepared

This approach follows the "Comprehensive Development Framework" (CDF) developed by the former President of the Bank, James D. Wolfenshon, in 1999, which proposed a holistic attitude to development, integrating social, structural, human, governance, and environmental elements in the economic and financial considerations. The WBG, therefore, promotes a cohesive development strategy that, together with appropriate institutional reforms, ensures the protection of human rights, anti-corruption policies, and greater attention to the environment. The evolution of this model is now embedded in the "Green, Resilient, and Inclusive Development" (GRID) approach, which promotes economic growth that goes hand in hand with environmental goals and inclusion. GRID focuses therefore on transitions in energy, agriculture, transport and cities, and it endorses risk management and preparation for pandemics, natural hazards, climate change and consequent financial shocks. [47]

These shifts in the WB "development model" have also informed its diagnostics (and lending) activities: the Bank, jointly with the IDA and the IFC, has indeed developed "Country Climate and Development Reports" (CCDRs) that help countries prioritize the most impactful actions that can reduce greenhouse gas emissions and boost adaptation and resilience, while delivering on broader development goals. [48] The reports suggest concrete priority actions to support low-carbon transition, inspire WBG operations, and help attract funding and direct financing for high-impact climate action.

5.4.5. Financing Activities

WB financial assistance consists of direct loans or guarantees to Member States, political subdivisions of a Member, or private companies. While all IMF members have access to its "General Resources Account" only in the event of balance of payments difficulties, WB Members are considered eligible for loans and guarantees only if the Bank, taking into account the market situation, "is satisfied that the borrower could not otherwise obtain

---

by governments in low-income countries in consultation with officials from the WB and IMF: these documents would provide the foundation for external assistance by the Fund and the IDA.

[47] World Bank Group, *Green, Resilient and Inclusive Development*, World Bank Group, 2021.

[48] World Bank Group, *The Development, Climate, and Nature Crisis: Solutions to End Poverty on a Livable Planet - Insights from World Bank Country Climate and Development Reports covering 42 economies*, World Bank Group, 2023.

the loan on terms reasonable for it" (Article III(4)(ii) of the IBRD Articles of Agreement). Since low-income countries can benefit from low-interest or interest-free loans by the IDA, the IBRD normally carries out its lending activity mainly in favor of middle-income countries.[49]

The loan is made if the Loan Committee submits a written report recommending the project after a thorough review of the application.[50] The Bank must then assess whether the potential borrower can meet the loan conditions, which are essentially designed to ensure that the loans will be used profitably and can be repaid. The IBRD must also review the repayment schedule for principal and interest, and certify that the project is technically viable and economically sustainable.[51] Such a loan is governed by a "Loan Agreement" between the IBRD and the State, which specifies: the amount of the loan; its disbursement in tranches; the repayment schedule; and the technical specifications of the project. If the borrower is a private entity, the State where the project is located or one of its administrative authorities must also enter into a "Guarantee Agreement" with the IBRD related to the repayment of principal, interest and other expenses related to the loan. All these arrangements are considered by the Bank as international agreements. Lending activities are conducted in accordance with the "General Conditions Applicable to Loan and Guarantee Agreements", which sets out the terms and conditions contained applicable to all financial products. These terms must be accepted by the borrower and, where applicable, by the guarantor.

---

[49] All 189 World Bank Member countries, along with 28 others with populations of more than 30,000 are classified by income level and geographic region for the presentation of key statistics. Key classifications available include geographic regions, income groups, and operational lending categories of the World Bank Group. Economies are currently divided into 4 income groupings: low, lower-middle, upper-middle, and high; income is measured using GNI per capita. The income groupings, however, have no operational implications for the WB.

[50] According to Article V(7) of the IBRD Articles of Agreement, "the committees required to report on loans under Article III, Section 4, shall be appointed by the Bank. Each such committee shall include an expert selected by the governor representing the member in whose territories the project is located and one or more members of the technical staff of the Bank".

[51] Under Article III(4)(iv) of the IBRD Articles of Agreement, the Bank shall assess that "rate of interest and other charges are reasonable and such rate, charges and the schedule for repayment of principal are appropriate to the project", while under Article III(4)(v) "the Bank shall pay due regard to the prospects that the borrower, and, if the borrower is not a member, that the guarantor, will be in position to meet its obligations under the loan; and the Bank shall act prudently in the interests both of the particular member in whose territories the project is located and of the members as a whole".

Loans might take different forms. First, Members might access the "Investment Policy Financing" facility (IPF), which aims at poverty reduction and sustainable development by providing financial support to specific projects with defined development objectives, activities and results. In these cases, the WB assesses the proposed project on various considerations, namely its technical aspects (including its suitability to the needs of the borrower); economic analysis, considering the project's objectives; financial management, considering the planning, budgeting, accounting, execution and reporting phases of the project.[52] The Bank also considers the procurement and environmental and social aspects of the proposed Project. IPF is focused on the medium to long-term (5 to 10 years) and supports a wide range of activities and sectors.

Second, the WB provides "Development Policy Financing" (DPF), which are policy-based loans or guarantees. Through these operations, the IBRD supports a Member country's program of policy and institutional actions that promote growth and sustainable poverty reduction. The Bank, in practice, determines whether specific policies are likely to have significant social consequences, especially on poor people and vulnerable groups, setting out a "Program Document" that establishes the measures to be implemented by the borrower, and indicators for monitoring and results' evaluation.[53] These transactions are governed by a "Development Policy Letter", which sets out the measures to be taken, by a "Loan agreement" and, where applicable, by a "Guarantee Agreement". This type of instrument has a shorter maturity (1 to 3 years) and allows rapid disbursement of financial resources to support macroeconomic policy interventions, such as structural reforms in a sector or the economy as a whole, and governance reforms. These loans are therefore approved only upon the maintenance of an adequate macroeconomic policy framework, as determined by the Bank with inputs from the IMF. Since July 1, 2023, all DPF operations are aligned with the goals of the Paris Agreement.[54]

Lastly, other financial services are known as "Program-for-Results"

---

[52] World Bank, *Bank Policy, Investment Policy Financing*, OPS5.03-POL.128, 10 June 2024.

[53] World Bank, *Bank Policy, Development Policy Financing*, OPS5.02-POL.105, 2 August 2017.

[54] The World Bank Group made a commitment to align all its financing operations with the goals of the *Paris Agreement* in its *Climate Change Action Plan 2021-2025*. These undertaking will entail an integrated vetting approach - screening, managing, and reducing climate risks for both mitigation and adaptation - for every project. Practically, all World Bank Group financed operations will have to support the deployment of lower-carbon options, whenever technically and economically feasible.

(PfR), which link the disbursement of funds directly to the delivery of defined outcomes connected to a project developed directly by the borrower;[55] and "Multiphase Programmatic Approach" (MPA), that allows countries to structure a long, large, or complex engagement as a set of smaller linked operations (or phases), under one program.[56] With regard to IDA, the majority of its resources are provided in the form of highly concessional loans (also known as credits) or grants. Loans can take the form of "Short Maturity Loans" (SMLs), with a maturity of 12 years and a grace period of 6 years. Other loans can mature after 30, 38, 40 or even 50 years, with longer grace periods and repayments ranging from 2 percent to 6.8 percent.[57]

Economic resources for loans by the IBRD arise mostly from the Members' quotas, grants, and trust funds financed by Members or by private entities, as well as through the emission of bonds and investment products on the world's financial markets. On the other part, IDA is funded largely by contributions from the governments of its richer Member countries, which meet every 3 years to replenish IDA funds.[58]

Lastly, the WB mandate maintains an exclusive economic and financial nature, in accordance with the "political neutrality clause" under Article IV(10) of the IBRD Articles of Agreement and under Article V(6) of the IDA Articles of Agreement. These provisions prohibit the organizations and their officials from interfering in the internal affairs ("political affairs") of States and from being influenced, in the performance of their duties, by their political orientation ("political character"). This rule states therefore that lending decisions must then be taken only on the basis of considerations of an economic character, evaluated impartially and in view of the statutory objectives, so as to avoid discrimination between Members (except the ones relating to their different economic conditions). Consequently, the WB has based its action on purely economic factors without considering issues such as democracy, human rights, and the maintenance of peace and security.

---

[55] World Bank, *Bank Policy, Program-for-Results Financing*, OPS5.04-POL.107, 25 March 2022.

[56] World Bank, *Multiphase Programmatic Approach*, 18 July 2017.

[57] See IDA, *Lending Terms*, effective as 1 October 2024.

[58] The most recent IDA replenishment (IDA20), which occurred in 2021, was the institution's largest replenishment ever, with 23.5 billions USD in contributions from donor countries supporting a total replenishment of 93 billions USD to cover the 3 years from mid-2022 to mid-2025.

5.4.6. The International Finance Corporation and Its Support to the Private Sector

The IFC is the largest global development institution focused on the private sector in developing countries.[59] Established in 1956, the Corporation is owned by 184 Member countries, each owning shares of the IFC proportional to the number of IBRD shares detained. As in the case of the IBRD, each Member receives votes consisting of share votes (one vote for each share of IFC's capital stock held by the Member) plus basic votes (calculated so that the sum of all basic votes is equal to 5.55 percent of the sum of basic votes and share votes for all Members). Its structure follows the tripartite model of the other WBG institutions, having a Board of Governors (whose Members are *ex officio* the IBRD Governors), a Board of Executive Directors, chaired by the IBRD President, and a President.

The purpose of the Corporation is to supplement the activities of the IBRD, by

> *"(i) in association with private investors, assist[ing] in financing the establishment, improvement and expansion of productive private enterprises which would contribute to the development of its member countries by making investments, without guarantee of repayment by the member government concerned, in cases where sufficient private capital is not available on reasonable terms; (ii) seek[ing] to bring together investment opportunities, domestic and foreign private capital, and experienced management; and (iii) seek[ing] to stimulate, and to help create conditions conducive to, the flow of private capital, domestic and foreign, into productive investment in member countries".* [60]

Under Article III of its Articles of Agreement, this organization finances investments in productive enterprises operating in the territory of Member States, whether private or public. Resources come essentially from three sources: Member States' quotas, which must be paid in full in USD or in convertible currencies; funds borrowed from the IBRD; and bonds issued in the global capital markets (Article II(3)(c) of the IFC Articles of Agreement).

The operations of the Corporations follow certain principles established by Article III(3) of the IFC Articles of Agreement: first, the IFC shall not undertake any financing for which private capital could be obtained on

---

[59] IFC, *IFC The Fists Six Decades: Leading the Way in Private Sector Development – A History*, International Finance Corporations, 2016.

[60] Article I of the IFC Articles of Agreement.

reasonable terms and shall finance projects located in the territory of a developing country which is also a Member State, unless such Member objects to such financing. In addition, the Corporation shall not assume responsibility for managing an enterprise in which it had invested and shall impose no conditions that the profit of any financing shall be spent in the territory of a particular country.

Investments by the IFC may take the form of loans, typically from 7 to 12 years; involve the acquisition of a share of the enterprise's equity (between 5 to 20 percent); or employ blended finance instruments, favoring the mobilization of private capital, providing guarantees and other structured financial products.

5.4.7. The Multilateral Investment Guarantee Agency

The Seoul Convention of 1988 establishes the Agency as an autonomous international organization with "full juridical personality" under international law and the domestic laws of its Members (Article 1) with the main objective of encouraging the flow of investments for productive purposes among its Member countries and in particular to its developing Member countries (Article 2). The reference to "investments for productive purposes" emphasizes the Agency's concentration on concrete projects and programs in all sectors of the economy.

The Agency has the common structure of international organizations: the Council of Governors represents its 182 Member States, and it is vested with all the powers prescribed by the Convention; the Board, composed of 25 Directors, shall be responsible for the general operations of the Agency;[61] the President and staff conduct the ordinary business. Each Member possesses a number of capital stock of the Agency, expressed in SDRs, paid in freely usable currencies. Shares also determine voting power: each State has allocated an equal number of membership votes, plus one subscription vote for each share of stock held by that State.

MIGA promotes its objectives by issuing guarantees "against non-commercial risks in respect to investments".[62] The idea of covering the risk of investment in developing countries materialized after these countries,

[61] Directors are elected through a system of electoral constituencies. The 6 larger shareholders (France, China, United Kingdom, United States, Japan, Germany) and Saudi Arabia constitute a single-State constituency. According to Article 42 of the Convention, each Director is entitled to cast the number of votes of the Members whose votes counted towards his/her election.

[62] Seoul Convention, Article 2(a).

following a period of relative closure of their economies, realized the positive effects of foreign investment and started concluding investment treaties.[63] In addition to guaranteeing investments in these Member countries against non-commercial risks, the Agency is to carry out complementary activities to promote investment flows.[64]

The Convention provides for coverage of the four categories of non-commercial risks. The currency transfer risk is broadly defined in Article 11(a)(i) of the Convention as "any introduction attributable to the host government of restrictions on the transfer outside the host country of its currency into a freely usable currency or another currency acceptable to the holder of the guarantee, including a failure of the host government to act within a reasonable period of time on an application by such holder for such transfer". It therefore encompasses all forms of new direct restrictions, including additions to existing restrictions, as well as indirect or disguised restrictions, whether such restrictions are imposed by law or in fact.[65] Article 11(a)(ii) defines the expropriation risk, including measures attributable to the host government such as nationalization, confiscation, sequestration, seizure, attachment and freezing of assets. Measures normally taken by governments to regulate their economic activities such as taxation, environmental and labor legislation as well as normal measures for the maintenance of public safety, are not intended to be covered by this provision unless they discriminate against the holder of the guarantee.[66] The

[63] See Chapter 3, Section 3.1.

[64] Seoul Convention, Article 2(b). The Agency has a responsibility under Article 23(a) of the Convention to conduct research and disseminate information on investment opportunities in developing Member countries, as well as to undertake other activities to promote foreign investment. In addition, the Agency, at the request of a Member, may provide technical assistance and advice with the objective of improving investment conditions. This could include advice on such matters as the drafting of investment codes and reviewing investment incentive programs. In carrying out its promotional activities, the Agency will be guided by the relevant investment agreements among its Members and will seek to remove impediments among its Members to investment flows. Also, Article 23(b)(i) places a duty on the Agency to encourage the amicable settlement of disputes between investors and host countries, providing information on available dispute settlement and conciliation mechanisms. The Agency is also directed to promote and facilitate the conclusion of investment protection treaties among its Members. For example, it could undertake studies on existing agreements and assist Member governments in the analysis of the implications of and benefits from such agreements.

[65] The restriction must be "attributable to the host government"; restrictions imposed by public agencies and other public organs of the host country are intended to be covered by this language.

[66] See Chapter 3, Section 3.3.1.

breach of contract risk is contained in Article 11(a)(iii). Indemnification is available only when an investor has no forum to pursue the contractual claim against the government or when recourse to such a forum is hampered by an unreasonable delay as defined in the guarantee contract or when, after obtaining a final decision in his favor, the investor is unable to enforce it. Finally, Article 11(a)(iv) encompasses the risk of war and civil disturbance, to be intended to include revolutions, insurrections, *coups d'état* and similar political events which are typically outside the control of the host government. Acts of terrorists and similar activities which are specifically directed against the holder of the guarantee are, however, not intended to be covered by this provision.[67]

Under Article 13 of the Convention, domestic natural and legal persons from a Member State other than the one hosting the investment are eligible for MIGA insurance coverage.[68] Eligible investments include equity interests, including medium or long-term loans made or guaranteed by holders of equity in the enterprise concerned, and such forms of direct investment as may be determined by the Board.[69] The coverage, which can be up to 90 percent of the value of the investment, is governed by an international guarantee contract between the Agency and the investor, specifying the duration, coverage, and types of risk. The investor may invoke the MIGA guarantee only after exhausting the legal remedies available in the host Country of the investment. Only in the event of an unfavorable outcome before domestic remedies, the investor may request payment to the Agency. Article 18 of the Convention provides that where the Agency compensates or agrees to compensate an investor under a contract of guarantee, it assumes the rights and claims that the investor acquired against the host country as a result of the event giving rise to the claim against the Agency (so-called "subrogation").

---

[67] The Seoul Convention provides additional flexibility by allowing the coverage of other specific non-commercial risks, but only at the joint request of the investor and the host country and with approval of the Board by special majority (Article 11(b) of the Convention). Such approval may be issued on a case-by-case basis or in the form of regulations specifying the cases to be covered under this provision.

[68] Additionally, the Board of Directors may extend eligibility to a natural person who is a national of the host country or a juridical person which is incorporated in the host country or the majority of whose capital is owned by its nationals, provided that the assets invested are transferred from outside the host Country.

[69] The investment must not only generate a profit for the investor but also contribute to the economic development of the host country; be consistent with its development objectives and priorities and comply with its laws. Also, to be eligible for MIGA coverage, the investment project does not need to be covered by government or private insurance.

5.5. The Relationship between the Bretton Woods Institutions and International Law

Through the years, IEL has progressively opened up to other areas and sub-areas within international law, making evident that IEL was built and continues to function within the wider framework of public international law[70]. Of course, as subjects of international law, the institutions of the WBG and the IMF are capable of possessing rights and duties under their constituent instruments, general rules of international law, and the treaties to which they have acceded. These include obligations in the domain of human rights, to be exercised separately from, or jointly with, their Member States.[71] In addition, these organizations are specialized agencies of the United Nations. The relationship agreement linking the institutions to the UN emphasizes – as is the case for the World Bank – the independent status of the institutions. However, this does not mean they are exempted from obligations arising from the UN Charter, including those relating to human rights.[72]

Notwithstanding, studies demonstrated that economic adjustment programs sponsored by these organizations generally have a negative impact on poor and marginalized people as they include, among other things, privatization of public services (healthcare, education, housing and water services), raising their fees and/or resulting in significant layoffs; subsidies for

[70] See Chapter 1, Section 1.1.

[71] The circumstances under which international organizations may be held responsible for internationally wrongful acts are exemplified by the International Law Commission's Draft Articles on the Responsibility of International Organizations (DARIO). In light of Article 4 DARIO, two conditions are required under international law for the responsibility of international organizations to be established: firstly, the breach of one of their international obligations, and, secondly, that the breach at issue is attributable to the organization. The acts and omissions of an international financial institutions may give rise to human rights violations also when they aid or assist (Article 14), or direct and control (Article 15) a State (or another international organization) in the commission of a wrongful act. See W. Van Genungten, *The World Bank Group, the IMF and Human Rights. A Contextualised Way Forward*, CUP, 2017, pp. 27-35.

[72] According to E. Sciso (ed.), *Accountability, Transparency and Democracy in the Functioning of Bretton Woods Institutions*, Springer, 2017, pp. viii, the IMF and the World Bank have, since 1947, been specialized agencies of the United Nations, based on an agreement concluded with the UN Economic and Social Council. Therefore, even though they are not formally parties to the Universal Covenants agreed among States, the Fund and the Bank are *de facto* held to promote the respect of the fundamental economic and social rights of the people who are affected by their interventions, in conformity with the relevant provisions of the universal instruments which apply in the field of their activities.

farming, education, healthcare, and water are often cut or eliminated; trade liberalization subjects domestic businesses, industries, and agricultural production to stiff international competition.[73]

Both institutions are, therefore, often the subject of severe criticism for obvious limitations in their structure, functioning, and actual operations, leading to the belief that international financial law is disconnected from the wider spectrum of international law. This conception is also favored by the organizations' common response to this criticism, as they – having a purely economic mandate – should not evaluate the internal political affairs of States. In practical terms, the "political prohibition" established by their Articles of Agreement would impede embracing human rights as a universal value and aligning with corresponding legal obligations.[74]

More specifically, the IMF has often been accused of imposing significant economic policy reforms on Members requesting its financial assistance: the effects of the conditionality attached to its financial activities have indeed been severe. Scholars, NGOs, the UN and certain monitoring bodies have argued that the organization does not assess the consequences of its measures on the populations of the affected States, preventing those States from investing in important sectors such as education, health, and public jobs.[75] The Fund, therefore, would operate without taking into account the economic and social conditions of the country it is asking to carry out certain reforms, offering standardized solutions that are not always linked to or applicable in the specific national context.

Additionally, austerity measures commonly feature in the prescribed conditionalities of IMF loans. Shaped by dominant free market ideologies and theories reflecting the neoliberal vision of the economy and society, these restrictive economic and social policies that are supposed to help

---

[73] M.R., Abouharb, D. Cingranelli, *Human Rights and Structural Adjustment*, CUP, 2009, p. 11.

[74] Office of the High Commissioner on Human Rights, UN Expert on Extreme Poverty, *The World Bank is a Human Rights-Free Zone*, 29 September 2015.

[75] Commission on Human Rights, *Joint Report by the Independent Expert on structural adjustment policies and the Special Rapporteur on foreign debt*, 14 January 2000, E/CN.4/2000/51, para. 1: "*For almost 20 years, the international financial institutions and creditor Governments were engaged in the self-deceptive and destructive game of managing third world economies from afar and forcing unpopular economic policies down the throats of powerless third world countries in the belief that the bitter medicine of macroeconomic adjustment would ultimately put these countries on a path to prosperity and a debt-free existence. Two decades later, many countries are in worse condition than when they started implementing IMF/World Bank structural adjustment programmes. The social and ecological costs of these harsh austerity programmes have been far-reaching, with many countries experiencing a dramatic decline in human development indices*".

consolidate public finances (taking in practice mainly the form of cuts in public spending) may have the effect of compromising a series of basic human rights, such as the right to adequate food, the right to health, the right to decent work, the right to education and the right to adequate housing, all enshrined in the International Covenant on Economic, Social and Cultural Rights (ICESCR) and in other conventional instruments.[76]

Failures of IMF intervention are exemplified by the case of Argentina and Greece. On the one part, the Latin American country, between the period 1991-2001, had to ensure the implementation of a series of structural and fiscal reforms in the face of the Fund's disbursement of economic aid. After having followed the IMF's directions, Argentina faced a very serious economic crisis in 2001, which, according to many, was caused precisely by the spending cuts imposed by the IMF. These measures have undermined the government's ability to intervene in key sectors such as health, education and security, as well as in the privatization of strategic national sectors, making the population even poorer and leading the State to default. Greece, on the other part, was the first of a number of EU Member States to receive conditional financial assistance to address its high sovereign debt. From May 2010, on the verge of financial collapse, Greece was forced to resort to outside assistance from the IMF and Eurozone Member States. Under multiple Memorandums of Understanding negotiated and monitored by the so-called "troika" – the European Commission, the European Central Bank and the IMF – loans were provided under the strict conditionality requirement of implementing austerity-based policies,[77] with the aim to redress imbalances in public finances, reduce external debt and restore competitiveness so as to prevent economic collapse and stabilize the Greek economy. However, poverty rates increased as a result of rising unemployment and cuts to social security benefits, showing the inefficacy of the IMF-led solutions.[78]

---

[76] Office of the High Commissioner for Human Rights, *Report on Austerity Measures and Economic and Social Rights*, E/2013/82, 2013.

[77] Terms included massive cuts to public sector staff and salaries, reductions in pensions, a reduction of the minimum wage by 22 percent, weakening of labor protections, myriad cuts to social benefits, as well as the introduction of a slew of new taxes impacting the poor and working people the most, as the increase of the VAT tax at 23 percent. Privatization of vast sections of the public sector was also a core aspect of the required measures.

[78] In its review of its general guidelines on conditionality, the IMF concluded that *"[F]und-supported programs are increasingly emphasizing social aspects"* and *"[s]ocial spending has been largely safeguarded under most Fund-supported programs"*, but it noted some exceptions, including that of Greece, stating that "in certain programs, successful

As for the World Bank system, the original Articles of Agreement literally forbid the Bank from dealing with any issues of political character, and the Bank considered human rights to be part of that. As far as human rights issues are concerned, the Bank had its first major clash in the 1960s, when the United Nations General Assembly passed a series of resolutions urging and requesting the Bank to stop lending to South Africa and Portugal because of their respective apartheid and colonial policies. Nevertheless, the Bank refused to do so on the grounds that it represented a non-political organization without the authority to impose sanctions upon Members for conduct unrelated to its purposes and approved a number of loans in defiance of the UN resolutions. However, despite this restrictive initial approach – which had led the World Bank to decline an invitation to participate in the drafting and subsequent ratification of the ICESCR – the Organization has gradually adhered to a new concept of economic development, which takes into account the close connection between economic growth and the protection of diverse interests, such as the implementation of economic, social and cultural rights.[79]

Indeed, as the main "player" in development financing, the activities of the WB and its institutions directly influence the fulfillment and enjoyment of human rights.[80] The change in the WB policy during the 1980s towards structural adjustment lending (in today's WB glossary, "Development Project Financing") imposed an evolution of the Bank's mandate from project-based interventions to economic reform and re-engineering of public sector policies and institutions, impacting the livelihoods of people considerably. Since then, the WB mission has evolved to serve a broader concept of development, being also concerned with the respect for human rights obligations as recognized by the UN General Assembly through the Declaration on the Right to Development of 1986, which, in its preamble, states that "*all human rights and fundamental freedoms are indivisible and interdependent and that, in order to promote development, equal attention and urgent consideration should be given to the implementation, promotion and protection*

---

crisis resolution has required significant cuts in expenditures, including in social sectors, and in real wages (the Greece program is a leading example)", see IMF, *Review of Conditionality*, 19 June 2012.

[79] G. Lehane, *Human Rights at the World Bank Group*, in Y. Radi (ed.), *Research Handbook on Human Rights and Investment*, Edward Elgar, 2018, pp. 188-191.

[80] See, for example, the findings of the World Bank Inspection Panel in *Uzbekistan: Second Rural Enterprise Support Project* (P109126) *and Additional Financing for the Second Rural Enterprise Support Project* (P126962), *Final Eligibility Report and Recommendation* (19 December 2014), where the complainants alleged violations of core human rights international conventions and the Bank's policies on child and forced labor.

of civil, political, economic, social and cultural rights".[81] This approach to development has since been confirmed by various decisions adopted by States and international organizations, evolving into the concept of sustainable development, which is today enshrined in the UN Sustainable Development Goals. These goals, along with other instruments, determine the playing field in which the IMF and the WB play a major role, with a constant balance between long-term social objectives and short-term market needs.

Decisive in the World Bank's support for this new programmatic concept were the studies and opinions prepared by the general counsels of the organization,[82] which broadened its objectives through a reinterpretation of its Statute.[83] This process culminated in a legal opinion affirming that the WB "*can and should take into account human rights because, given the way international law has evolved with the respect to the concepts of sovereignty and interference, the Bank would not fall foul to the political prohibition of the Articles*".[84]

The Bank has therefore gradually broadened its scope to include new areas in its decision-making, such as environmental protection, sustainable development, good governance, democracy and the rule of law, cultural development, post-conflict reconstruction, anti-corruption programs and, of course, the protection of human rights and fundamental freedoms, as directly involved in the funded project.

Clearly, the IMF and the WB have engaged (in different ways) in the human rights debate, embracing social and environmental rights and thus silently overcoming their "political prohibition." The work of such international organizations, which was originally limited to the financial and economic sphere, is now recognized to affect social policies of aid-recipient States and, in cases where conditionality is characterized by austerity, the enjoyment of human rights, not only inadequately protected but in some cases even violat-

---

[81] United Nations General Assembly, *Declaration on the Right to Development*, A/RES/41/28, 4 December 1986.

[82] While these opinions are not binding and do not constitute an official interpretation of the IBRD Articles of Agreement (which, under Article IX(a), is reserved to the Board of Directors), they are considered authoritative and can be informally applied by the organization, having important practical effects.

[83] See I.F.I. Shihata *Legal Memorandum of the Vice-President and General Counsel of IBRD, Issues of Governance in Borrowing Members – The Extent of Their Relevance Under the Bank's Articles of Agreement*, 5 February 1991; I.F.I. Shihata, *Prohibition of Political Activities in the Bank's Work: Legal Opinion by the Senior Vice President & General Counsel*, 12 July 1995.

[84] R. Dañino, *Legal Opinion on Human Rights and the Work of the World Bank. Senior Vice-President and General Counsel*, 27 January 2006.

ed. However, it can be said that both organizations have developed policies and strategies to better include social (and environmental) issues in their lending and policy-advice activities, including institutional reforms.

5.5.1. The IMF and Human Rights

Compared to the WBG, the Fund is less pronounced in linking its activities to obligations stemming from international law, especially in the human rights field. The IMF almost denies having such obligations. The closest reference to an official IMF definition on the subject of its obligations under human rights law is found in a 2005 paper by its former general counsel, which contends that rules on human rights do not apply to the Fund, even if the organization contributes to the realization of the rights set out in the ICESCR.[85]

However, it can be said that in the last decade the IMF is clearly rethinking this stance, following the evolution of the international legal system and the reinforcement of global concerns such as human rights, environmental and climate concerns, equality and democracy. Still, the IMF still does not use a specific "human rights language" and has not adopted a specific policy regarding human rights in its financing activities.

Notwithstanding, in several IMF publications, one can find references to human rights issues: in a Staff Discussion Note of January 2019, for example, researchers from the Fund address the 17 SDGs and the implication of the Fund's activities for the fulfillment of the current development agenda.[86] Also, the Fund has expanded its work on inequality, inclusive growth, and jobs: for example, the gender gap and women's economic empowerment are the subjects of several IMF policies and strategic notes.[87] Lastly, the IMF adopted its first-ever "Strategy to Help Members Address Climate Change Related Policy Challenges",[88] tackling urgent concerns regarding energy transition and environmental safeguards.

These innovations demonstrate a new awareness of the multiple social

---

[85] F. Gianviti, *Economic, Social and Cultural Rights and the International Monetary Fund*, in IMF, *Current Developments in Monetary and Financial Law*, International Monetary Fund, 2009, p. 3.

[86] IMF (V. Gaspar, D. Amaglobeli, M. Garcias-Escribano, D. Prady, M. Soto), *Fiscal Policy and Development: Human, Social, and Physical Investments for the SDGs*, International Monetary Fund, 23 January 2019.

[87] IMF, *Strategy Towards Mainstreaming Gender*, 2022.

[88] IMF, *IMF Strategy to Help Members Address Climate Change Related Policy Challenges: Priorities, Modes of Delivery, and Budget Implications*, 2021.

and environmental impacts of the IMF mandate.[89] However, it does not seem that the Fund is following the path adopted by other organizations and by the World Bank in the development of a specific sustainability/human rights policy or with the creation of an expert body on the human rights dimensions of IMF programs. Both solutions could make a major contribution to further embedding human rights in the policies and programs of this organization.

5.5.2. The World Bank "Environmental and Social Framework"

Starting in the 1980s, the World Bank began an internal reform process that led to the adoption of a series of internal rules (variously named but, for environmental and social issues, known as "Operational Policies" or "Safeguard Policies") designed to prevent or mitigate negative consequences of the World Bank's activities on the environment or on people. These rules constituted the closest thing to a real policy on sustainable development and fundamental rights. Although initially conceived as documents setting out some "aspirational" objectives or guiding principles, these policies became increasingly prescriptive, becoming *de facto* instructions from the World Bank to its staff in all stages of the design and implementation of a project financed by the organization. Additionally, it was common practice to incorporate these commitments and standards in the Loan Agreements with the borrowers, thus recognizing an "external" dimension to these purely internal standards.[90]

These policies failed, however, to create a complete framework for the protection of the individual or the environment. They expressed a static list of concerns, linked to the details of a project. What was lacking, therefore, was the overall, integrated vision of development that would have made it possible to consider other concerns, in particular the rights of individuals.

On 4 August 2016, after a long consultation process, the Executive Directors of the World Bank approved the new "Environmental and Social Framework" (ESF) with the intention of replacing most of the previously applicable rules and policies.[91] As of 1 October 2018, the new ESF applies

[89] A. Caliari, *IMF Human Rights Accountability: A Pragmatic Way to Break the Deadlock*, American University Washington College of Law Perspectives, 2014, p. 4.

[90] As a consequence, the borrower was mandated to take the necessary measures to comply with all the contractual conditions, whether financial, environmental or social, which are therefore as binding as any other clause or provision in the contract.

[91] D. Van Den Meerssche, *Accountability in International Organisations: Reviewing the World Bank's Environmental and Social Framework*, in E. Sciso (ed.), *Accountability,*

to all operations financed by the WB: however, for a period of 7 years, the old policies will be applicable in parallel to projects approved before the effective date of its entry into force.

With the ESF, the WB has reorganized its approach to social and environmental issues in a three-tier structure. First, a "Vision for Sustainable Development" was adopted. The Vision is a statement that contains the WB's "aspirations" in relation to sustainable development and, above all, outlines a change of perspective in the Bank's policies, delineating other areas of intervention which were absent in the old policies (climate change, the protection of biodiversity and the reference – albeit in a vague wording – to human rights). In addition to the Vision, the Framework includes the "Environmental and Social Policy for Investment Financing" (ESP), which outlines the mandatory requirements applicable to the World Bank, and 10 "Environmental and Social Standards" (ESSs) addressed to borrowers.[92] With this new articulation, responsibilities are therefore clearly distinguished between the WB and its borrowers. On the one hand, the Bank will be in charge of conducting adequate due diligence on the project, reviewing information, data, and documents submitted by the borrowers, and guiding them in the planning and implementation of the project. On the other hand, borrowers will remain responsible for the proposal and design phases of the project, which must, however, contain an adequate "Environmental and Social Assessment" (ESA) aimed at identifying all risks associated with the realization of the project and throughout its life cycle.

The ESF provides for a material expansion of the content of these standards compared to the pre-existing policy. Indeed, several new topics appear in the new framework, such as the rights of workers in the "ESS2 Labor and Working Conditions", which incorporates the main international core labor standards as set out in the Conventions and Recommendations adopted by the International Labor Organization (ILO). Other topics that have gained increased attention are climate change, the rights of indigenous peoples and the protection of biodiversity.

However, upon closer inspection, some features of the ESF may un-

---

Transparency and Democracy in the Functioning of Bretton Woods Institutions, Springer, 2017, pp. 157-187.

[92] These standards are: ESS1 *Assessment and Management of Environmental and Social Risks and Impacts*; ESS2 *Labor and Working Conditions*; ESS3 *Resource Efficiency and Pollution Prevention and Management*; ESS4 *Community Health and Safety*; ESS5 *Land Acquisition, Restrictions on Land Use and Involuntary Resettlement*; ESS6 *Biodiversity Conservation and Sustainable Management of Living Natural Resources*; ESS7 *Indigenous Peoples/Sub-Saharan African Historically Underserved Traditional Local Communities*; ESS8 *Cultural Heritage*; ESS9 *Financial Intermediaries*; ESS10 *Stakeholder Engagement and Information Disclosure*.

dermine its effectiveness. There is a certain flexibility in its application based on para. 7 of the ESP, according to which "*The Bank will only support projects that are consistent with, and within the boundaries of, the Bank's Articles of Agreement and are expected to meet the requirements of the ESSs in a manner and within a timeframe acceptable to the Bank*". This means that the Bank can pursue a project even if, at the end of its due diligence, it does not meet – at that specific moment in time – the requirements encapsulated in the ESSs. This approach risks weakening the application of these rules over time and, potentially, disregarding the development objectives.

It must be noted that other WBG organizations have also adopted benchmarks and parameters to assess their performance on social and environmental issues. The IFC in 2006 adopted its own "Performance Standards on Social and Environmental Sustainability", now updated in an "IFC's Sustainability Framework".[93] The new framework is comprised of the Sustainability Policy, the Performance Standards, and the Access to Information Policy and articulates the organization's strategic commitment to sustainable development. Also, MIGA, following a first policy implemented in 2007, approved a "Policy on Environmental and Social Sustainability" in 2013.[94] Both documents constitute internal rules of the organizations outlining the procedures to be followed when the implementation of a project may have social or environmental impacts.

5.6. Accountability of International Financial Institutions

Given the continued human rights impacts of policies implemented on loan conditionalities, a need to ensure the accountability of the IMF and the World Bank arose. The idea behind accountability is therefore that institutions, whether private or public, need to be held responsible for their actions when operating internationally, both from a legal and political point of view. Therefore, apart from the introduction of specific frameworks to assess likely short and long-term human impacts on the poor and disadvantaged, there has been a need to create effective "accountability mechanisms" to control the activity of the IMF and of the institutions of the WBG.

A key reason why these mechanisms are necessary is that, under international law, international organizations such as the IMF and the institutions of the WBG enjoy jurisdictional immunity, i.e. they cannot be sued by pri-

[93] IFC, *Policy on Environmental and Social Sustainability*, 1 January 2012.

[94] MIGA, *Policy on Environmental and Social Sustainability*, 1 October 2013.

vate parties before national courts. Such immunity is necessary to shield organizations from unilateral intervention by Member States, so as to ensure their ability to function autonomously and effectively and is therefore inspired by the principle of functional necessity.[95] This rationale has resulted in a difference in scope between States' immunity and organizations' immunity. Indeed, the law of State immunity has developed the doctrine of restrictive immunity, according to which States are entitled to jurisdictional immunity only with regard to their sovereign acts (*acta iure imperii*) while the forum State is not barred from exercising jurisdiction over a foreign State for commercial acts (*acta jure gestionis*). In the case of international organizations, by contrast, it has been argued that the functional necessity foundation necessarily leads to absolute immunity.

Suing an international organization before national courts may prove impossible even when it does not enjoy absolute immunity. An example is the case of *Jam v. IFC* before the US Supreme Court.[96] This dispute arose out of the construction of a coal-fired power plant in Gujarat, India, that was financed by the IFC. A group of local farmers, fishermen, and villagers in India brought suit against the IFC in federal court in Washington, D.C., claiming that the power plant had polluted the surrounding areas. The question presented in *Jam* was whether US law affords international organizations absolute immunity from suit in the United States, or whether international organizations instead are only entitled to the more limited or "restrictive" immunity that applies to foreign States under the domestic provisions. The Court, resting on a narrow issue of statutory interpretation, decided that international organizations located in the US territory enjoy only the same immunity to which foreign sovereigns are currently entitled, that is, restrictive immunity. In so ruling, the Court reversed decades of precedent and practice affording international organizations absolute immunity from suit.[97] However, in the end, the Indian petitioners were still unable to sue the IFC and obtain compensation. This is because, in a subsequent decision, the Court of Appeals of the DC Circuit found that it

[95] This is, for example, the justification of IBRD's immunity. Indeed, Article VII(1) of the IBRD Articles of Agreement states: "To enable the Bank to fulfil the functions with which it is entrusted, the status, immunities and privileges set forth in this Article shall be accorded to the Bank in the territories of each member". The same wording is used by Article IX(1) of the IMF Articles of Agreement.

[96] Supreme Court of the United States, *Budha Ismail Jam v. the International Financial Corporation (IFC)*, 27 February 2019.

[97] P. Rossi, "The International Law Significance of "Jam v. IFC": Some Implications for the Immunity of International Organizations", in *Diritti umani e diritto internazionale*, 2019, pp. 305-318.

lacked jurisdiction over damages that occurred in India.[98]

To summarize, immunity and other jurisdictional obstacles (such as the territorial competences of courts or the complex qualification of a loan for development purposes as commercial activity) may hinder the recourse to domestic jurisdiction in cases involving the activities of international financial organizations. Moreover, even if judgments may serve the purpose of recognizing compensation to victims of human rights violations connected to financial activities of the IMF or of the WBG institutions, the complexities of human rights impacts impose that any assessment should accompany each stage of the project cycle, also involving the adoption of neutralizing measures or modifications to the project. Accountability mechanisms, as conceived, can serve this purpose.

These mechanisms, therefore, create an independent process to address complaints and resolve disputes regarding the negative social and environmental impacts of a financed project. They formally serve as a tool to collect, evaluate, and resolve community complaints related to investments and projects. In practical terms, although the structure and approach vary, accountability mechanisms consist of a set of procedures to resolve grievances, review compliance with internal social and environmental rules, and provide remedies when investments and projects cause harm. In particular, they provide an opportunity to efficiently address complaints and settle disputes at an early stage in a project's life cycle, solving relatively small disputes before they escalate into widespread grievances that require expensive and time-consuming remediation measures. In addition, accountability mechanisms are sources of knowledge and learning that translate into better projects; they allow to detect problems in a project's design, implementation, or viability, correct them at the outset, and prevent them from occurring in future projects, helping international financial institutions to diagnose weaknesses in its operations, management, or systems and determine how to improve them.[99]

5.6.1. The IMF Independent Evaluation Office

The idea of establishing an independent evaluation office at the IMF goes back at least to January 1993 when the Executive Board considered a management proposal for a separate evaluation office. However, despite exten-

---

[98] *Jam v. IFC*, 3 F.4th 405, 6 July 2021.

[99] J.P.A. Lorenzo, "Accountability Mechanisms of Multilateral Development Banks and the Law of International Responsibility", in *International and Comparative Law Quarterly*, 2024, pp. 209-245.

sive discussions, a consensus to proceed with the proposal was not reached at that time. Rather than establishing an independent evaluation office, an understanding was reached to continue with existing practices of self-evaluation by the operational departments; to conduct internal evaluations by the Office of Internal Audit and Inspection (OIA) in response to specific needs; and at the same time, to undertake two to three independent evaluations per year by outside experts.

At its 2000 Spring Meeting, however, the IMFC endorsed the Executive Board's decision to establish an Independent Evaluation Office (IEO) as a means to enhance the learning culture within the Fund, help build the Fund's external credibility, promote a greater understanding of the work of the Fund, and support the Executive Board's institutional governance and oversight responsibilities.[100] On the basis of the discussion and input received from the public, the Executive Directors drafted the "Terms of Reference" for IEO, which were discussed and approved by the Executive Board on September 14, 2000, and became operational a year later.

According to its Terms, IEO and its staff are independent of Fund management: a Director, appointed by the Executive Board, heads the IEO. The Director's term of appointment is for a period of 4 years, renewable for a second term of up to 3 years.[101] The Office has been established to systematically conduct objective and independent evaluations on issues (and on the basis of criteria) of relevance to the mandate of the Fund. Its evaluations span from a general consideration of IMF programs and approach to its response to specific situations (such as the Covid-19 pandemic or the crises in Greece, Ireland and Portugal in the 2010s). The scope for independent evaluation is clearly circumscribed to *ex post* evaluation to avoid interference with ongoing operations. Therefore, there are no strictly and precisely defined restrictions on what IEO could evaluate.

In carrying out its mandate, including in the preparation of its work program, IEO will be free to consult with whomever and whichever groups it deems necessary, both within and outside the Fund.[102]

---

[100] IMF, *IMF Executive Board Report to the IMFC on the Establishment of the Independent Evaluation Office (EVO) and its Terms of Reference*, 12 September 2001.

[101] IMF, *Terms of Refence of the EVO – Director*, 12 September 2001. The Director of EVO will be responsible for the preparation of the Work Program. The content of the Work Program should focus on issues of importance to the Fund's membership and of relevance to the mandate of the Fund.

[102] The IMF requests its staff to comply with IEO requests to obtain information that is relevant to its work program, and it is encouraged to provide the IEO with all

The Executive Board has the ultimate authority to determine whether or not the results of a particular EVO evaluation will be published. However, given the mandate of EVO and the importance of transparency to the credibility of an independent evaluation office, there would be an expectation that the work of EVO (including its Annual Reports) would be published (within the constraints imposed by the need to respect the confidentiality of information provided to the Fund by its Members).

The role of IEO is of fundamental importance inside the IMF. Indeed, it provides an independent and credible assessment of the performance of the organization and its activities, which helps generate more broadly-based public support for the organization and its work.[103] Moreover, IEO inputs can help the Fund and its staff seek constant improvement and delineate its priorities. For example, the IEO launched an early-stage evaluation to assess the IMF's approach to climate change.[104] The evaluation will focus on the initial implementation of the "2021 Climate Strategy" focusing on how the Fund has adapted its surveillance, lending, and capacity development activities to help Member States countries address the challenges created by climate change, and to draw early lessons from the experience of the IMF's engagement on climate change that could enhance the effectiveness of the institution's response.

5.6.2. The World Bank Accountability Mechanism

The effects of the WB activities on the local communities and the environment of the countries in which it operates have provoked strong protests towards the organizations. Therefore, since the 1990s, there has been a call to develop mechanisms for monitoring the Bank's activities.

information and documents they are aware of that would be pertinent to an evaluation, even if such information is not specifically requested by the IEO. There are only a few exceptions to the requirement that staff comply with IEO information requests. These exceptions are: (i) information subject to attorney-client privilege; (ii) documents containing personal information about Fund employees or candidates for employment; and (iii) confidential communications that fall within officials "zone of privacy" (confidential communications of management with persons or institutions outside the Fund, and within and between their immediate offices). See IMF, *Office Memorandum Staff Cooperation with the Independent Evaluation Office*, 2017.

[103] The Fund, indeed, is not always understood by the public at large, particularly with regard to how these institutions use public funds and how they make important, indeed critical, decisions that affect the destiny of countries and their respective populations, see M.J. Schwartz, R.C. Rist, *The International Monetary Fund and the Learning Organization. The Role of Independent Evaluation*, International Monetary Fund, 2016, p. 20.

[104] IEO, *Draft Issue Paper. The IMF and Climate Change*, 30 September 2024.

The need arose after the financing by the Bank of the *Sardar Sarovar dam* in 1985 with a contribution of 450 million USD: the project entailed a resettlement of numerous indigenous communities living in the area. Protests by the communities, activists, civil society and academics demanded World Bank accountability for the displacement of millions and initially sought to verify the claims regarding the benefits of the dams, while some reports documented Indian police shooting and killing individuals during forced relocation. Shaken by the unfavorable media coverage, the World Bank announced it would institute an Independent Review of the Sardar Sarovar projects: the "Morse Commission" issued its report in June 1992. The report exposed the Bank's violation of its own policies and recommended drastic reform of the relocation programs and environmental assessment.[105] Furthermore, the follow-up report found that the violations identified in the Narmada River case were not an anomaly, but a systemic part of the Bank's culture. The Indian government, following the report, soon canceled the remaining loans, thus ending support from the World Bank for the Sardar Sarovar dam.

This controversy led to the creation of the Inspection Panel (IP) in 1993, established in 1993 pursuant to Resolution No. IBRD 93-10 and Resolution No. IDA 93-6.[106] The Panel's creation was presented as groundbreaking because it envisaged, for the first time, a form of direct, if limited, recourse for affected persons to seek review of implementation of Bank-financed projects under certain circumstances, and therefore a mechanism for individuals to hold an international organization accountable.[107]

After several years, in 2020, the World Bank Executive Directors approved a package of reforms for the IP. The WB Accountability Mechanism (AM) was therefore created by the Board of Executive Directors on 8 September 2020. This Mechanism comprises two constituent parts: the Inspection Panel and the Dispute Resolution Service (DRS).[108] The Mechanism is managed by an Accountability Mechanism Secretary, nominated by the President of the WB and appointed by the Board of Executive Direc-

[105] World Bank, *Office Memorandum India: Sardar Sarovar (Namada) Projects – Morse Review*, 5 May 1992.

[106] The activities of the IP are now regulated by *Resolution No. IBRD 2020-0004* and *Resolution No. IDA 2020-0003*, 8 September 2020 ("IP Resolution").

[107] R. Mackenzie, C.P.R. Romano, Y. Shany, P. Sands, *The Manual on International Courts and Tribunals*², OUP, 2010, pp. 464-465.

[108] See World Bank, *Resolution No. IBRD 2020 – 0005 and Resolution No. IDA 2020 – 0004*, 8 September 2020, para. 2.

tors of the IBRD. The Accountability Mechanism Secretary is appointed for a term of 5 years and may not serve for more than one term. The Accountability Mechanism Secretary will be prohibited from working for the World Bank Group in any capacity following the conclusion of his/her appointment. [109] The Secretary oversees all administrative matters and record-keeping for the Accountability Mechanism and manages its work program, budget and staff.

5.6.2.1. The Inspection Panel

The Panel consists of three members of different nationalities from IBRD Member States. The President of the Bank, after consultation with the Executive Directors, nominates the members of the Panel, to be appointed by the Board of Executive Directors. Each member of the Panel is appointed for a period of five years, provided that no member may serve for more than one term. [110] Members of the Panel may be removed from office only by decision of the Executive Directors, for cause. The IP Resolution establishes that, to guarantee the independence of the Panel, its members may not serve on the Panel until two years have elapsed since the end of their service in the WBG.

The Panel receives requests for inspection presented to it by an affected party in the territory of the borrower which is not a single individual (i.e., a community of persons such as an organization, association, society or other grouping of individuals), or by the local representative of such party or by another representative in the exceptional cases where the party submitting the request contends that appropriate representation is not locally available and the Executive Directors so agree at the time they consider the request for inspection. Also, any Executive Director may ask the Panel for an investigation in special cases of serious alleged violations of the Bank's policies and procedures, while the Board of Executive Directors may at any time instruct the Panel to investigate. [111]

The affected party must demonstrate that its rights or interests have been or are likely to be directly affected by an action or omission of the WB as a result of a failure of the organization to follow its operational policies and procedures with respect to the design, appraisal and/or implemen-

---

[109] *Ibid.*, para. 3.

[110] The Panel functions under the coordination of a Chairperson, elected by the Panel for a period of one year; he/she works on a full-time basis from the headquarters of the WB in Washington DC.

[111] See World Bank, *Resolution No. IBRD 2020 – 0005 and Resolution No. IDA 2020 – 0004*, 8 September 2020, para. 13.

tation of a project financed by the WB, provided in all cases that such failure has had, or threatens to have, a material adverse effect.[112]

Under para. 15 of the IP Resolution, the Panel will not hear complaints related to actions which are the responsibility of other parties, such as a borrower, or potential borrower, and which do not involve any action or omission on the part of the Bank; related to procurement; related to projects closed, or after the 95 percent of the loan has been disbursed, or 15 months after the closing date of the loan financing the project; on matters over which the Panel has already made its recommendation upon having received a prior request, unless justified by new evidence or circumstances not known at the time of the prior.

5.6.2.2. Procedural Steps before the Inspection Panel

The first step of the procedure is for an affected party to present a written request for inspection stating all relevant facts, including the harm suffered and the nature of the alleged actions or omissions by the WB. The party should also mention the action already taken to bring the issue to the WB officials and their response.

Within 21 business days of being notified of a request for inspection, the management of the World Bank shall provide the Panel with a response, also providing the evidence that it has complied with the WB's relevant policies; or that there are serious failures exclusively attributable to its own actions or omissions, but that it intends to comply; or that the existing failures are not attributable in whole or in part to the World Bank.

Within 21 business days of receiving the response from the management, the Panel shall determine whether the request meets the eligibility criteria and shall make a recommendation to the Board of Executive Directors as to whether the matter should be investigated. If the Panel so recommends, the Board of Executive Directors will authorize an investigation without making a judgment on the merits of the complainants' request, and without discussion except with respect to the eligibility crite-

---

[112] See, for example, World Bank Inspection Panel, *Uganda, Transport Sector Development Project - Additional financing* (P121097), Investigation Report, 4 August 2016), where the Panel then assessed the social implications of the project on local communities in detail, with a particular focus on the issues of gender-based violence and child protection, finding that the Bank had failed to uphold its social assessment and supervision obligations. In the case, the complainants reported lack of participation, inadequate compensation, poor health and safety measures, fear of retaliation, child sexual abuse, teenage pregnancies caused by road workers, increased spread of sexually transmitted infections, sexual harassment of female employees and inadequate compensation for resettled people.

ria.[113] The investigation is conducted by at least one member of the Panel, as decided by the Chairperson, and may include consultations and in-country visits.

The Panel shall submit its investigation report to the Executive Directors and the President of the WB. The report shall consider all relevant facts and shall conclude with findings on whether there is a serious Bank failure to observe its operational policies and procedures with respect to project design, appraisal and/or implementation. The report will include all relevant facts that are needed to understand fully the context and basis for its findings and conclusions.

Within 6 weeks of receiving the Panel's findings, management will submit a report indicating its recommendations in response to such findings to the Executive Directors for their consideration ("Management Report and Recommendation"). This document shall include a "Management Action Plan", listing the actions that management proposes for addressing the Panel's findings of non-compliance and for which it seeks the Executive Directors' approval, determined in consultation with the affected parties and the borrower. Thereafter, the Executive Board will have to decide whether to adopt changes to the current project based on the Panel's indications.

According to para. 42 of the IP Resolution, the Panel has no right to present its view on the action plan nor on its monitoring. Indeed, the management is responsible for monitoring the implementation of the action plan, under the supervision of the Executive Directors and through the submission of progress reports.[114]

5.6.2.3. The Dispute Resolution Service

The purpose of the DRS is to facilitate a voluntary and independent dispute resolution option for requesters and borrowers in the context of Inspection Panel requests for inspection: this option is available after the

[113] Following this authorization, the Accountability Mechanism Secretary shall offer to the parties the opportunity to opt for the DRS; if the Parties do not agree to engage in a dispute resolution process, the Panel shall commence the investigation.

[114] According to paras. 48-49 of the IP Resolution, the Executive Directors may approve, as an additional reassurance tool for avoiding reputational risks, independent risk-based verification of the implementation of the management action plan by the Panel and/or Group Internal Audit. Verification will focus solely on the Bank's actions as outlined in the management action plan, and will assess the status (including completion) of specific management actions, based on timelines of agreed actions to avoid premature review of actions.

Board of Executive Directors has approved the recommendation of the Inspection Panel to investigate a request.

The availability of this function is offered to the parties by the Accountability Mechanism Secretary, that informs the Board, the Inspection Panel and management whether or not the parties voluntarily agree to pursue dispute resolution, within 30 business days after the Directors' approval of the investigation. The maximum length of the dispute resolution process is one year from such date. If the parties agree to use the dispute resolution process, the IP shall hold its investigation; if the parties do not agree to pursue dispute resolution, the Panel will commence its investigation in accordance with para. 34 of the IP Resolution.

In this process, parties select a mediator, that can also be chosen from a pool of candidates maintained by the DRS who are qualified to deliver dispute resolution services in a culturally appropriate manner. The parties agree on the objectives, scope, participants, methods, stages and timelines of the dispute resolution process. The method, in particular, may include consultative dialogue, information sharing, joint fact-finding, mediation, conciliation and other approaches.[115]

The dispute resolution process concludes if (i) the parties reach an agreement; (ii) one or both parties withdraw from the dispute resolution process; or (iii) after the expiration of the dispute resolution period. If the Parties reach an agreement, such agreement is incorporated in a Dispute Resolution Agreement signed by the parties, containing a time-bound implementation schedule for agreed actions.

Upon conclusion of the dispute resolution process, the Accountability Mechanism Secretary issues a report to the Board of Executive Directors, the Inspection Panel and the Bank management informing them of the outcome. The IP, having received the report, takes the steps set forth in para. 33 of the IP Resolution: therefore, if the parties have reached an agreement and signed a Dispute Resolution Agreement, the case shall be considered closed, and the Panel shall issue a memorandum closing the case and take no further action with respect to the request. Otherwise, the Panel shall commence its investigation.

[115] The scope of the dispute resolution is of course limited to project-related issues raised in the request for inspection and identified as the issues to be investigated in the IP report to the Board of Executive Directors recommending the investigation.

5.6.3. The IFC/MIGA Compliance Advisory Ombudsman

Since the establishment of the Inspection Panel, other WBG organizations have also created internal compliance mechanisms. The Office of the Compliance Advisor Ombudsman (CAO) was established in 1999 to address complaints related to IFC/MIGA activities and to enhance the environmental and social outcomes of these projects. Its goal is to promote dialogue, in a fair, objective and constructive manner, between individuals, groups of individuals or organizations affected by a project and the two institutions.

During its first period of establishment CAO's activities were not comparable to those of the IP, as it was only an informal conciliatory and consultative mechanism for resolving conflicts between stakeholders. Now, the CAO performs investigative functions.[116] All its activities are led by a Director General, with no previous working experience with the WBG, appointed for 5 years, subject to renewal for another 5 years.

CAO operates through three complementary functions, which all contribute to delivering on this mandate: a dispute resolution function; a compliance function, carrying out reviews of IFC/MIGA compliance with its environmental and social policies, assessing related harm, and recommending remedial actions to address non-compliance and harm where appropriate; an advisory function to IFC/MIGA and their Boards with the purpose of improving IFC's/MIGA's systemic performance on environmental and social sustainability and reducing the risk of harm.[117]

According to its Policy, any individual or group, or representative they authorize to act on their behalf, believing they are or may be harmed by a project (or sub-project) may lodge a complaint with CAO.[118] Complaints may relate to environmental and social harm regarding any aspect of the planning, implementation, or impact of a project. There are no formal requirements for lodging a complaint with CAO, but complaints should include certain information on the complainants, on the project and on the harm suffered.[119]

---

[116] IFC/MIGA, *Independent Accountability Mechanism (CAO) Policy*, 28 June 2001. This Policy became effective on 1 July 2021.

[117] This function entails advice on broader IFC/MIGA environmental and social policies, processes and approaches, guidance documents, strategic issues, trends, and systemic concerns, therefore it does not focus on specific Projects. This function may be initiated directly by the Ombudsman or upon request by the Boards of the IFC/MIGA or their officials.

[118] Complaints should be submitted in writing and may be presented in any language and should be delivered to the CAO office in Washington DC or electronically.

[119] See IFC/MIGA, *Independent Accountability Mechanism (CAO) Policy*, paras. 33-

The first step that CAO takes after receiving a complaint is to acknowledge its receipt and to screen it against the eligibility criteria. CAO will deem the complaint eligible if: the complaint relates to an active project; the issues raised in the complaint pertain to its mandate; and the complainant is or may be affected by the harm raised in the complaint. CAO will deem the complaints ineligible when they are clearly fraudulent, frivolous, malicious, or generated to gain competitive advantage; they contain allegations of fraud and/or corruption, referring these allegations to the World Bank Group Integrity Vice Presidency; complaints relating to non-active projects or non-IFC/MIGA projects.

If the complaint is eligible, CAO will conduct its assessment, engaging with IFC/MIGA teams, the complainant and the client. This evaluation shall be completed within 90 business days and does not entail any judgment on the merits. [120]

CAO will then produce an assessment report that includes: a broad summary of the information gathered and the Parties' perspectives of the issues raised in the complaint during the assessment, including views from other stakeholders as deemed relevant; the decision of the Parties to pursue a dispute resolution process or if the complaint will proceed to the compliance function; and a copy of the complaint and any client response that may be provided, redacted to protect the confidentiality of the complainant where appropriate. [121]

During the assessment process, the complainant and the client decide whether they would like to initiate CAO's dispute resolution or compliance function. If both parties agree to undertake dispute resolution, CAO will facilitate this process. If there is no agreement, the complaint will proceed to CAO's compliance function.

The dispute resolution function entails a process through which parties may find mutually satisfactory solutions to the issues raised in the complaint. In consultation with the parties, different methods might be used, including mediation; facilitation and information sharing; joint fact-finding;

34, In addition, CAO suggests providing information on whether anything has been done by the complainants to attempt to resolve the problem, including any contact with IFC/MIGA staff, the Client, or the host government, and what aspects remain unresolved.

[120] The CAO Director General may extend the assessment timeframe by a period not exceeding 30 business days if, after the 90 business days, the Parties confirm that resolution of the complaint is likely; or either Party expresses interest in dispute resolution, and there is potential that the other Party will agree.

[121] CAO will provide a draft assessment report to the parties and IFC/MIGA for factual review and comment for at least 10 business days prior to finalizing the report.

dialogue and negotiation. Where the Parties have reached an agreement through the dispute resolution process, CAO will monitor the implementation of the agreement and will conclude the dispute resolution process and close the case if the agreed terms have been implemented to the parties' mutual satisfaction. Instead, in case of the conclusion of the dispute resolution process with partial or no agreement, CAO will enquire whether the complainant wishes to transfer the complaint to the compliance function. The case will be transferred if the complainant provides explicit consent, or otherwise the case will be closed.

The purpose of the CAO compliance function is to carry out reviews of IFC/MIGA's compliance with its environmental and social policies. This process follows a three-step approach: compliance appraisal, which determines whether further investigation is warranted. If warranted, the appraisal is followed by compliance investigation and compliance monitoring. A compliance appraisal will consider issues raised in the complaint or identified during the CAO assessment phase, but not those resolved during a CAO dispute resolution process. [122] The outcome is a final report determining whether a compliance investigation is necessary, or to merge, defer, or close the case. In practical terms, compliance investigation determines whether IFC/MIGA has complied with its policies and whether there is harm related to IFC/MIGA deviating in a material way from relevant directives and procedures. Where CAO finds non-compliance and related harm, it makes recommendations for IFC/MIGA to consider when developing remedial actions.

According to the procedure, CAO circulates a draft investigation report within one year of the disclosure of the appraisal report; the complainants and the IFC/MIGA have 20 business days from the receipt of the draft report to provide written comments. After considering the comments, CAO finalizes the compliance investigation report in 20 business days. The final investigation report is submitted to management and circulated to the Board of the relevant institution for information.

Within 50 business days of receiving CAO's compliance investigation report and findings, management is required to submit a report ("Man-

[122] According to the *Policy*, para. 80-84, CAO may also initiate a compliance appraisal of one or more projects in response to an internal request from the CAO Director General, the Presidents, the Boards, or managements of IFC/MIGA. Such internal request may be made in circumstances where: (i) an appraisal is deemed necessary to review environmental and social compliance issues of systemic importance to IFC/MIGA; (ii) concerns exist regarding particularly severe harm; or (iii) project-affected people may be subject to, or fear, reprisals, preventing them from lodging a complaint with CAO.

agement Report") to the Board for consideration, stating the actions proposed in response to CAO's findings ("Management Action Plan" - MAP) and time-bound remedial actions proposed. After the Board has approved a MAP, CAO will monitor its implementation.

The Ombudsman will close the compliance monitoring process when it determines that substantive commitments as set out in the MAP have been effectively fulfilled; or, if not all substantive commitments have been effectively fulfilled, when CAO determines that there is no reasonable expectation of further action to address non-compliance findings. In either case, it prepares a final monitoring and closure report and circulates it for information to the Boards, the Presidents, the management of IFC/MIGA, the complainants, and the client before making it public.

5.7. Final Remarks

International financial law is adopting a more cohesive approach to international law, gradually incorporating standards and rules developed in other sub-sectors of international law. Indeed, the Articles of Agreement of the IMF and of the IBRD, as drafted originally at Bretton Woods, have not remained static but rather have been developed or adapted to meet changing or new needs by means of modified or novel practices and policies, or by amendment in the institutional structure of these organizations.

Indeed, the system designed seemed unable to address some of the greatest challenges of our time including human rights, environmental protection, and the safeguarding of cultural diversity. From a substantive perspective, international financial law has been seen as having an increasing impact on sovereign policy objectives. Its inability to connect economic factors and human and social objectives has been one of the main shortcomings of this body of law. This disconnection probably depended also on the lack of a specialized dispute resolution mechanism. Indeed, courts and arbitral tribunals have often been presented with questions involving coordination and compatibility between rules and principles pertaining to international law, providing guidance for other courts, international organizations and States on how to balance competing obligations. In this field, nobody has this power.

Therefore, the legitimacy of the international legal system in general and international economic governance in particular has been discussed intensively. Specifically, the IMF's operational paradigm has often been criticized, since it always emphasized fiscal discipline, macroeconomic stability, and liberalization. The IMF indeed prioritized handling balance of payments issues and guaranteeing exchange rate stability. However, changing global economic dynamics and the rising complexity of financial crises extended the IMF's responsibilities. The Fund has adopted a significant shift towards incorporating respect for sovereign autonomies and universal human rights precepts, mostly through lessons learned from its previous experiences and highlighted by the IEO. The adoption of a specific climate change policy, for example, testifies to the new awareness by the Fund of its role in orienting the economic policies of States. Notwithstanding, it still appears that IMF activities are mostly disconnected from the general spectrum of international law, since principles and rules regarding peace, environment, and rights continue to find limited space in its decisions and functions.

The case of the World Bank Group is different. Indeed, the Group and its various institutions have been more open to concerns coming from other sectors of international law, incorporating rules and standards in their policies. This approach can be easily identified with regard to environmental law. Rules and principles, such as the precautionary approach, the principle of prevention and the necessity of conducting environmental impact assessments, are clearly established in the internal rules of the Bank, establishing clear obligations on the WB and its staff but also on borrowers, which in the end have the effect of imposing environmental obligations on Member States and, also, on sub-contractors. The same can be said for human rights, even if their application in Bank policies can be limited to certain categories (such as indigenous peoples or workers) or to specific rights (housing, right to water, right to health) that can more easily be affected by projects financed by the Bank. [123] The fundamental integration of other rules and principles of international law has also entailed the accountability of the WBG organizations towards affected communities through the Inspection Panel first and the Accountability Mechanism and CAO nowadays. These bodies, even if they do not have any judicial or arbitral functions, have surely contributed to demonstrating that international financial law should not be perceived as a self-contained system; rather, it should be conceived as a part of public international law.

---

[123] See Inspection Panel, *Uganda - Uganda, Transport Sector Development Project - Additional financing (P121097),* Investigation Report, 4 August 2016.

References

Abouharb, M.R., Cingranelli, D. (2009). *Human Rights and Structural Adjustment*, Cambridge University Press.

Abrams, A. (2009). *The IMF Council of Governors*, in R. Lamdany, L. Martinez-Diaz (eds.). *Studies of IMF Governance. A Compendium*, International Monetary Fund.

Adinolfi, G (2012). *Poteri e interventi del Fondo monetario internazionale*, Giappichelli.

Adinolfi, G., Vellano, M. (2013). *La crisi del debito sovrano degli Stati dell'Area euro*, Giappichelli.

Ascensio, H (2020). *Droit international économique*, Presses Universitaire de France.

Aufricht, H. (1964). *The International Monetary Fund - Legal Basis, Structure, Functions*, Stevens & Sons.

Bismuth, R., Carreau, D., Hamann, A., Juillard P. (2017). Droit international economique, 6th ed., Dalloz.

Caliari, A. (2014). *IMF Human Rights Accountability: A Pragmatic Way to Break the Deadlock*, American University Washington College of Law Perspectives.

Collins, D. (2019). *Foundations of International Economic Law*, Edward Elgar.

Choukroune, L., Nedumpara, J.J. (2021). *International Economic Law. Text, Cases, Materials*, Cambridge University Press.

Denters, E., Viterbo, A. (2013). *International Monetary Fund*, Springer.

Gianviti F. (1989). *The International Monetary Fund and the external debt*, in *Recueil des Cours* vol. 215, Brill, The Hague.

Han L. (2024). International Economic Law in Contemporary World. Springer.

IFC (2016). *IFC The Fists Six Decades: Leading the Way in Private Sector Development – A History*, International Finance Corporation.

Lehane, G. (2018). *Human Rights at the World Bank Group*, in Y. Radi (ed.). *Research Handbook on Human Rights and Investment*, Edward Elgar.

Lorenzo, J.P.A. (2024). "Accountability Mechanisms of Multilateral Development Banks and the Law of International Responsibility", in *International and Comparative Law Quarterly*, pp. 209-245.

Lowenfeld, A. (2008). *International Economic Law*, 2nd ed., Oxford University Press.

Mackenzie, R., Romano, C.P.R., Shany, Y., Sands, P. (2010). *The Manual on International Courts and Tribunals*, 2nd ed., Oxford University Press.

Manderieux, L., Vellano, M. (2017). *Étique globale, bonne gouvernance et droit international économique*, Giappichelli.

Marrella, F. (2023). *Manuale di diritto del commercio internazionale*, Cedam.

Mauro, M.R. (2019). *Diritto internazionale dell'economia. Teoria e prassi delle relazioni economiche internazionali,* ESI.

Mauro, M.R. (2022). "Istituzioni finanziarie internazionali e democrazia: alla ricerca di un nuovo multilateralismo", in S. Cafaro (ed.), *Beni e valori comuni nelle dimensioni internazionale e sovranazionale,* Editoriale Scientifica.

Mauro, M.R. (2023). "La riforma delle organizzazioni internazionali economiche: verso un multilateralismo inclusivo e sostenibile", in P. Gargiulo, I. Ingravallo, P. Rossi, *L'ONU nei nuovi assetti sistemici internazionali: le riforme necessarie. Pace e sicurezza internazionali, sviluppo sostenibile, tutela dei diritti umani*, Editoriale Scientifica, pp. 295-314.

Mola, L. (2012). *Sovereign Immunity, Insolvent States and Private Bondholders: Recent National and International Case Law, in the Law and Practice of International Courts and Tribunals*, Brill, pp. 525-554.

Monyae, D., Ndzendze, B. (2021). *The BRICS Order. Assertive or Complementing the West?*, Springer.

Rossi, P. (2019). "The International Law Significance of "Jam v. IFC": Some Implications for the Immunity of International Organizations", in *Diritti umani e diritto internazionale*, pp. 305-318.

Sciso, E. (ed.) (2017). *Accountability, Transparency and Democracy in the Functioning of Bretton Woods Institutions*, Springer, pp. 157-187.

Van Genungten, W. (2017). *The World Bank Group, the IMF and Human Rights. A Contextualised Way Forward*, Cambridge University Press.

Viterbo, A. (2018). "Immunità dalla giurisdizione della Banca mondiale e diritto di accesso al giudice", in *Diritti umani e diritto internazionale*, pp. 397-420.

Viterbo, A (2020). *Sovereign Debt Restructuring. The Role and Limits of Public International Law,* Giappichelli.

Yamazawa, I. (2021). *Asia Pacific Economic Cooperation (APEC). Challenges and Tasks for the Twenty First Century*, Routledge.

INDEX

A

Accountability of international financial institutions, 234
Appellate Body, 161
  current challenges, 17, 167
Applicable law to investment disputes, 117
Arbitration,
  in the WTO context, 165-166, 168
  international commercial, 30
  investor-State, 25, 100
Awards, 124
  ICSID, 124
  non-ICSID, 127

B

Bilateral Investment Treaties (BITs), 34, 59
  intra-EU, 61
Bretton Woods, 2
  institutions, 18, 139, 196, 226

C

Compliance Advisory Ombudsman (CAO), 244
Corporate duties, 26
Corporate rights, 25
Corporations, 22
Customary international law, 31, 38
  and treaties, 40
  and WTO law, 152
  as a source of international investment law, 56

D

Dispute Settlement Body (DSB), 159

E

Enabling clause, 14, 191
Equality of States, 13
Expropriation, 23, 70

F

Fair and equitable treatment (FET), 45, 76
Foreign investments
  notion, 63
  rules on the treatment of, 67
Fragmentation, 1, 142
Full protection and security, 88

G

GATT 1947, 138
GATT 1994, 145
General exceptions, 184
General international law,
  and international economic law, 1-4
  and international financial law, 226

and international investment law, 56
and WTO law, 148, 152
General principles, 43
common to domestic legal systems, 43
of international law, 44
G20, 198

H

Human rights
and corporations, 26-30
and foreign investments, 94-98
and the IMF, 231
and the World Bank, 232

I

Inspection Panel, 240
International Bank for Reconstruction and Development (IBRD), 18, 212
and the WTO, 143
internal structure, 214
International Development Association (IDA), 18, 216
International Finance Corporation (IFC), 18, 222
International Investment Agreements (IIAs), 34, 61
International Monetary Fund (IMF), 203
and the WTO, 143
functions, 207
internal structure, 204
lending activities, 208
International organizations, 16
acts of, 49
Interpretation,
of ICSID awards, 128
of IIAs, 96
of non-ICSID awards, 131
of treaties, 36
of WTO law and general international law, 148
Investment arbitration claims
consent as the basis of, 107
jurisdiction and admissibility of, 111
jurisdiction *ratione loci*, 115
jurisdiction *ratione materiae*, 113
jurisdiction *ratione personae*, 115
jurisdiction *ratione temporis*, 116
Investor-State Dispute Settlement (ISDS)
fundamental notions, 98
ICSID framework, 104
non-ICSID frameworks, 106

J

Judicial decisions, 46
Judicial precedents
in international law, 47
in investment arbitration, 126
in the WTO system, 154

L

Liberalization, 142, 169
Like products, 171, 178

M

Membership
ICSID, 104
International Bank for Reconstruction, 212
International Development Association, 216
WTO, 143
Most favored nation treatment (MFN)
in international investment law, 83
in the WTO context, 170
Multilateralization, 145, 169

N

National treatment (NT)
in international investment law, 80
in the WTO context, 175
Nationalization, 12, 70, 224

Non-Governmental Organizations (NGOs), 29, 52
and the WTO, 143

P

Panels, 160
Plurilateral trade agreements, 148
Post-award remedies, 128-132
Private entities, 22
Public interests
and foreign investments, 94
and the WTO system, 184

R

Regional integration, 189
Regional Trade Agreements (RTAs), 148

S

Security exceptions, 186
Self-contained regime, 1-4, 127, 148, 248
Single undertaking principle, 147
Soft law, 28, 50
Sources
of international economic law, 30
of international investment law, 56
of the WTO, 144
States, 9, 10
Subjects of international economic law, 8
Sustainable development, 142, 230, 232

T

Treaties, 31-36

U

Umbrella clauses, 36, 91
United Nations, 20

W

Withdrawal
from the IMF, 205
from the WTO, 144
of consent to investor-State arbitration, 62, 110
World Bank, 211
accountability mechanism, 238
financing activities, 218
functions, 217
WTO
accession and withdrawal, 143
dispute settlement system, 158
institutional structure, 155
jurisdiction, 162
objective and functions, 142

Made in the USA
Monee, IL
13 September 2026

62977454R00146